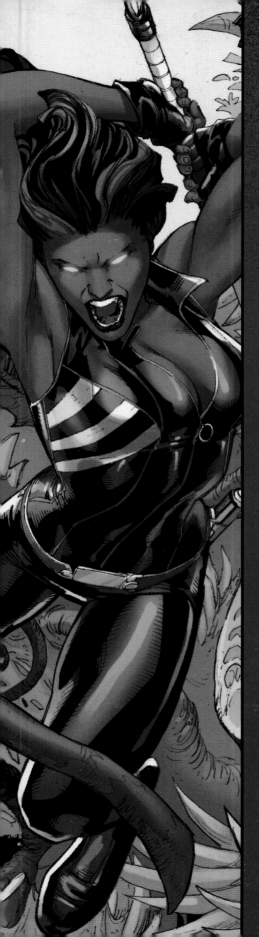

RED SHE-HULK

HELL HATH NO FURY

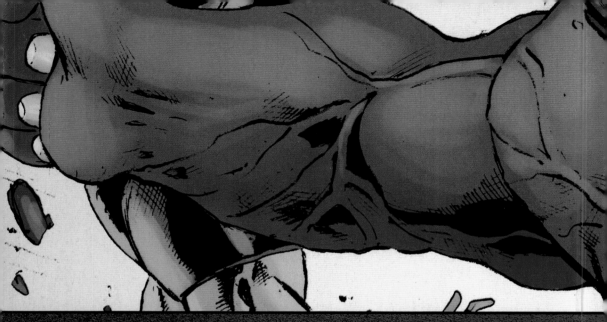

RED SHE-HULK

HELL HATH NO FURY

WRITER
JEFF PARKER

ARTISTS
CARLO PAGULAYAN
WELLINTON ALVES

COLOR ARTISTS
VAL STAPLES (#58-59 & #61-62)
JAVIER TARTAGLIA (#60)

LETTERER
VC'S CLAYTON COWLES

COVER ARTISTS
CARLO PAGULAYAN & VAL STAPLES (#58-60)
JANA SCHIRMER (#61-62)

ASSISTANT EDITOR
JON MOISAN

EDITOR
MARK PANICCIA

COLLECTION EDITOR: CORY LEVINE

ASSISTANT EDITORS: ALEX STARBUCK & NELSON RIBEIRO
EDITORS, SPECIAL PROJECTS: JENNIFER GRÜNWALD & MARK D. BEAZLEY
SENIOR EDITOR, SPECIAL PROJECTS: JEFF YOUNGQUIST
SVP OF PRINT & DIGITAL PUBLISHING SALES: DAVID GABRIEL
BOOK DESIGN: JEFF POWELL & CORY LEVINE

EDITOR IN CHIEF: AXEL ALONSO
CHIEF CREATIVE OFFICER: JOE QUESADA
PUBLISHER: DAN BUCKLEY
EXECUTIVE PRODUCER: ALAN FINE

RED SHE-HULK VOL. 1: HELL HATH NO FURY. Contains material originally published in magazine form as RED SHE-HULK #58-62. First printing 2013. ISBN# 978-0-7851-6531-6. Published by MARVEL WORLDWIDE, INC., a subsidiary of MARVEL ENTERTAINMENT, LLC. OFFICE OF PUBLICATION: 135 West 50th Street, New York, NY 10020. Copyright © 2012 and 2013 Marvel Characters, Inc. All rights reserved. All characters featured in this issue and the distinctive names and likenesses thereof, and all related indicia are trademarks of Marvel Characters, Inc. No similarity between any of the names, characters, persons, and/or institutions in this magazine with those of any living or dead person or institution is intended, and any such similarity which may exist is purely coincidental. Printed in the U.S.A. ALAN FINE, EVP - Office of the President, Marvel Worldwide, Inc. and EVP & CMO Marvel Characters B.V.; DAN BUCKLEY, Publisher & President - Print, Animation & Digital Divisions; JOE QUESADA, Chief Creative Officer; TOM BREVOORT, SVP of Publishing; DAVID BOGART, SVP of Operations & Procurement, Publishing; RUWAN JAYATILLEKE, SVP & Associate Publisher, Publishing; C.B. CEBULSKI, SVP of Creator & Content Development; DAVID GABRIEL, SVP of Print & Digital Publishing Sales; JIM O'KEEFE, VP of Operations & Logistics; DAN CARR, Executive Director of Publishing Technology; SUSAN CRESPI, Editorial Operations Manager; ALEX MORALES, Publishing Operations Manager; STAN LEE, Chairman Emeritus. For information regarding advertising in Marvel Comics or on Marvel.com, please contact Niza Disla, Director of Marvel Partnerships, at ndisla@marvel.com. For Marvel subscription inquiries, please call 800-217-9158. Manufactured between 2/14/2013 and 3/9/2013 by QUAD/GRAPHICS, VERSAILLES, KY, USA.

10 9 8 7 6 5 4 3 2 1

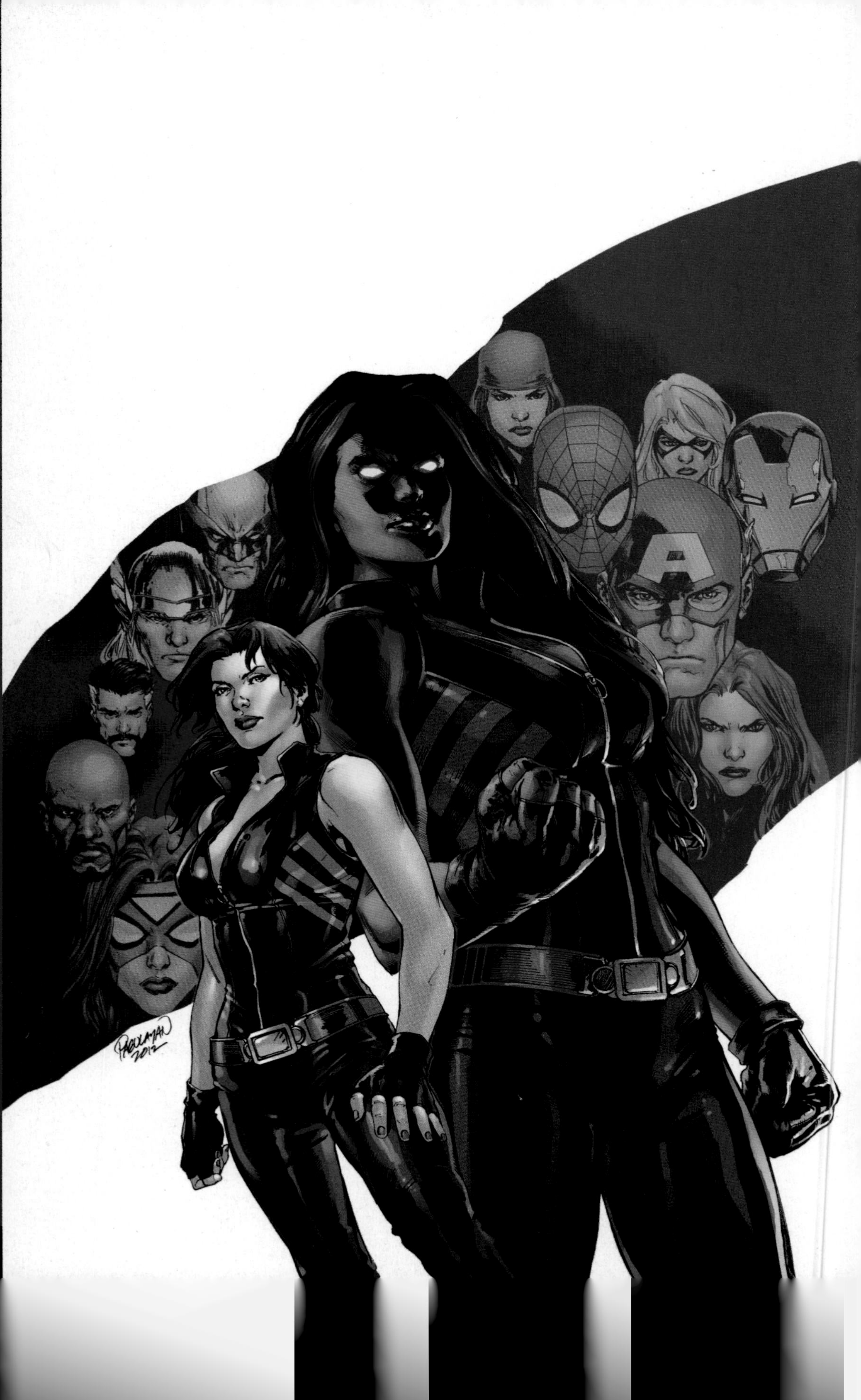

RED SHE-HULK

X-51 CAPSULE PROFILE:

[E]LIZABETH "BETTY" ROSS
[A]KA
[RE]D SHE-HULK

[M]Y CURRENT MISSION
[R]EQUEST DEALS WITH THE
[W]OMAN KNOWN PUBLICLY
[A]S RED SHE-HULK OR IN
[S]OME NEWS STORIES "THE
[R]ED WOMAN" OR
["]HELLION." TO MY
[U]NDERSTANDING ONLY A
[V]ERY FEW BESIDES ME
[K]NOW HER HUMAN FORM
[I]S BETTY ROSS, DAUGHTER
[O]F WAR HERO AND LONG-
[T]IME HULK ENEMY
[G]ENERAL THADDEUS
["]THUNDERBOLT" ROSS.
[S]HE WAS ONE OF THE
[P]EOPLE AT THE PRIME
[G]AMMA EVENT, THE BOMB
[T]EST THAT CREATED THE
[H]ULK. IT HAS BEEN
[P]OSITED THAT ANYONE
[P]RESENT AT THAT BLAST
[W]AS GENETICALLY
[P]REDISPOSED TO
[C]OMPLETE GAMMA-
[M]UTATION, AND
[T]HEREFORE PRIME
[T]ARGETS FOR LATER
[E]XPERIMENTATION...

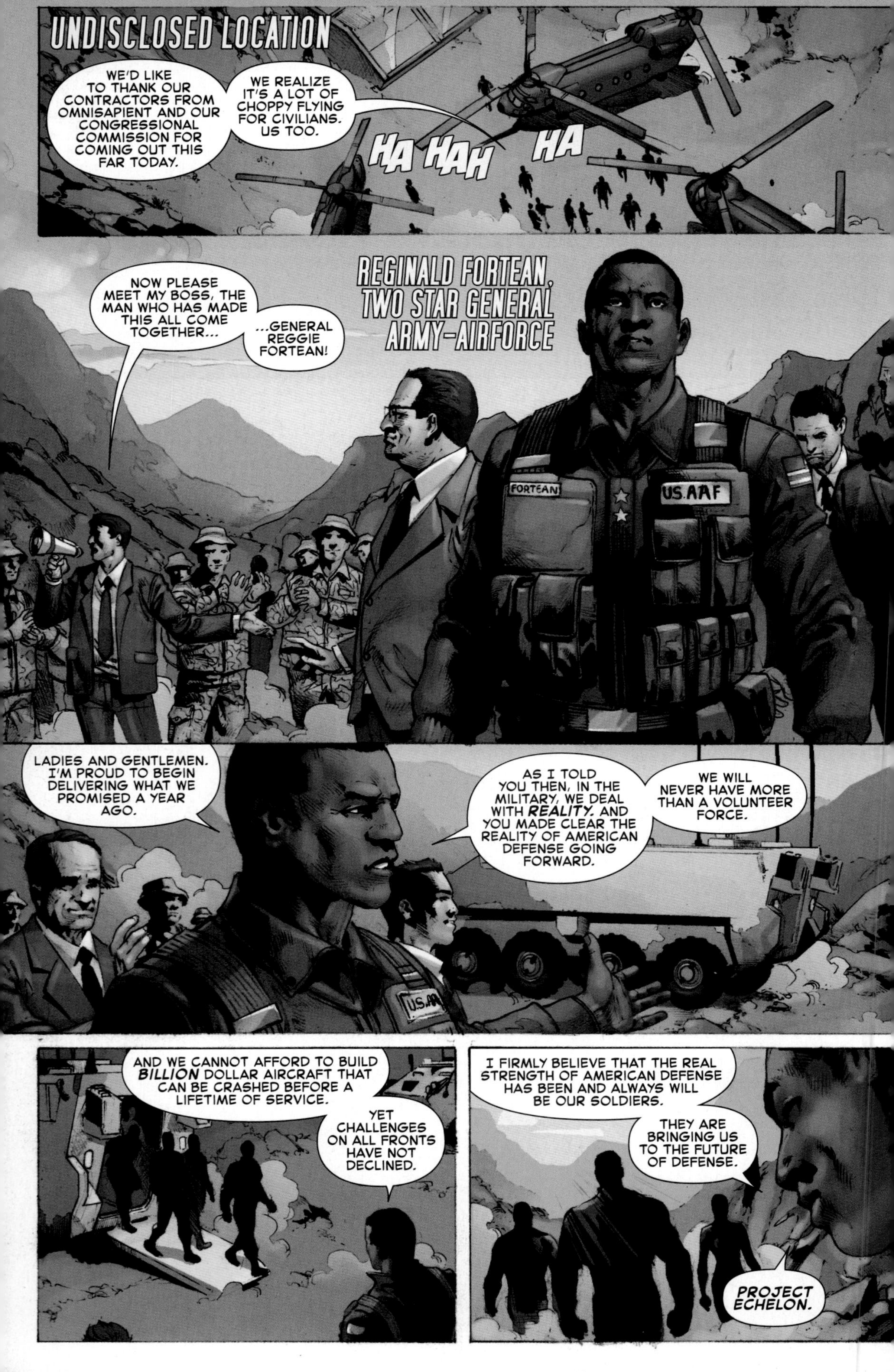
UNDISCLOSED LOCATION
WE'D LIKE TO THANK OUR CONTRACTORS FROM OMNISAPIENT AND OUR CONGRESSIONAL COMMISSION FOR COMING OUT THIS FAR TODAY.
WE REALIZE IT'S A LOT OF CHOPPY FLYING FOR CIVILIANS. US TOO.
HA HAH HA
NOW PLEASE MEET MY BOSS, THE MAN WHO HAS MADE THIS ALL COME TOGETHER...
...GENERAL REGGIE FORTEAN!
REGINALD FORTEAN, TWO STAR GENERAL ARMY-AIRFORCE
FORTEAN
US.AAF
LADIES AND GENTLEMEN. I'M PROUD TO BEGIN DELIVERING WHAT WE PROMISED A YEAR AGO.
AS I TOLD YOU THEN, IN THE MILITARY, WE DEAL WITH REALITY. AND YOU MADE CLEAR THE REALITY OF AMERICAN DEFENSE GOING FORWARD.
WE WILL NEVER HAVE MORE THAN A VOLUNTEER FORCE.
AND WE CANNOT AFFORD TO BUILD BILLION DOLLAR AIRCRAFT THAT CAN BE CRASHED BEFORE A LIFETIME OF SERVICE.
YET CHALLENGES ON ALL FRONTS HAVE NOT DECLINED.
I FIRMLY BELIEVE THAT THE REAL STRENGTH OF AMERICAN DEFENSE HAS BEEN AND ALWAYS WILL BE OUR SOLDIERS.
THEY ARE BRINGING US TO THE FUTURE OF DEFENSE.
PROJECT ECHELON.

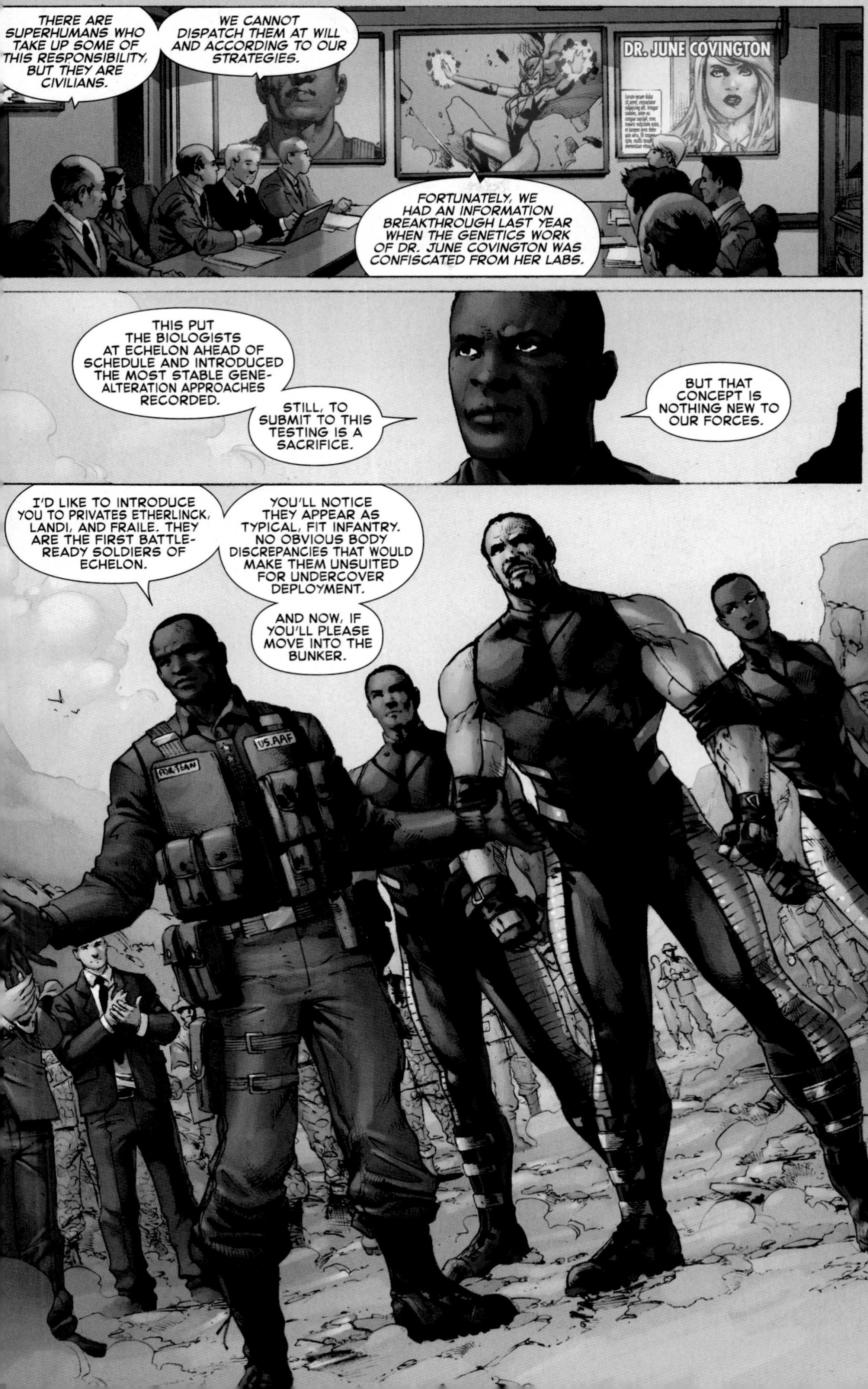
THERE ARE SUPERHUMANS WHO TAKE UP SOME OF THIS RESPONSIBILITY, BUT THEY ARE CIVILIANS.
WE CANNOT DISPATCH THEM AT WILL AND ACCORDING TO OUR STRATEGIES.
DR. JUNE COVINGTON
FORTUNATELY, WE HAD AN INFORMATION BREAKTHROUGH LAST YEAR WHEN THE GENETICS WORK OF DR. JUNE COVINGTON WAS CONFISCATED FROM HER LABS.
THIS PUT THE BIOLOGISTS AT ECHELON AHEAD OF SCHEDULE AND INTRODUCED THE MOST STABLE GENE-ALTERATION APPROACHES RECORDED.
STILL, TO SUBMIT TO THIS TESTING IS A SACRIFICE.
BUT THAT CONCEPT IS NOTHING NEW TO OUR FORCES.
I'D LIKE TO INTRODUCE YOU TO PRIVATES ETHERLINCK, LANDI, AND FRAILE. THEY ARE THE FIRST BATTLE-READY SOLDIERS OF ECHELON.
YOU'LL NOTICE THEY APPEAR AS TYPICAL, FIT INFANTRY. NO OBVIOUS BODY DISCREPANCIES THAT WOULD MAKE THEM UNSUITED FOR UNDERCOVER DEPLOYMENT.
AND NOW, IF YOU'LL PLEASE MOVE INTO THE BUNKER.
US.AAF
FORTEAN

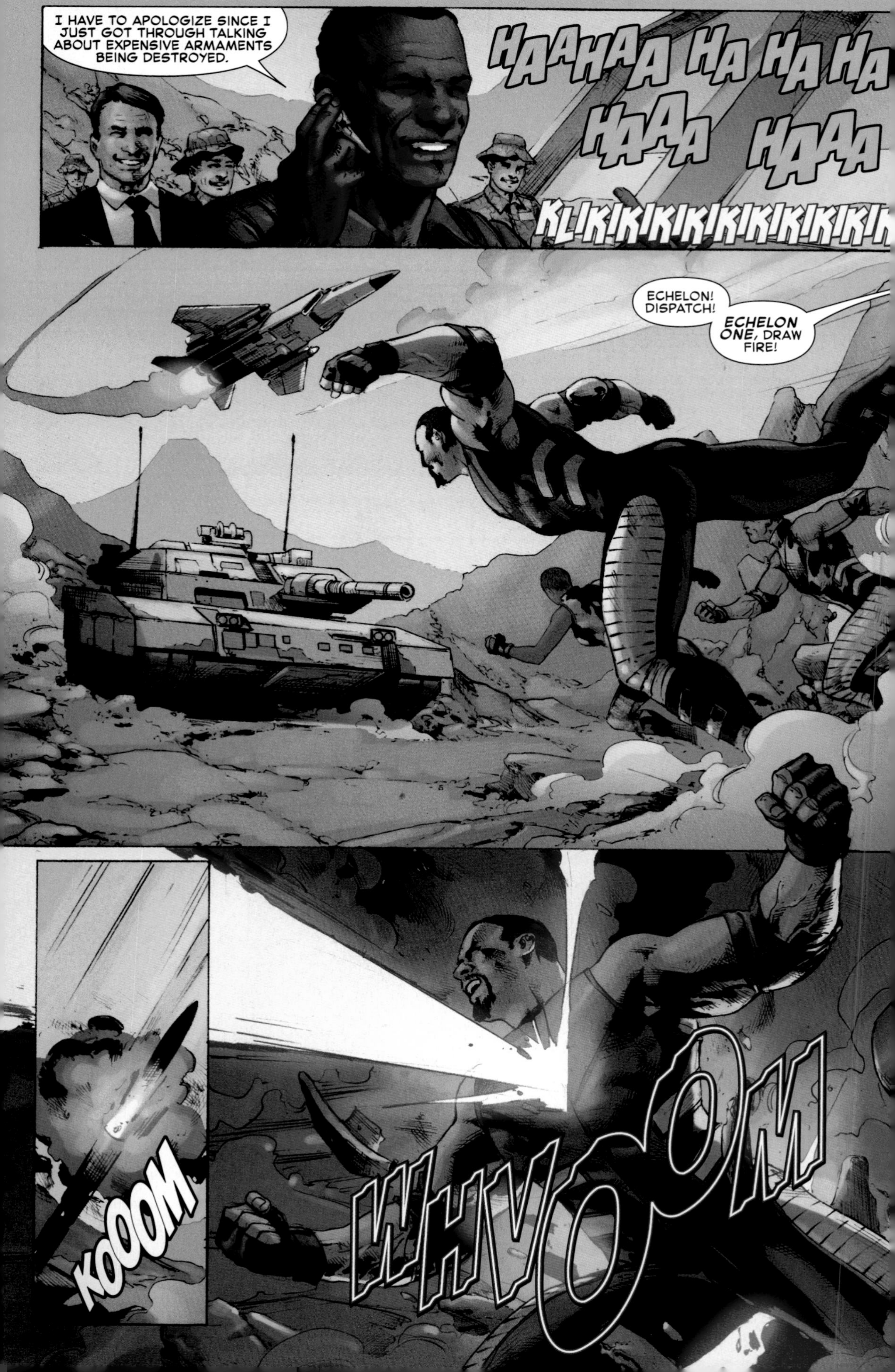
I HAVE TO APOLOGIZE SINCE I JUST GOT THROUGH TALKING ABOUT EXPENSIVE ARMAMENTS BEING DESTROYED.
HAAHAA HA HA HA
HAAAA HAAAA
KLIKIKIKIKIKIKIKIKIKIKIKIKI
ECHELON! DISPATCH!
ECHELON ONE, DRAW FIRE!
KOOOM
WHVOOOM

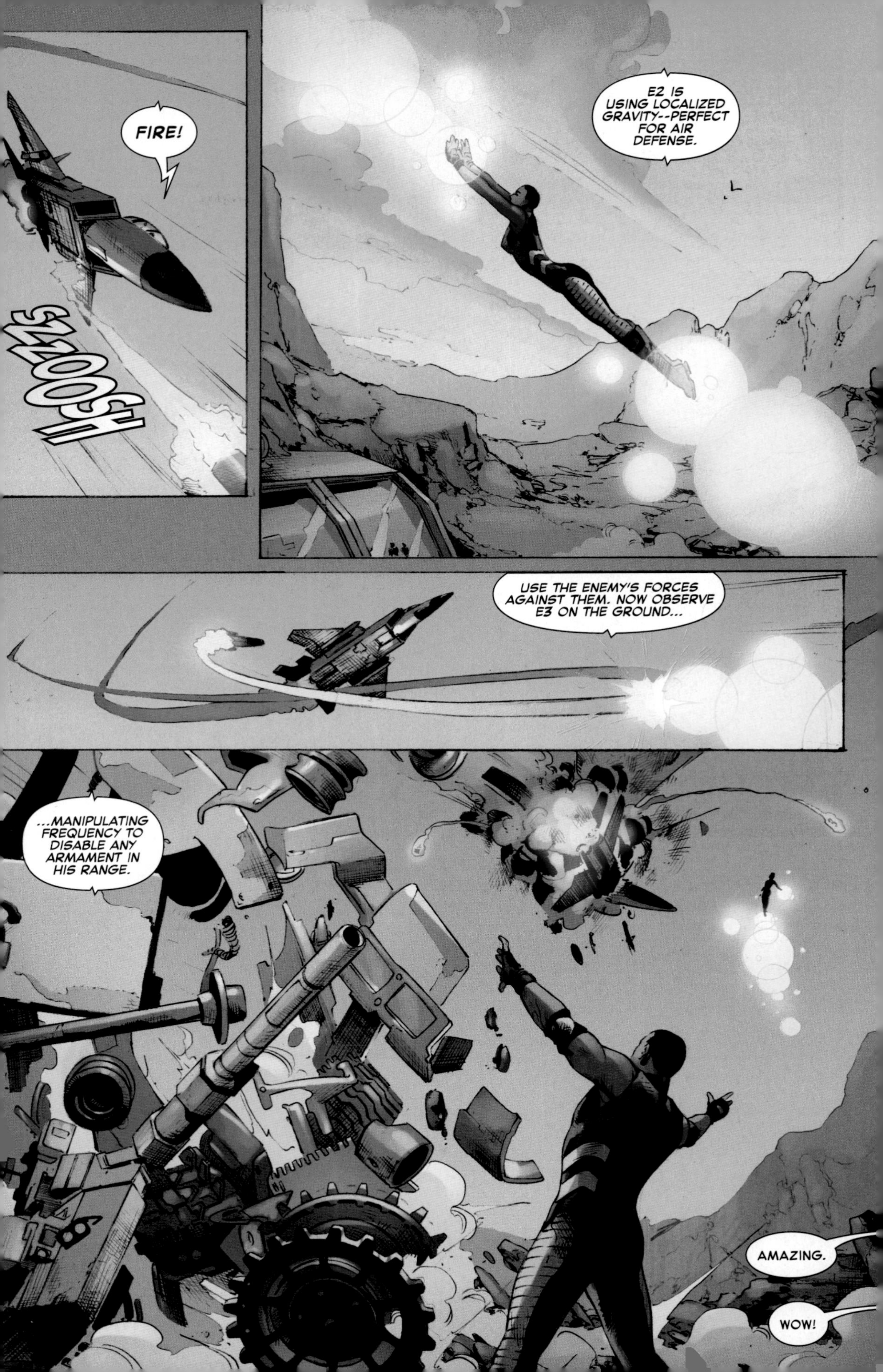

FIRE!
FWOOSH
E2 IS USING LOCALIZED GRAVITY--PERFECT FOR AIR DEFENSE.
USE THE ENEMY'S FORCES AGAINST THEM. NOW OBSERVE E3 ON THE GROUND...
...MANIPULATING FREQUENCY TO DISABLE ANY ARMAMENT IN HIS RANGE.
AMAZING.
WOW!

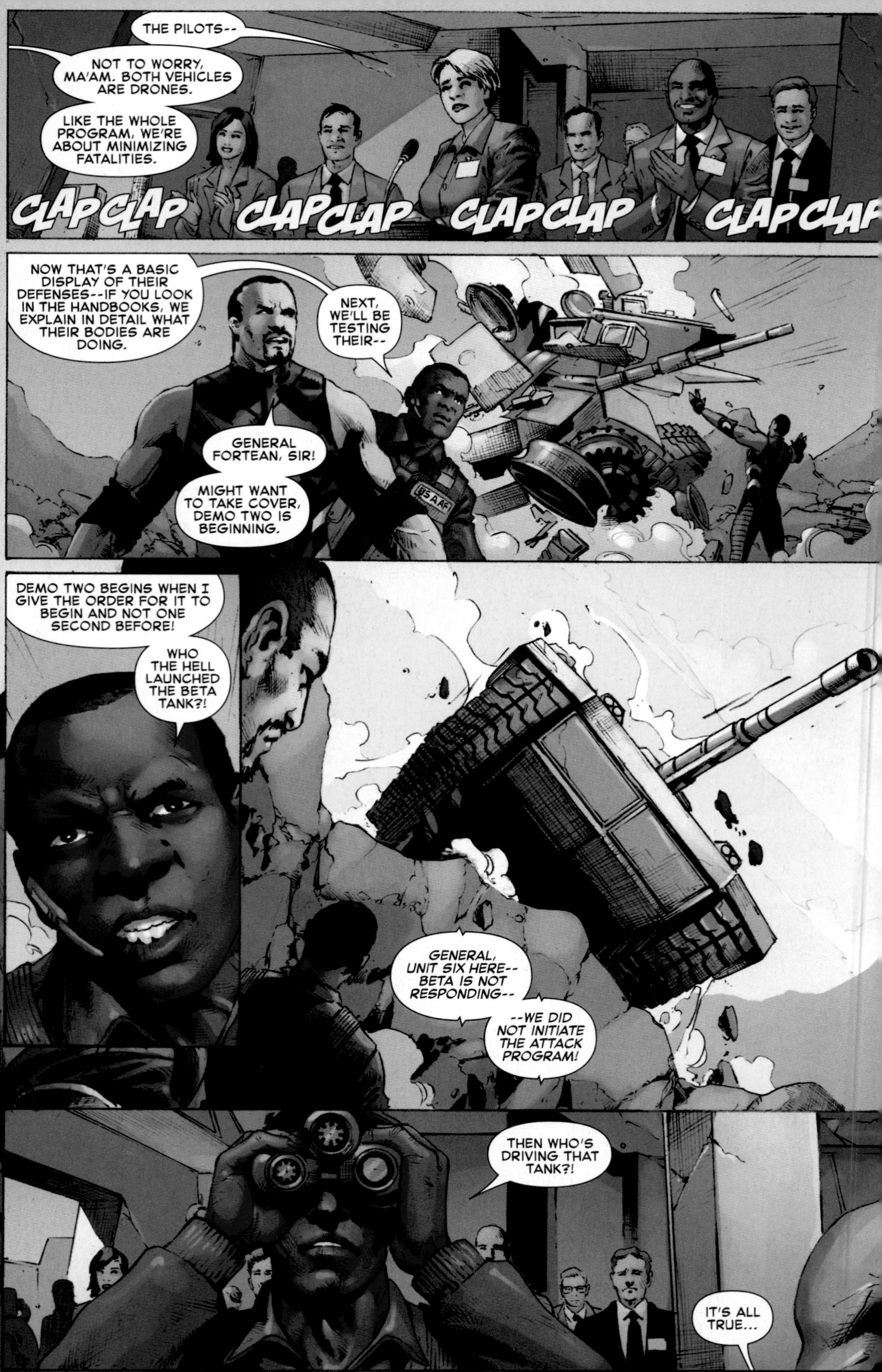
THE PILOTS--
NOT TO WORRY, MA'AM. BOTH VEHICLES ARE DRONES.
LIKE THE WHOLE PROGRAM, WE'RE ABOUT MINIMIZING FATALITIES.
CLAP CLAP CLAP CLAP CLAP CLAP CLAP CLAP
NOW THAT'S A BASIC DISPLAY OF THEIR DEFENSES--IF YOU LOOK IN THE HANDBOOKS, WE EXPLAIN IN DETAIL WHAT THEIR BODIES ARE DOING.
NEXT, WE'LL BE TESTING THEIR--
GENERAL FORTEAN, SIR!
MIGHT WANT TO TAKE COVER, DEMO TWO IS BEGINNING.
USAAF
DEMO TWO BEGINS WHEN I GIVE THE ORDER FOR IT TO BEGIN AND NOT ONE SECOND BEFORE!
WHO THE HELL LAUNCHED THE BETA TANK?!
GENERAL, UNIT SIX HERE-- BETA IS NOT RESPONDING--
--WE DID NOT INITIATE THE ATTACK PROGRAM!
THEN WHO'S DRIVING THAT TANK?!
IT'S ALL TRUE...

...YOU'RE REALLY DOING IT.
EVEN GENERAL ROSS RESISTED MEDDLING WITH HUMANITY TO WIN THE ARMS RACE. BUT YOU'VE GONE TOO FAR. NOW YOU'RE TAKING THE STEPS TO ERASE YOURSELVES FROM THE PLANET.
YOU WANT TO SEE WHAT SUPERHUMAN IS?
SUPERHUMAN IS HULK!
HELL HATH NO FURY

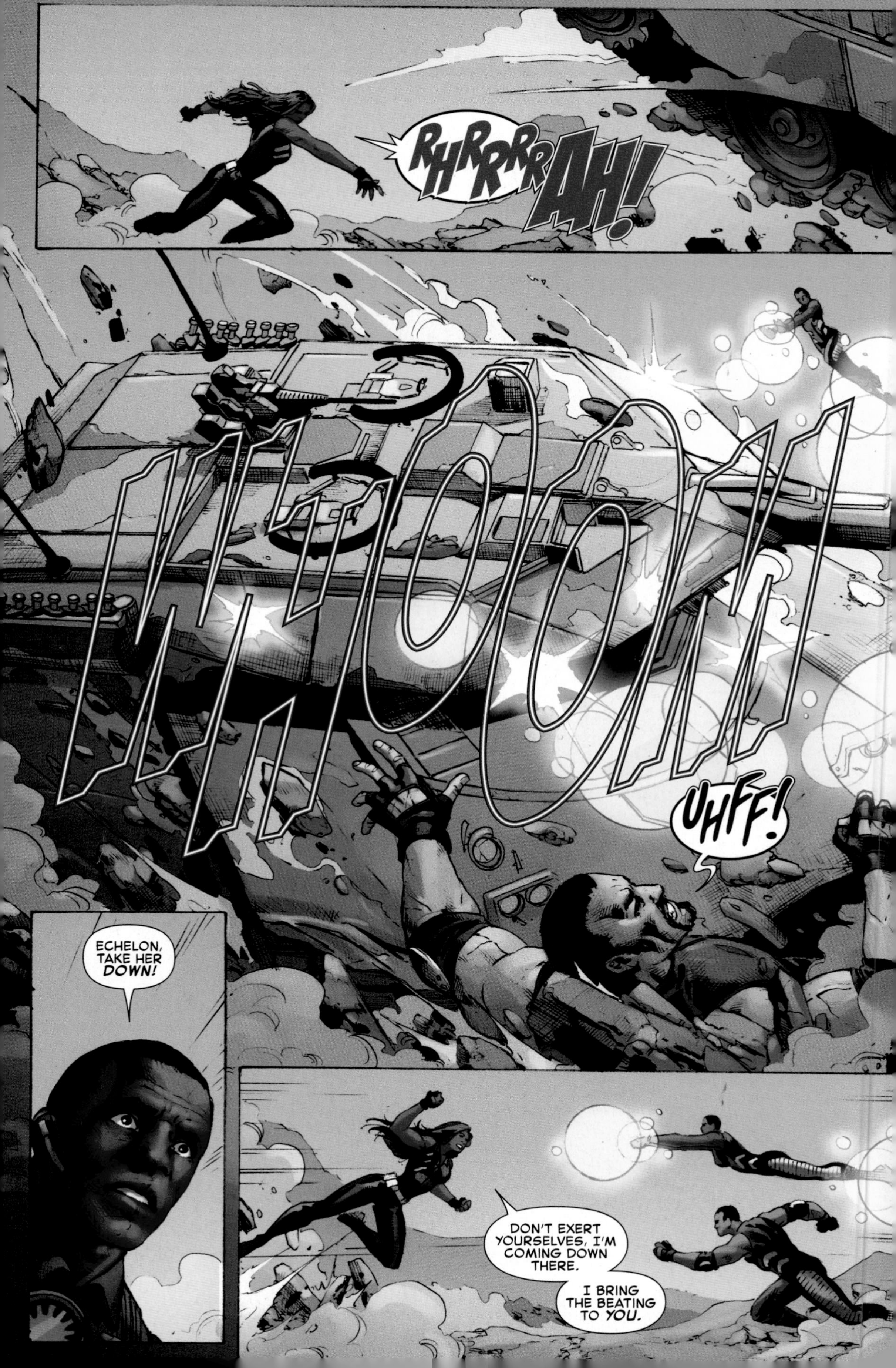
RHRRRRAH!
WHOOOM
UHFF!
ECHELON, TAKE HER DOWN!
DON'T EXERT YOURSELVES, I'M COMING DOWN THERE.
I BRING THE BEATING TO YOU.

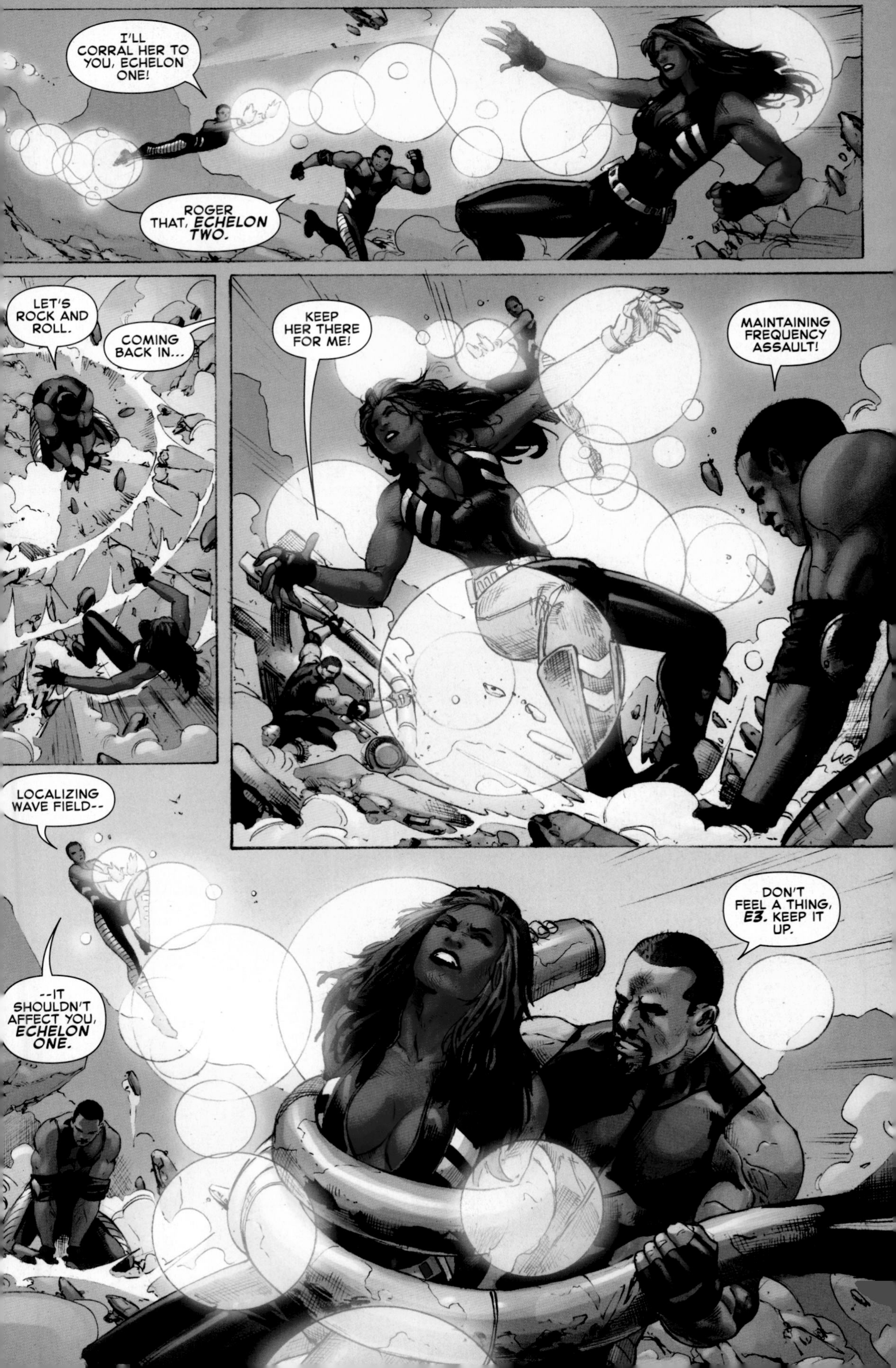
I'LL CORRAL HER TO YOU, ECHELON ONE!
ROGER THAT, *ECHELON TWO.*
LET'S ROCK AND ROLL.
COMING BACK IN...
KEEP HER THERE FOR ME!
MAINTAINING FREQUENCY ASSAULT!
LOCALIZING WAVE FIELD--
--IT SHOULDN'T AFFECT YOU, *ECHELON ONE.*
DON'T FEEL A THING, *E3.* KEEP IT UP.

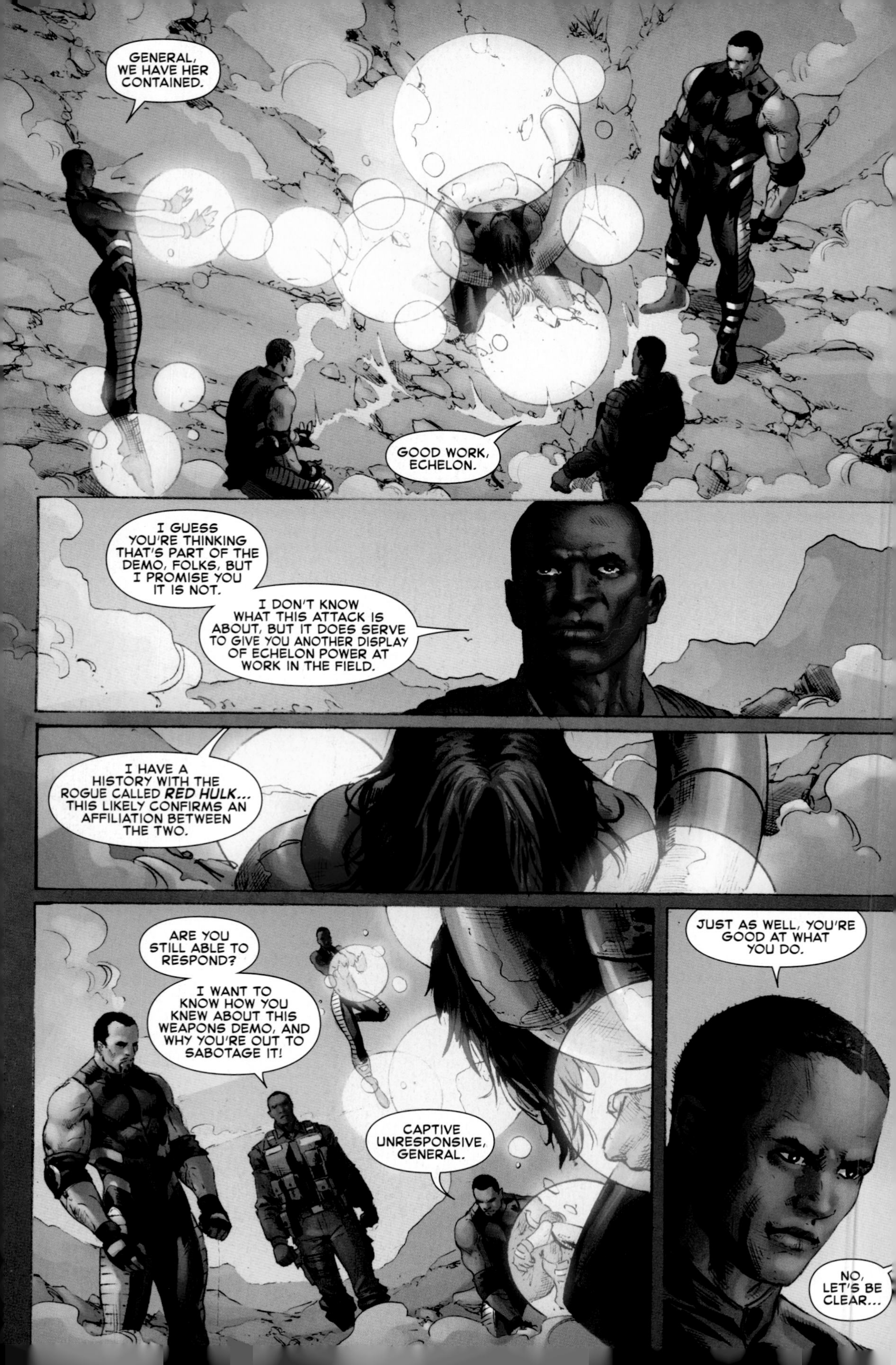
GENERAL, WE HAVE HER CONTAINED.
GOOD WORK, ECHELON.
I GUESS YOU'RE THINKING THAT'S PART OF THE DEMO, FOLKS, BUT I PROMISE YOU IT IS NOT.
I DON'T KNOW WHAT THIS ATTACK IS ABOUT, BUT IT DOES SERVE TO GIVE YOU ANOTHER DISPLAY OF ECHELON POWER AT WORK IN THE FIELD.
I HAVE A HISTORY WITH THE ROGUE CALLED RED HULK... THIS LIKELY CONFIRMS AN AFFILIATION BETWEEN THE TWO.
ARE YOU STILL ABLE TO RESPOND?
I WANT TO KNOW HOW YOU KNEW ABOUT THIS WEAPONS DEMO, AND WHY YOU'RE OUT TO SABOTAGE IT!
CAPTIVE UNRESPONSIVE, GENERAL.
JUST AS WELL, YOU'RE GOOD AT WHAT YOU DO.
NO, LET'S BE CLEAR...

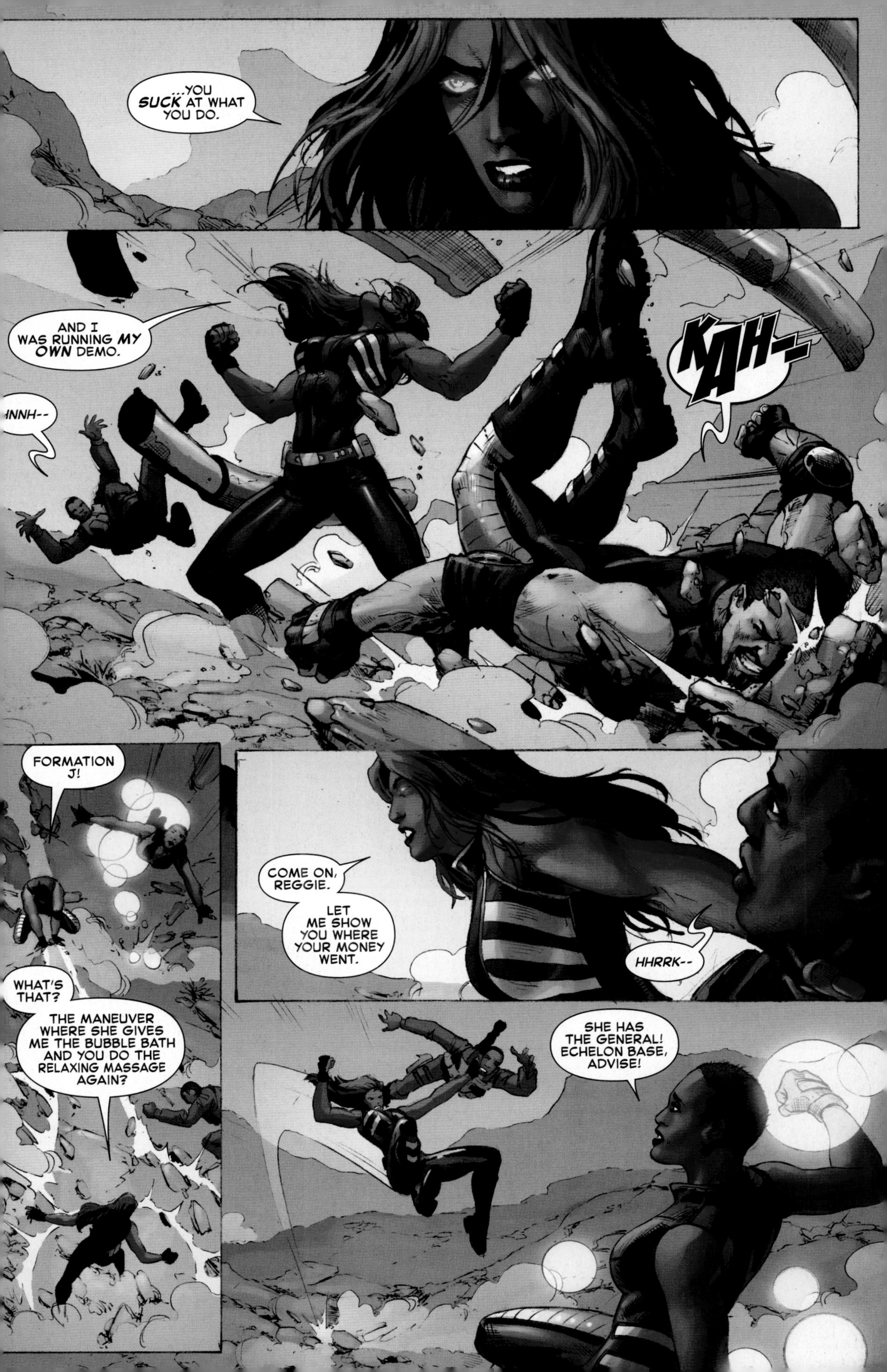
...YOU SUCK AT WHAT YOU DO.
AND I WAS RUNNING MY OWN DEMO.
HNNH--
KAH--
FORMATION J!
COME ON, REGGIE.
LET ME SHOW YOU WHERE YOUR MONEY WENT.
HHRRK--
WHAT'S THAT?
THE MANEUVER WHERE SHE GIVES ME THE BUBBLE BATH AND YOU DO THE RELAXING MASSAGE AGAIN?
SHE HAS THE GENERAL! ECHELON BASE, ADVISE!

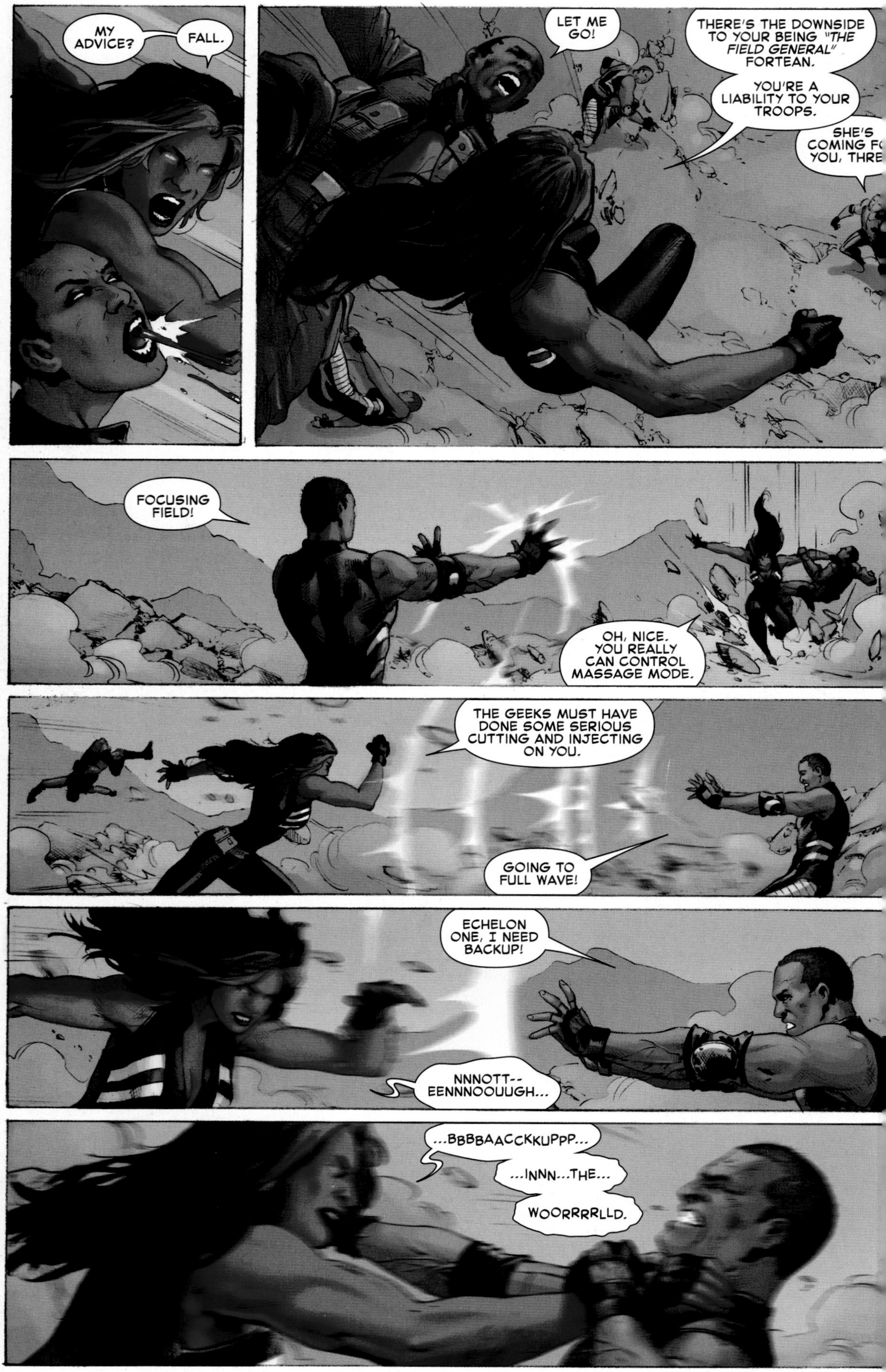
MY ADVICE?
FALL.
LET ME GO!
THERE'S THE DOWNSIDE TO YOUR BEING "THE FIELD GENERAL" FORTEAN.
YOU'RE A LIABILITY TO YOUR TROOPS.
SHE'S COMING F
YOU, THRE
FOCUSING FIELD!
OH, NICE. YOU REALLY CAN CONTROL MASSAGE MODE.
THE GEEKS MUST HAVE DONE SOME SERIOUS CUTTING AND INJECTING ON YOU.
GOING TO FULL WAVE!
ECHELON ONE, I NEED BACKUP!
NNNOTT-- EENNNOOUUGH...
...BBBBAACCKKUPPP...
...INNN...THE...
WOORRRRLLD.

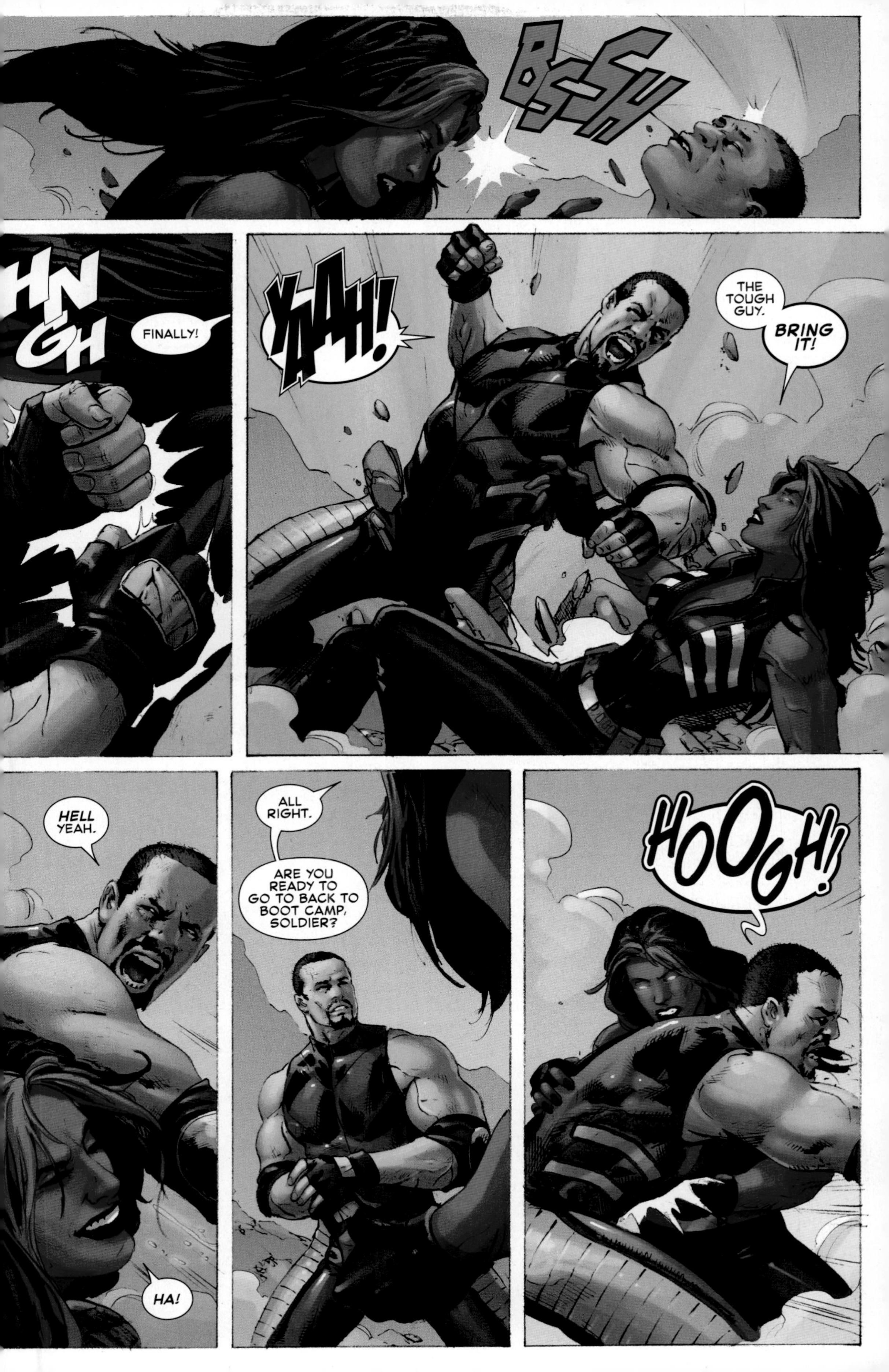
BSSH
HNGH
FINALLY!
YAAAH!
THE TOUGH GUY.
BRING IT!
HELL YEAH.
HA!
ALL RIGHT.
ARE YOU READY TO GO TO BACK TO BOOT CAMP, SOLDIER?
HOOGH!

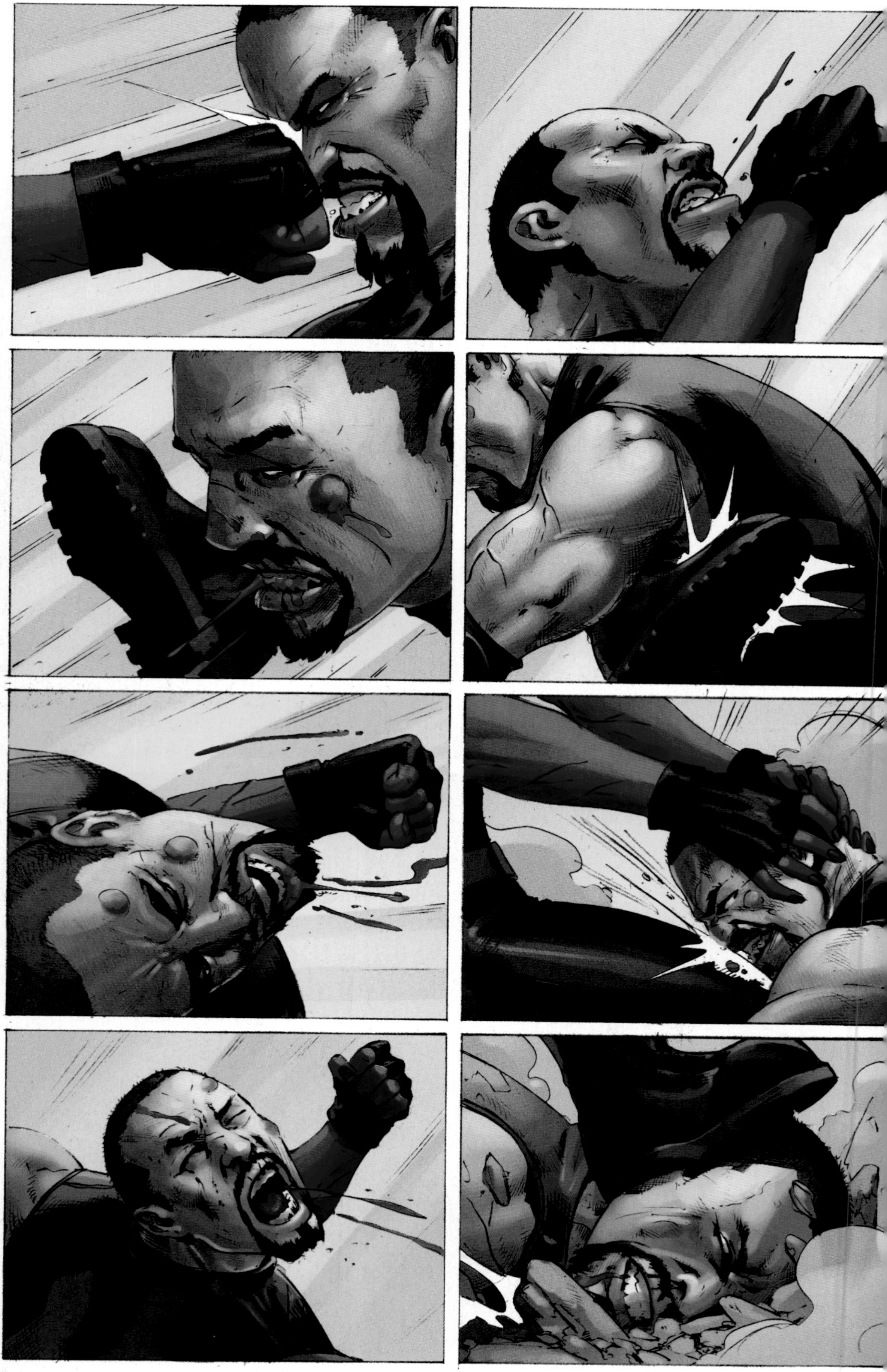

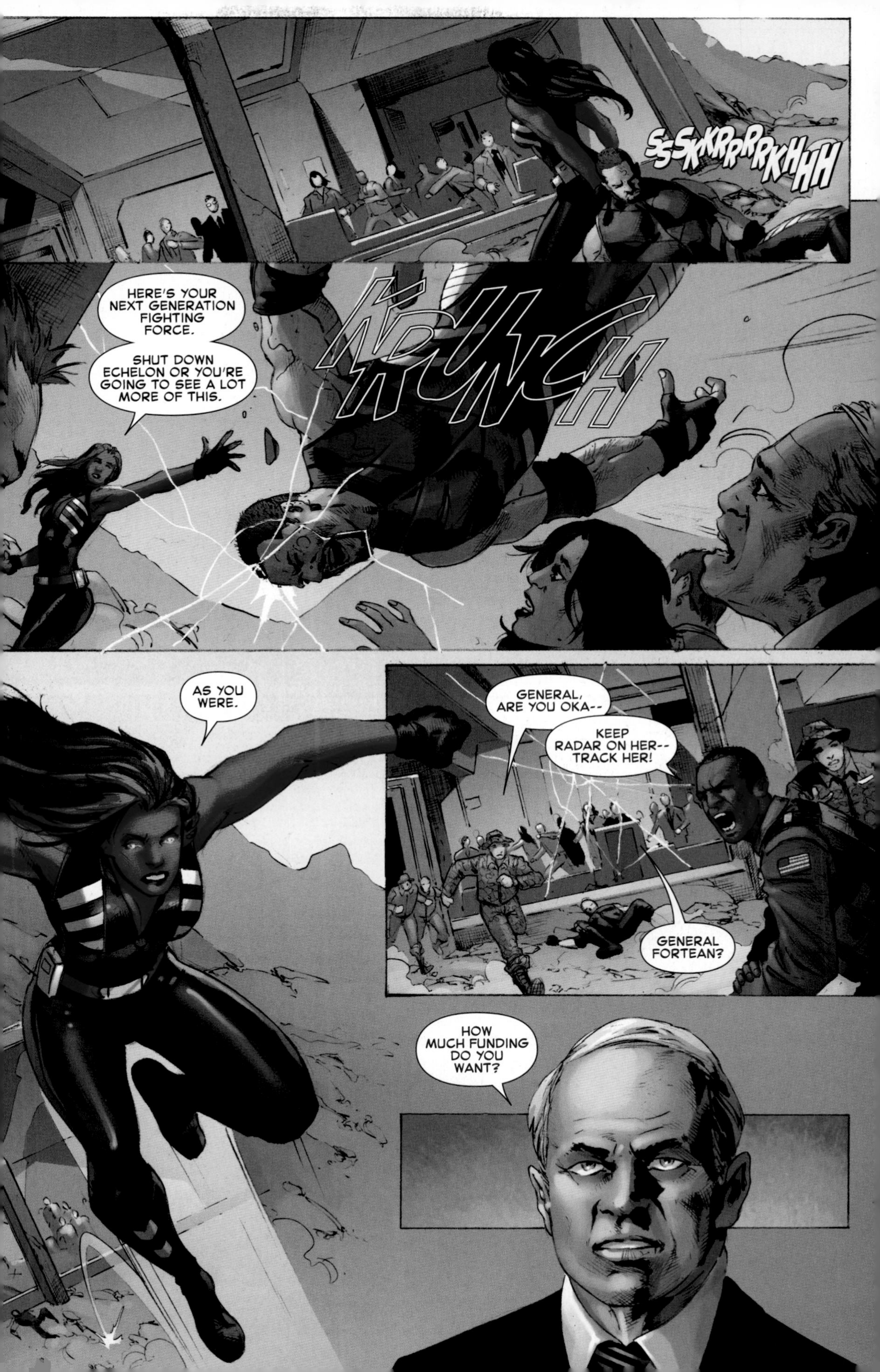
SSSKKRRRRKHHH
HERE'S YOUR NEXT GENERATION FIGHTING FORCE.
SHUT DOWN ECHELON OR YOU'RE GOING TO SEE A LOT MORE OF THIS.
KRUNCH
AS YOU WERE.
GENERAL, ARE YOU OKA--
KEEP RADAR ON HER-- TRACK HER!
GENERAL FORTEAN?
HOW MUCH FUNDING DO YOU WANT?

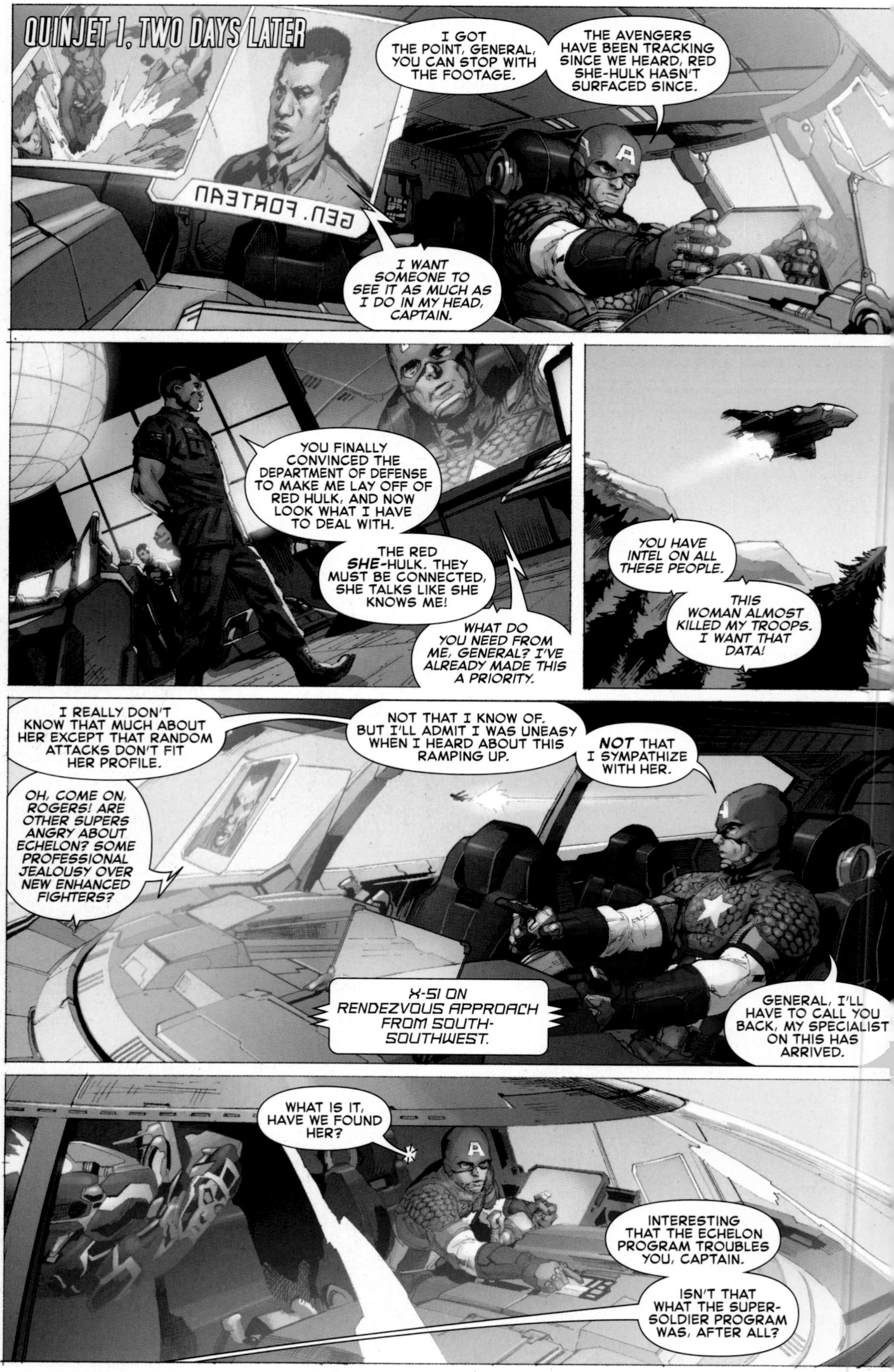
QUINJET 1, TWO DAYS LATER
I GOT THE POINT, GENERAL, YOU CAN STOP WITH THE FOOTAGE.
THE AVENGERS HAVE BEEN TRACKING SINCE WE HEARD, RED SHE-HULK HASN'T SURFACED SINCE.
GEN. FORTEAN
I WANT SOMEONE TO SEE IT AS MUCH AS I DO IN MY HEAD, CAPTAIN.
YOU FINALLY CONVINCED THE DEPARTMENT OF DEFENSE TO MAKE ME LAY OFF OF RED HULK, AND NOW LOOK WHAT I HAVE TO DEAL WITH.
THE RED SHE-HULK. THEY MUST BE CONNECTED, SHE TALKS LIKE SHE KNOWS ME!
WHAT DO YOU NEED FROM ME, GENERAL? I'VE ALREADY MADE THIS A PRIORITY.
YOU HAVE INTEL ON ALL THESE PEOPLE.
THIS WOMAN ALMOST KILLED MY TROOPS. I WANT THAT DATA!
I REALLY DON'T KNOW THAT MUCH ABOUT HER EXCEPT THAT RANDOM ATTACKS DON'T FIT HER PROFILE.
OH, COME ON, ROGERS! ARE OTHER SUPERS ANGRY ABOUT ECHELON? SOME PROFESSIONAL JEALOUSY OVER NEW ENHANCED FIGHTERS?
NOT THAT I KNOW OF. BUT I'LL ADMIT I WAS UNEASY WHEN I HEARD ABOUT THIS RAMPING UP.
NOT THAT I SYMPATHIZE WITH HER.
X-51 ON RENDEZVOUS APPROACH FROM SOUTH-SOUTHWEST.
GENERAL, I'LL HAVE TO CALL YOU BACK, MY SPECIALIST ON THIS HAS ARRIVED.
WHAT IS IT, HAVE WE FOUND HER?
INTERESTING THAT THE ECHELON PROGRAM TROUBLES YOU, CAPTAIN.
ISN'T THAT WHAT THE SUPER-SOLDIER PROGRAM WAS, AFTER ALL?

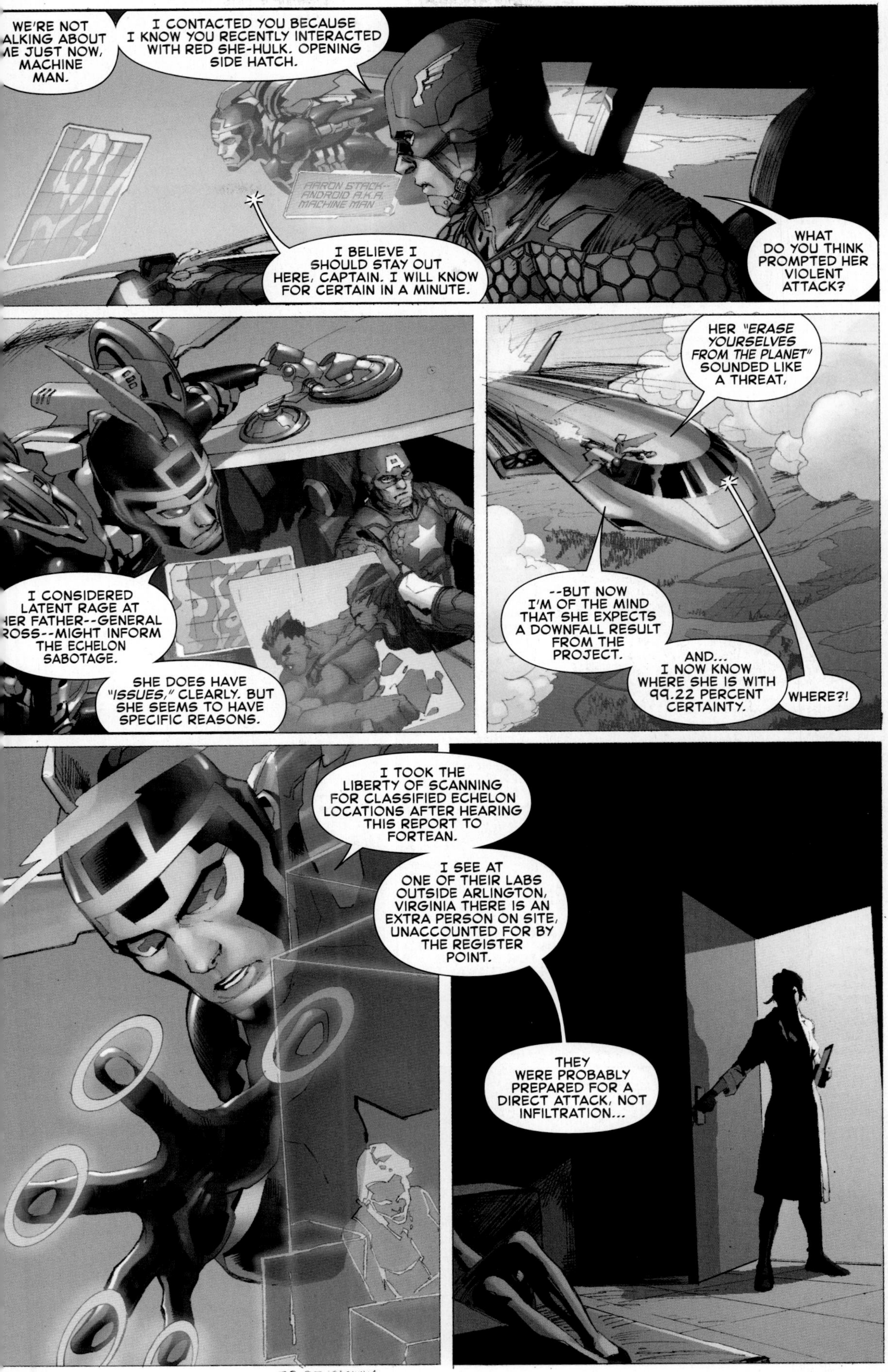
WE'RE NOT ALKING ABOUT ME JUST NOW, MACHINE MAN.
I CONTACTED YOU BECAUSE I KNOW YOU RECENTLY INTERACTED WITH RED SHE-HULK. OPENING SIDE HATCH.
AARON STACK-- ANDROID A.K.A. MACHINE MAN
I BELIEVE I SHOULD STAY OUT HERE, CAPTAIN. I WILL KNOW FOR CERTAIN IN A MINUTE.
WHAT DO YOU THINK PROMPTED HER VIOLENT ATTACK?
I CONSIDERED LATENT RAGE AT HER FATHER--GENERAL ROSS--MIGHT INFORM THE ECHELON SABOTAGE.
SHE DOES HAVE "ISSUES," CLEARLY. BUT SHE SEEMS TO HAVE SPECIFIC REASONS.
HER "ERASE YOURSELVES FROM THE PLANET" SOUNDED LIKE A THREAT,
--BUT NOW I'M OF THE MIND THAT SHE EXPECTS A DOWNFALL RESULT FROM THE PROJECT.
AND... I NOW KNOW WHERE SHE IS WITH 99.22 PERCENT CERTAINTY.
WHERE?!
I TOOK THE LIBERTY OF SCANNING FOR CLASSIFIED ECHELON LOCATIONS AFTER HEARING THIS REPORT TO FORTEAN.
I SEE AT ONE OF THEIR LABS OUTSIDE ARLINGTON, VIRGINIA THERE IS AN EXTRA PERSON ON SITE, UNACCOUNTED FOR BY THE REGISTER POINT.
THEY WERE PROBABLY PREPARED FOR A DIRECT ATTACK, NOT INFILTRATION...

PLS PUT GLOWING PERSPECTIVE GRID LINES

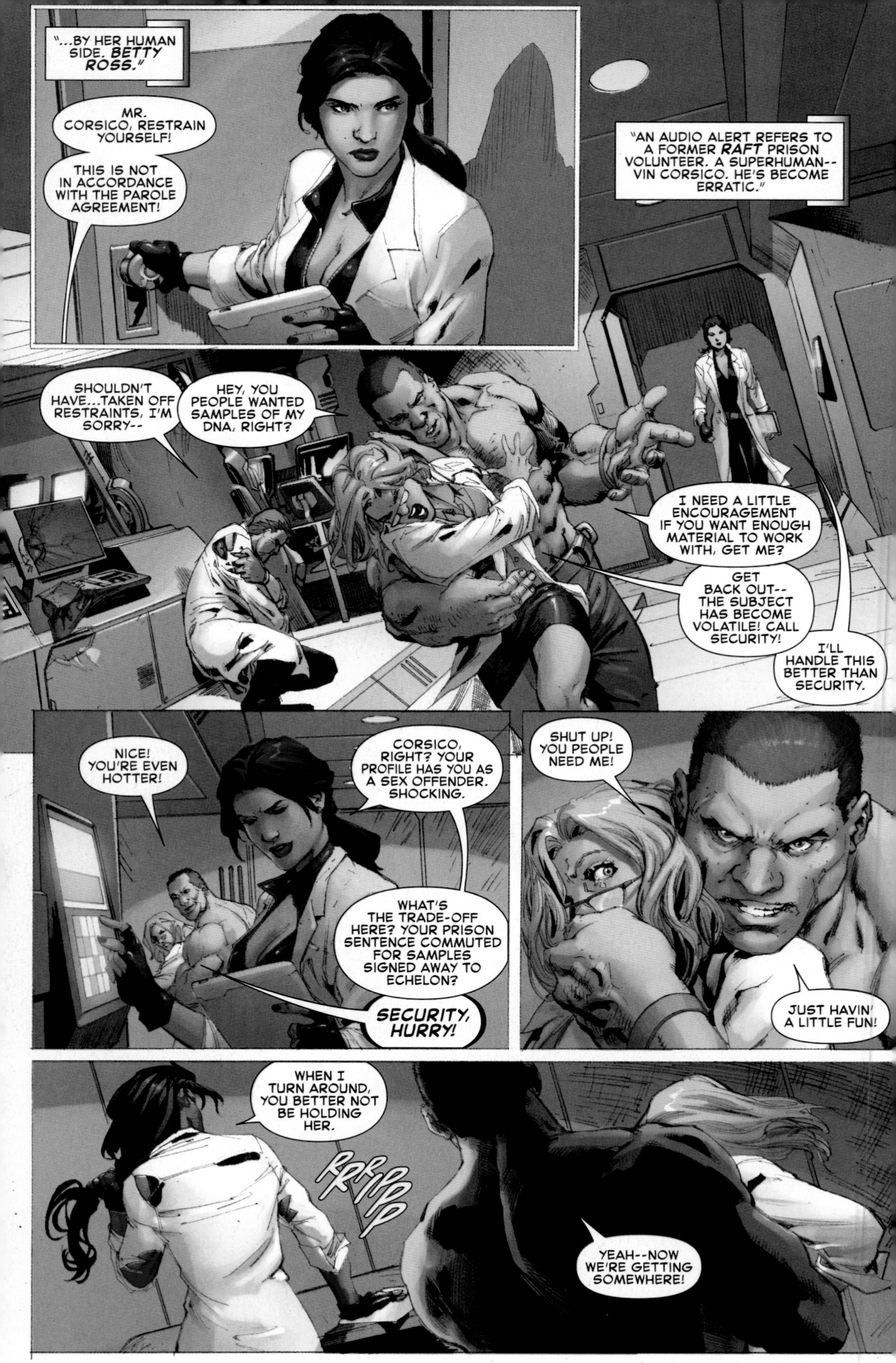
"...BY HER HUMAN SIDE. BETTY ROSS."
MR. CORSICO, RESTRAIN YOURSELF!
THIS IS NOT IN ACCORDANCE WITH THE PAROLE AGREEMENT!
"AN AUDIO ALERT REFERS TO A FORMER RAFT PRISON VOLUNTEER. A SUPERHUMAN--VIN CORSICO. HE'S BECOME ERRATIC."
SHOULDN'T HAVE...TAKEN OFF RESTRAINTS, I'M SORRY--
HEY, YOU PEOPLE WANTED SAMPLES OF MY DNA, RIGHT?
I NEED A LITTLE ENCOURAGEMENT IF YOU WANT ENOUGH MATERIAL TO WORK WITH, GET ME?
GET BACK OUT--THE SUBJECT HAS BECOME VOLATILE! CALL SECURITY!
I'LL HANDLE THIS BETTER THAN SECURITY.
NICE! YOU'RE EVEN HOTTER!
CORSICO, RIGHT? YOUR PROFILE HAS YOU AS A SEX OFFENDER. SHOCKING.
WHAT'S THE TRADE-OFF HERE? YOUR PRISON SENTENCE COMMUTED FOR SAMPLES SIGNED AWAY TO ECHELON?
SECURITY, HURRY!
SHUT UP! YOU PEOPLE NEED ME!
JUST HAVIN' A LITTLE FUN!
WHEN I TURN AROUND, YOU BETTER NOT BE HOLDING HER.
RRRIPPP
YEAH--NOW WE'RE GETTING SOMEWHERE!

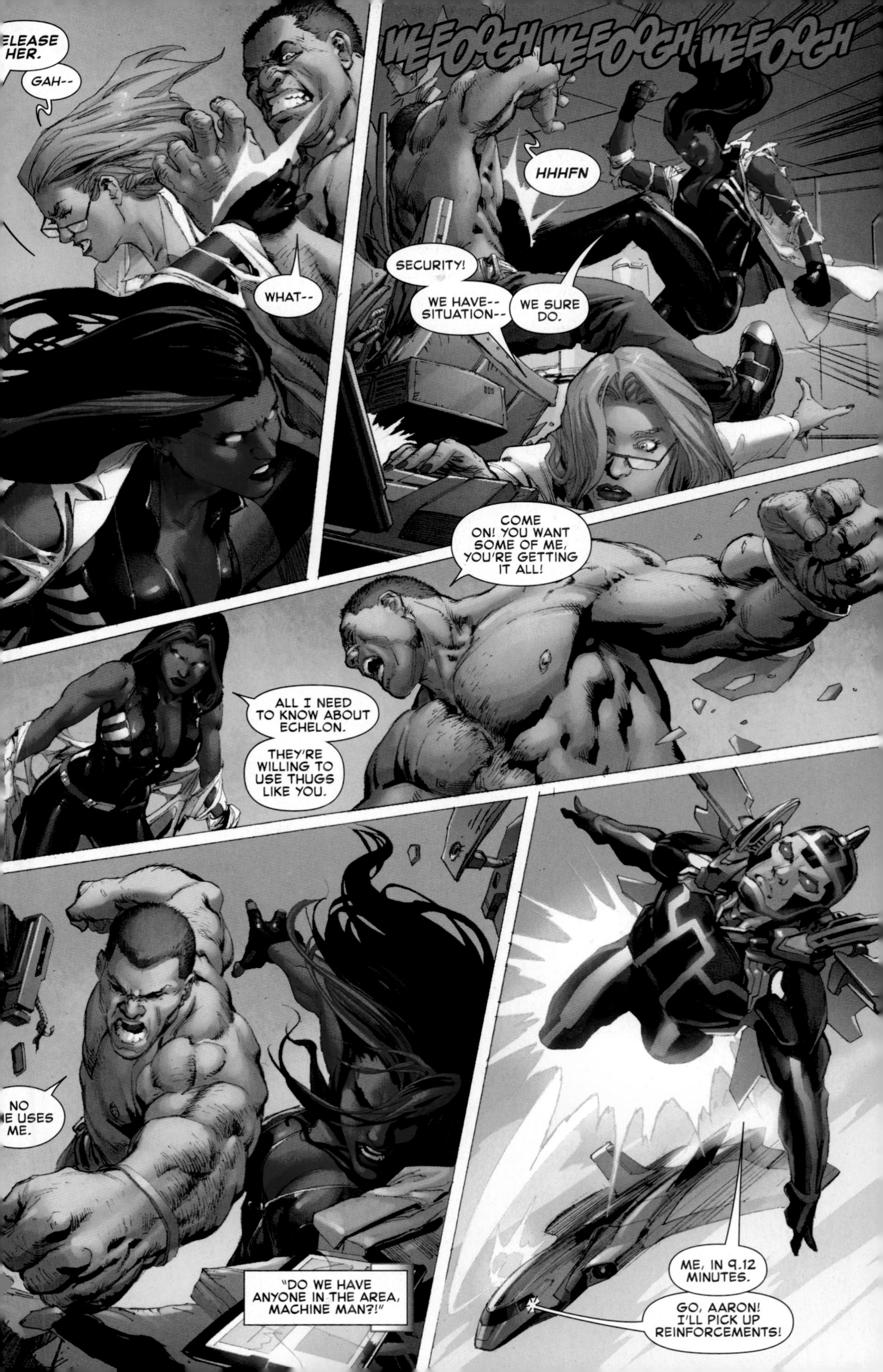
ELEASE HER.
GAH--
WHAT--
WEEOOGH WEEOOGH WEEOOGH
HHHFN
SECURITY!
WE HAVE-- SITUATION--
WE SURE DO.
COME ON! YOU WANT SOME OF ME, YOU'RE GETTING IT ALL!
ALL I NEED TO KNOW ABOUT ECHELON.
THEY'RE WILLING TO USE THUGS LIKE YOU.
NO E USES ME.
"DO WE HAVE ANYONE IN THE AREA, MACHINE MAN?!"
ME, IN 9.12 MINUTES.
GO, AARON! I'LL PICK UP REINFORCEMENTS!

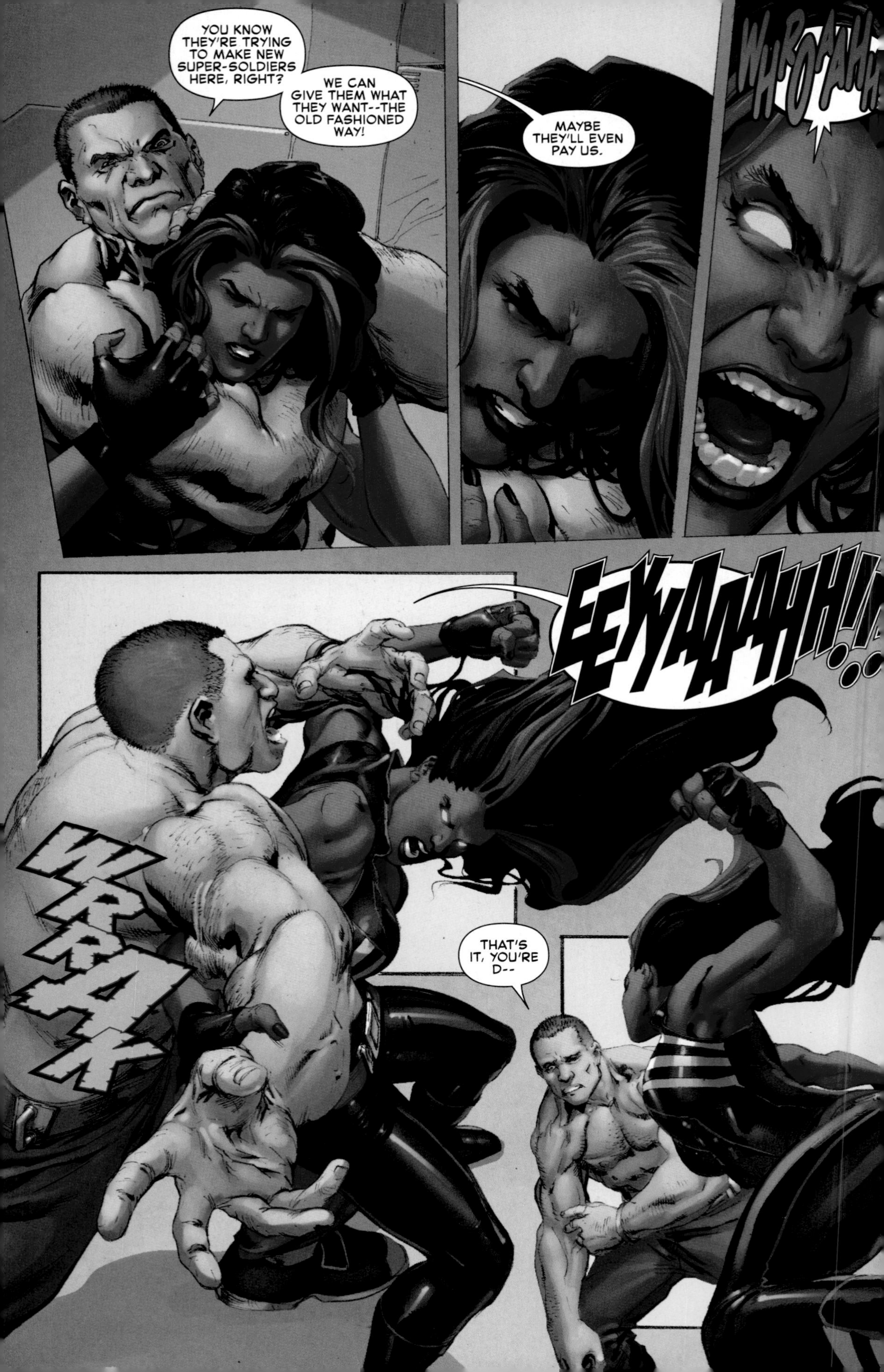
YOU KNOW THEY'RE TRYING TO MAKE NEW SUPER-SOLDIERS HERE, RIGHT?
WE CAN GIVE THEM WHAT THEY WANT--THE OLD FASHIONED WAY!
MAYBE THEY'LL EVEN PAY US.
WHOAHH
EEYAAAHH!!
WRAK
THAT'S IT, YOU'RE D--

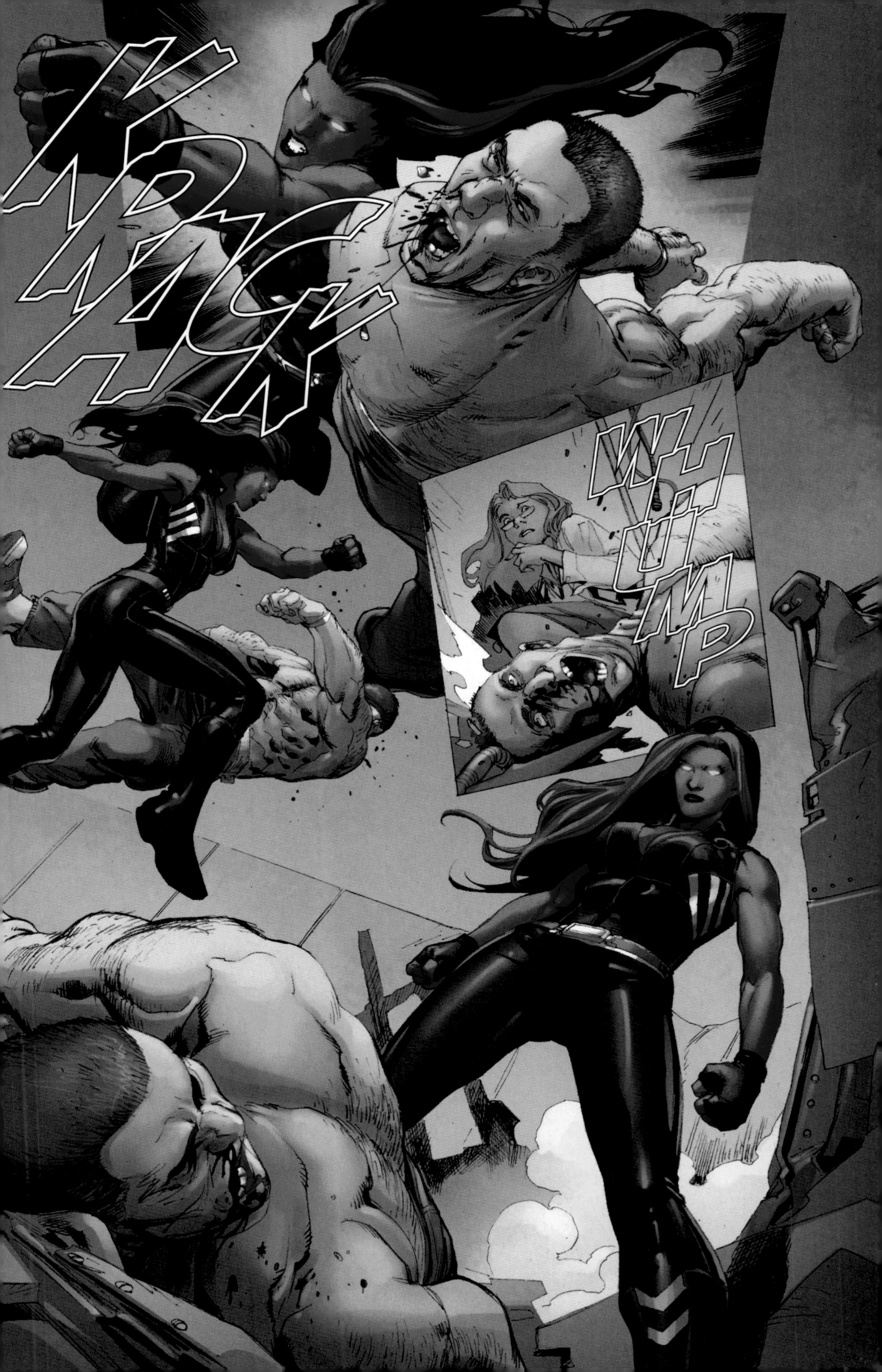
WHUMP

RED SHE-HULK
BY THE AUTHORITY OF THE AVENGERS...
...YOU ARE UNDER ARREST FOR MURDER!
A FUGITIVE... FOREVER?

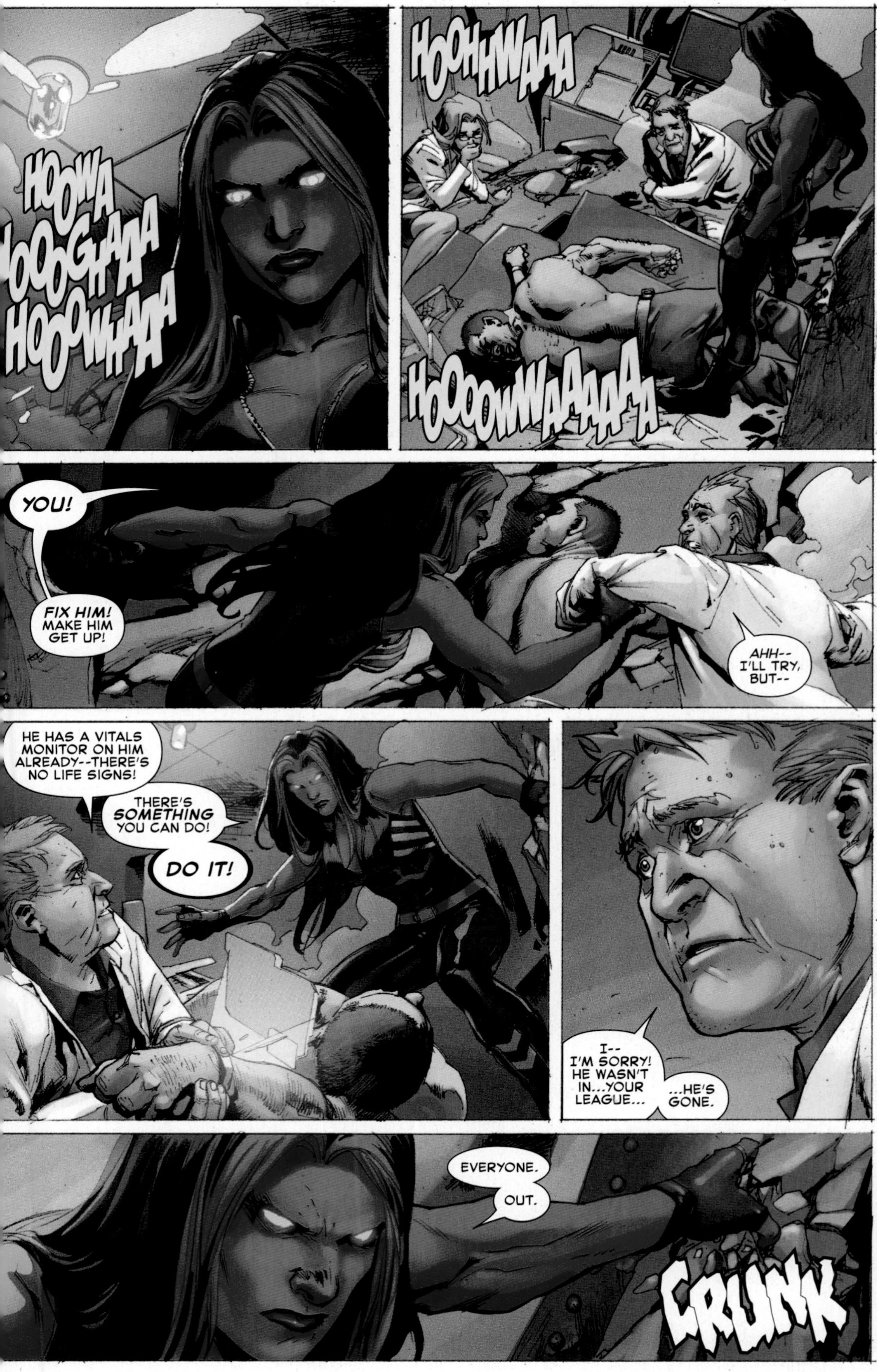
HOOWA
HOOOGHAAA
HOOOWHAAA
HOOHHWAAA
HOOOOWWAAAAAA
YOU!
FIX HIM! MAKE HIM GET UP!
AHH-- I'LL TRY, BUT--
HE HAS A VITALS MONITOR ON HIM ALREADY--THERE'S NO LIFE SIGNS!
THERE'S SOMETHING YOU CAN DO!
DO IT!
I-- I'M SORRY! HE WASN'T IN...YOUR LEAGUE...
...HE'S GONE.
EVERYONE.
OUT.
CRUNK

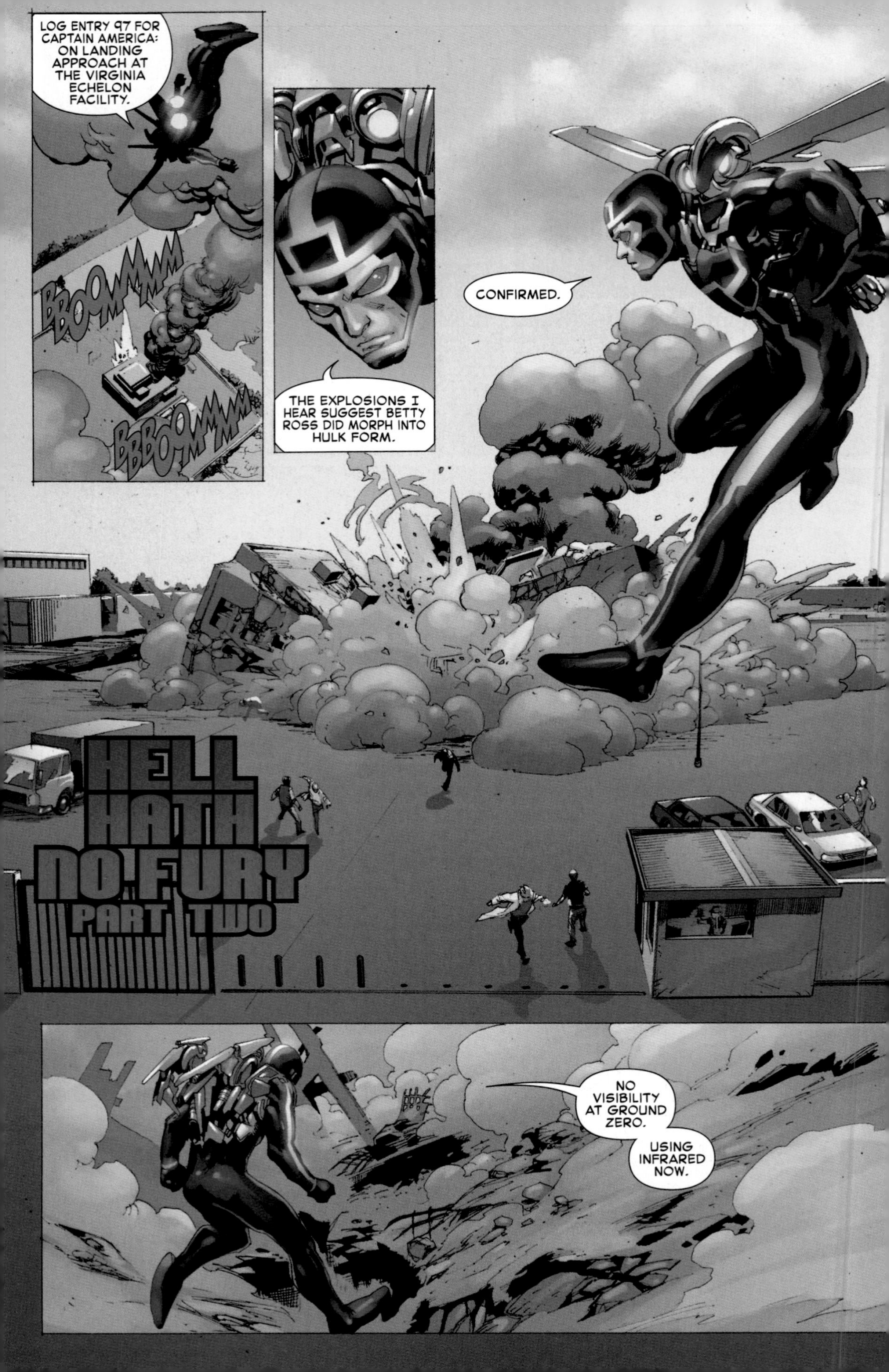
LOG ENTRY 97 FOR CAPTAIN AMERICA: ON LANDING APPROACH AT THE VIRGINIA ECHELON FACILITY.
BBOOMMMMM
BBBOOMMMMM
THE EXPLOSIONS I HEAR SUGGEST BETTY ROSS DID MORPH INTO HULK FORM.
CONFIRMED.
HELL HATH NO FURY
PART TWO
NO VISIBILITY AT GROUND ZERO.
USING INFRARED NOW.

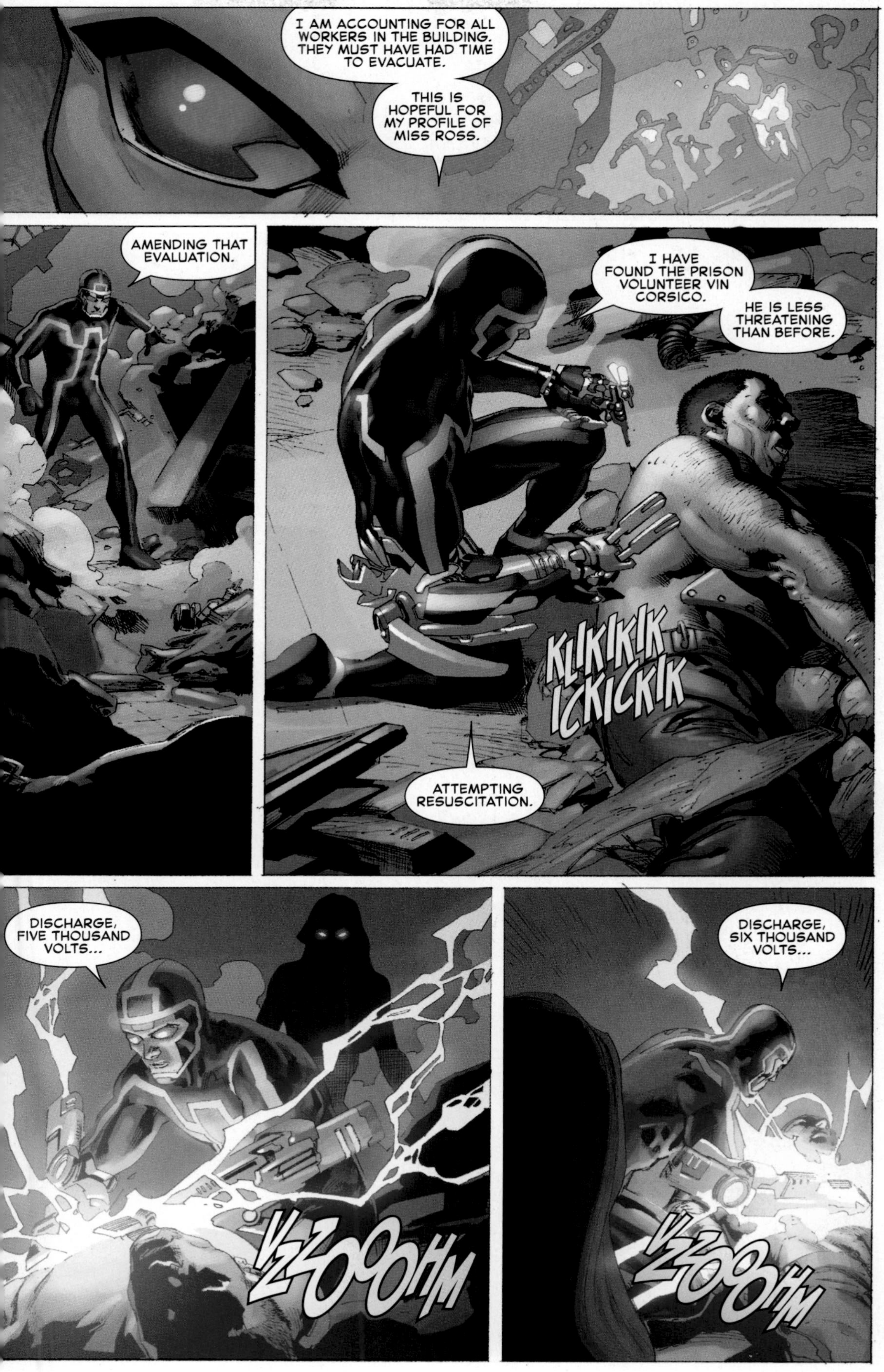
I AM ACCOUNTING FOR ALL WORKERS IN THE BUILDING. THEY MUST HAVE HAD TIME TO EVACUATE.
THIS IS HOPEFUL FOR MY PROFILE OF MISS ROSS.
AMENDING THAT EVALUATION.
I HAVE FOUND THE PRISON VOLUNTEER VIN CORSICO.
HE IS LESS THREATENING THAN BEFORE.
KLIKIKIK ICKICKIK
ATTEMPTING RESUSCITATION.
DISCHARGE, FIVE THOUSAND VOLTS...
VZZOOOHM
DISCHARGE, SIX THOUSAND VOLTS...
VZZOOOHM

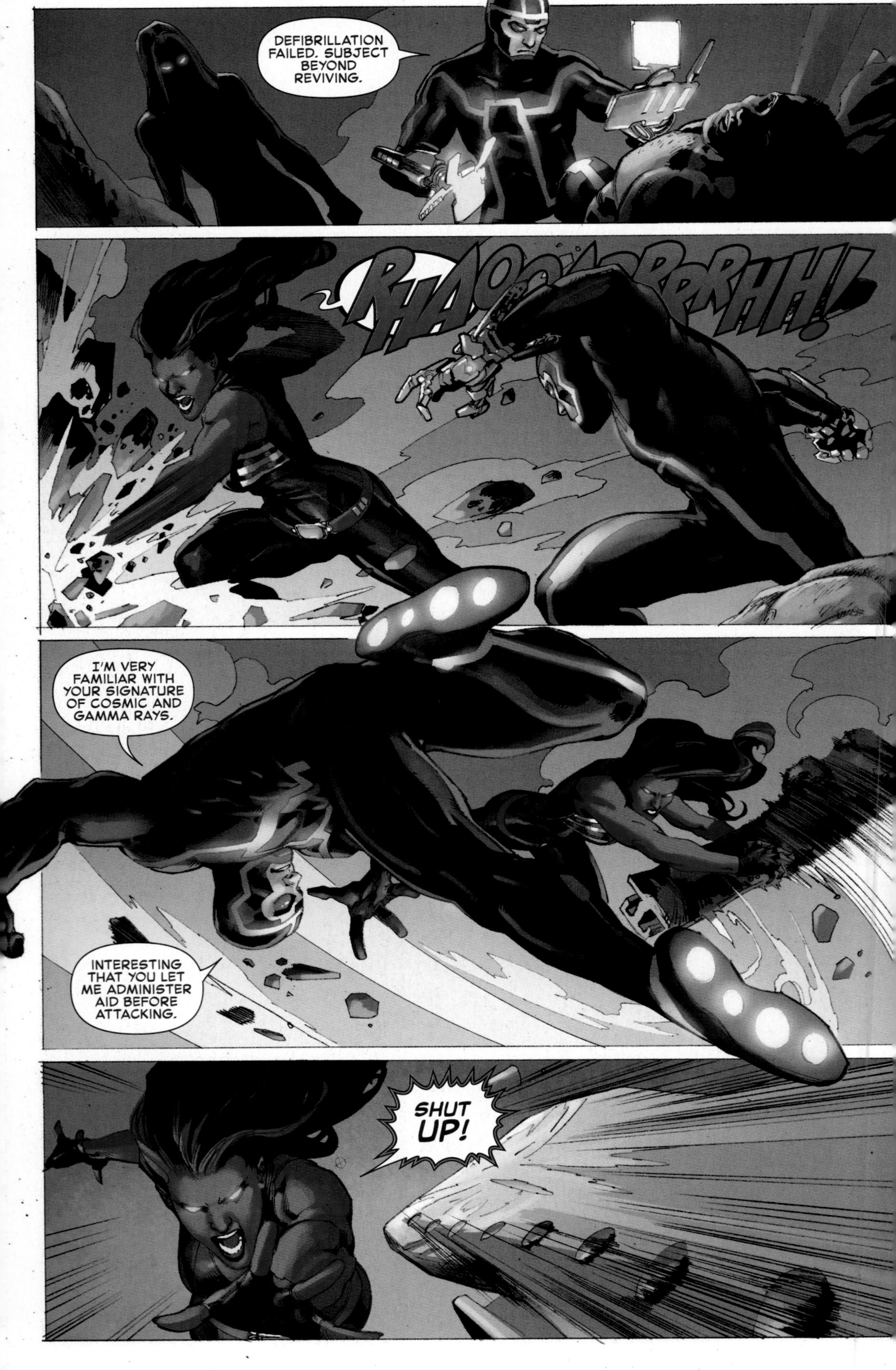
DEFIBRILLATION FAILED. SUBJECT BEYOND REVIVING.
RHAOOAARRRHH!
I'M VERY FAMILIAR WITH YOUR SIGNATURE OF COSMIC AND GAMMA RAYS.
INTERESTING THAT YOU LET ME ADMINISTER AID BEFORE ATTACKING.
SHUT UP!

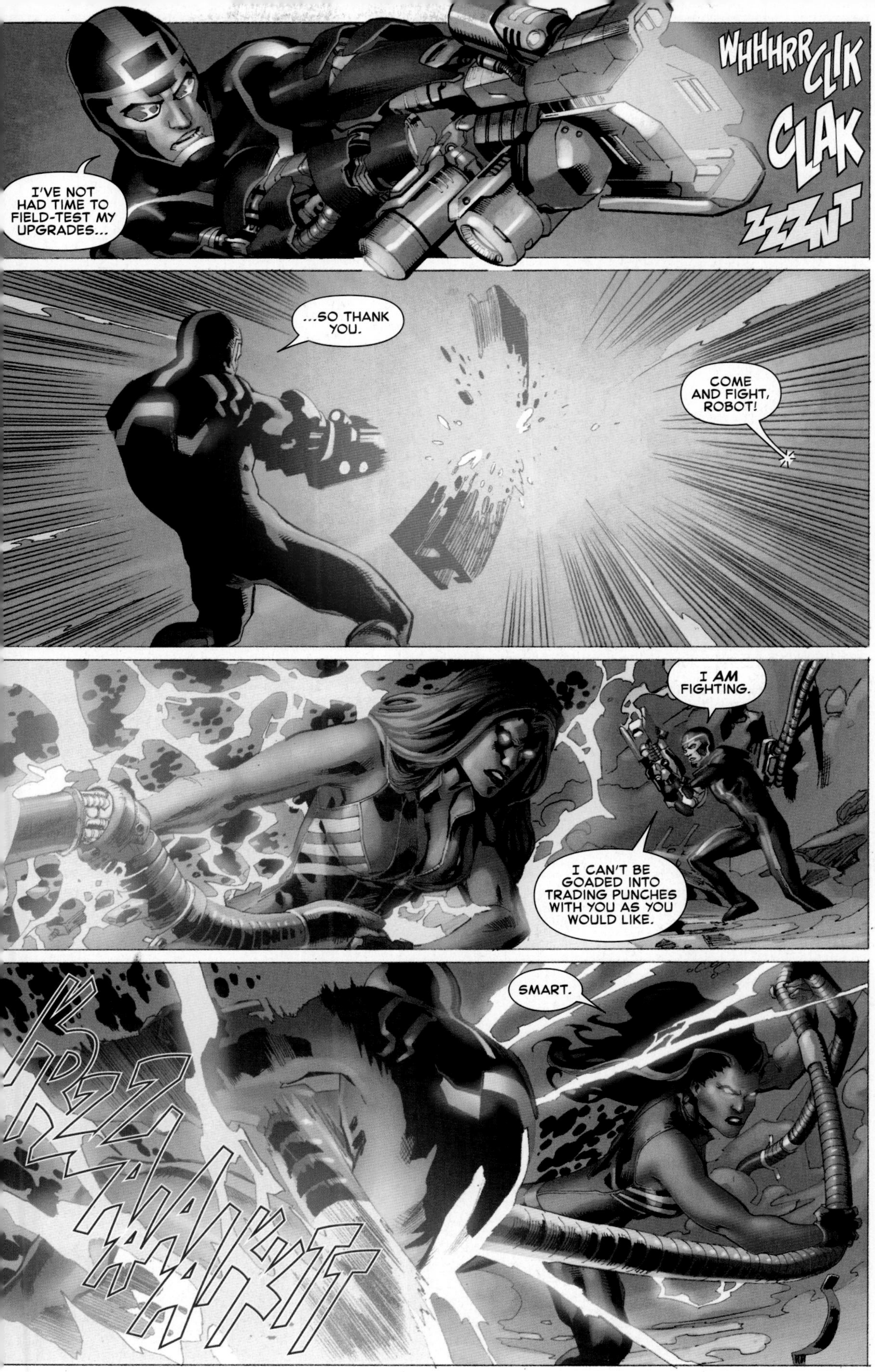
WHHHRR CLIK
CLAK
ZZZNT
I'VE NOT HAD TIME TO FIELD-TEST MY UPGRADES...
...SO THANK YOU.
COME AND FIGHT, ROBOT!
I AM FIGHTING.
I CAN'T BE GOADED INTO TRADING PUNCHES WITH YOU AS YOU WOULD LIKE.
SMART.

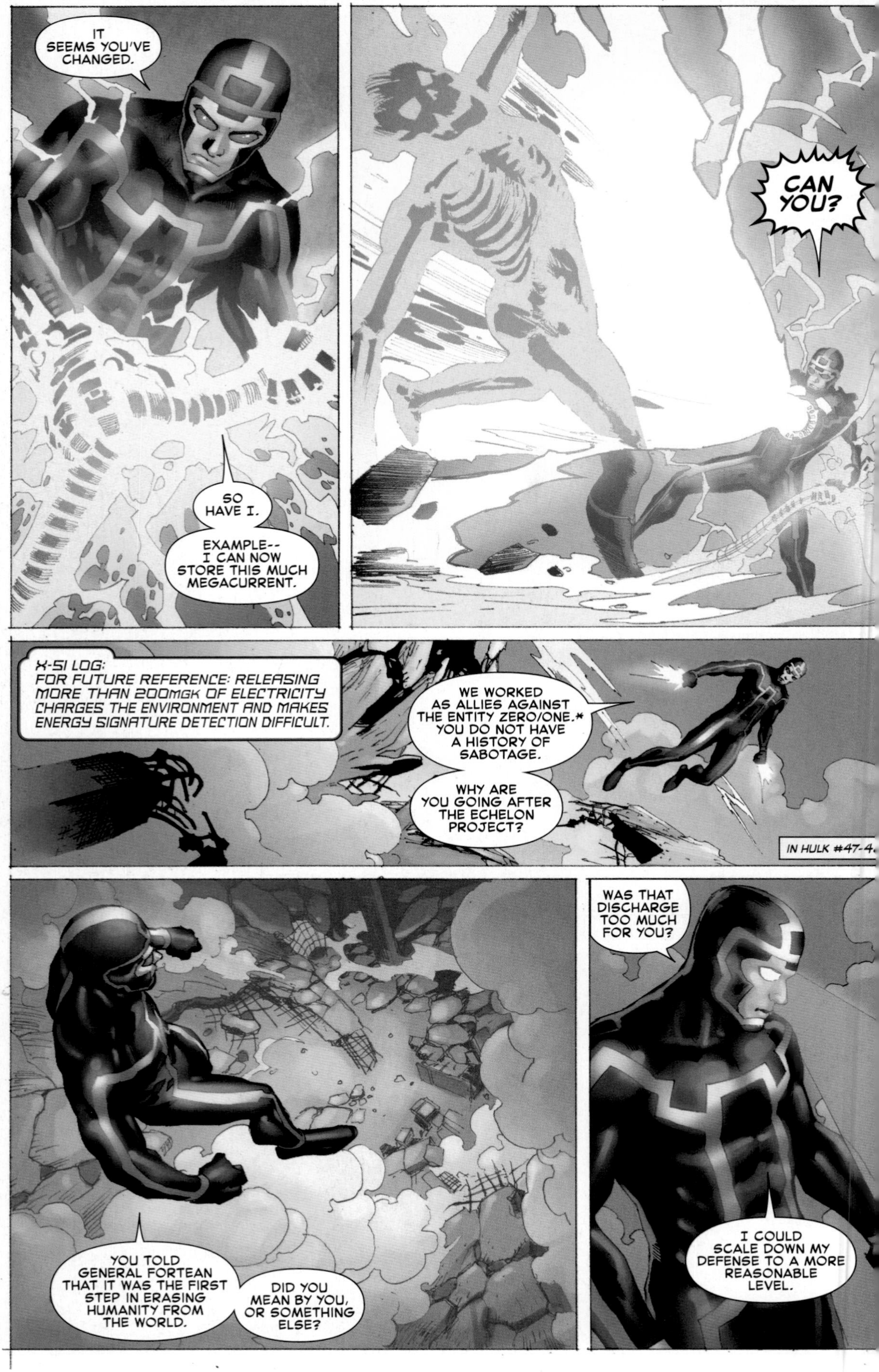
IT SEEMS YOU'VE CHANGED.
CAN YOU?
SO HAVE I.
EXAMPLE-- I CAN NOW STORE THIS MUCH MEGACURRENT.
X-51 LOG: FOR FUTURE REFERENCE: RELEASING MORE THAN 200MGK OF ELECTRICITY CHARGES THE ENVIRONMENT AND MAKES ENERGY SIGNATURE DETECTION DIFFICULT.
WE WORKED AS ALLIES AGAINST THE ENTITY ZERO/ONE.* YOU DO NOT HAVE A HISTORY OF SABOTAGE.
WHY ARE YOU GOING AFTER THE ECHELON PROJECT?
IN HULK #47-4
YOU TOLD GENERAL FORTEAN THAT IT WAS THE FIRST STEP IN ERASING HUMANITY FROM THE WORLD.
DID YOU MEAN BY YOU, OR SOMETHING ELSE?
WAS THAT DISCHARGE TOO MUCH FOR YOU?
I COULD SCALE DOWN MY DEFENSE TO A MORE REASONABLE LEVEL.

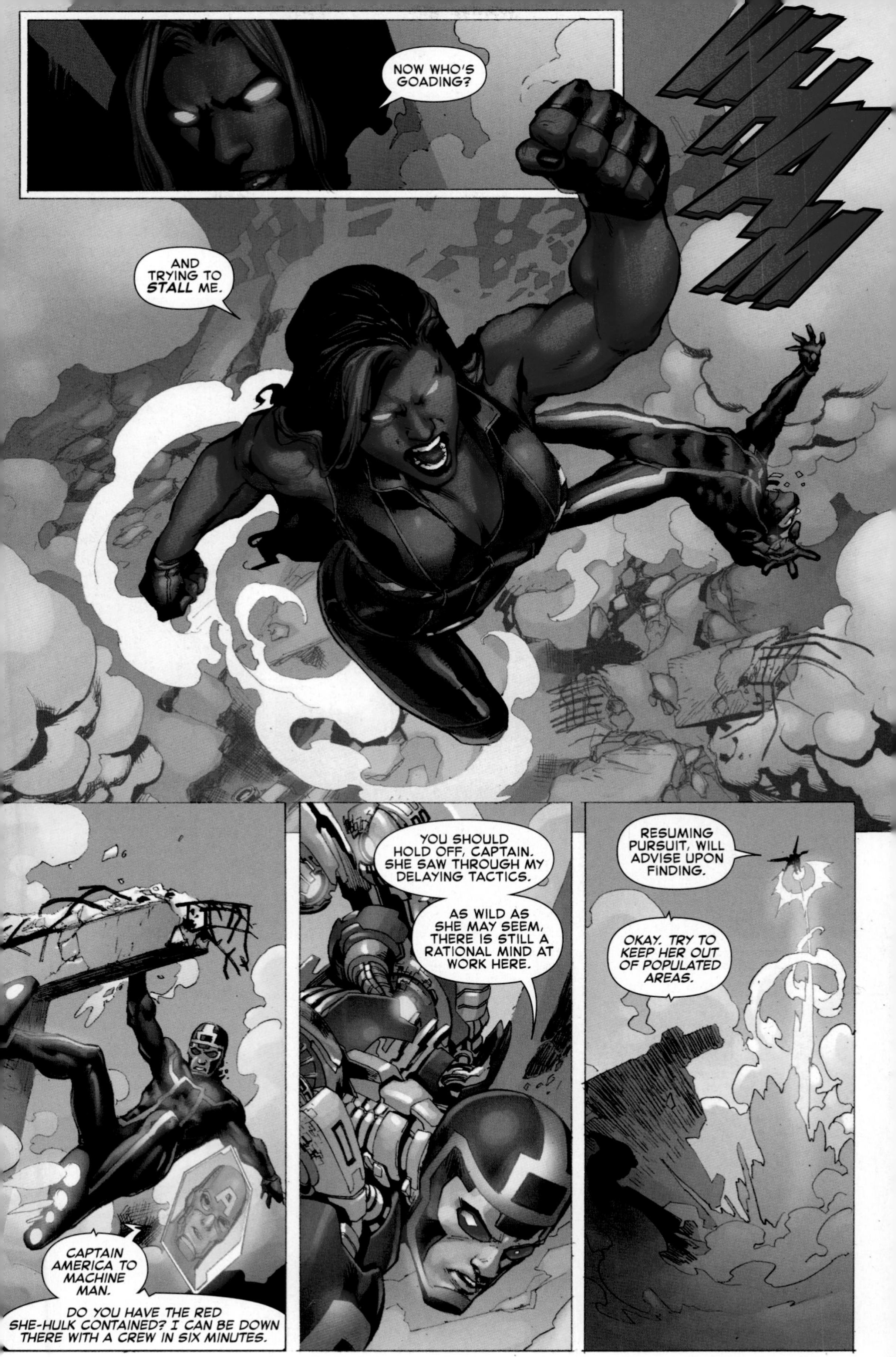
NOW WHO'S GOADING?
WHAM
AND TRYING TO STALL ME.
CAPTAIN AMERICA TO MACHINE MAN.
DO YOU HAVE THE RED SHE-HULK CONTAINED? I CAN BE DOWN THERE WITH A CREW IN SIX MINUTES.
YOU SHOULD HOLD OFF, CAPTAIN. SHE SAW THROUGH MY DELAYING TACTICS.
AS WILD AS SHE MAY SEEM, THERE IS STILL A RATIONAL MIND AT WORK HERE.
RESUMING PURSUIT, WILL ADVISE UPON FINDING.
OKAY. TRY TO KEEP HER OUT OF POPULATED AREAS.

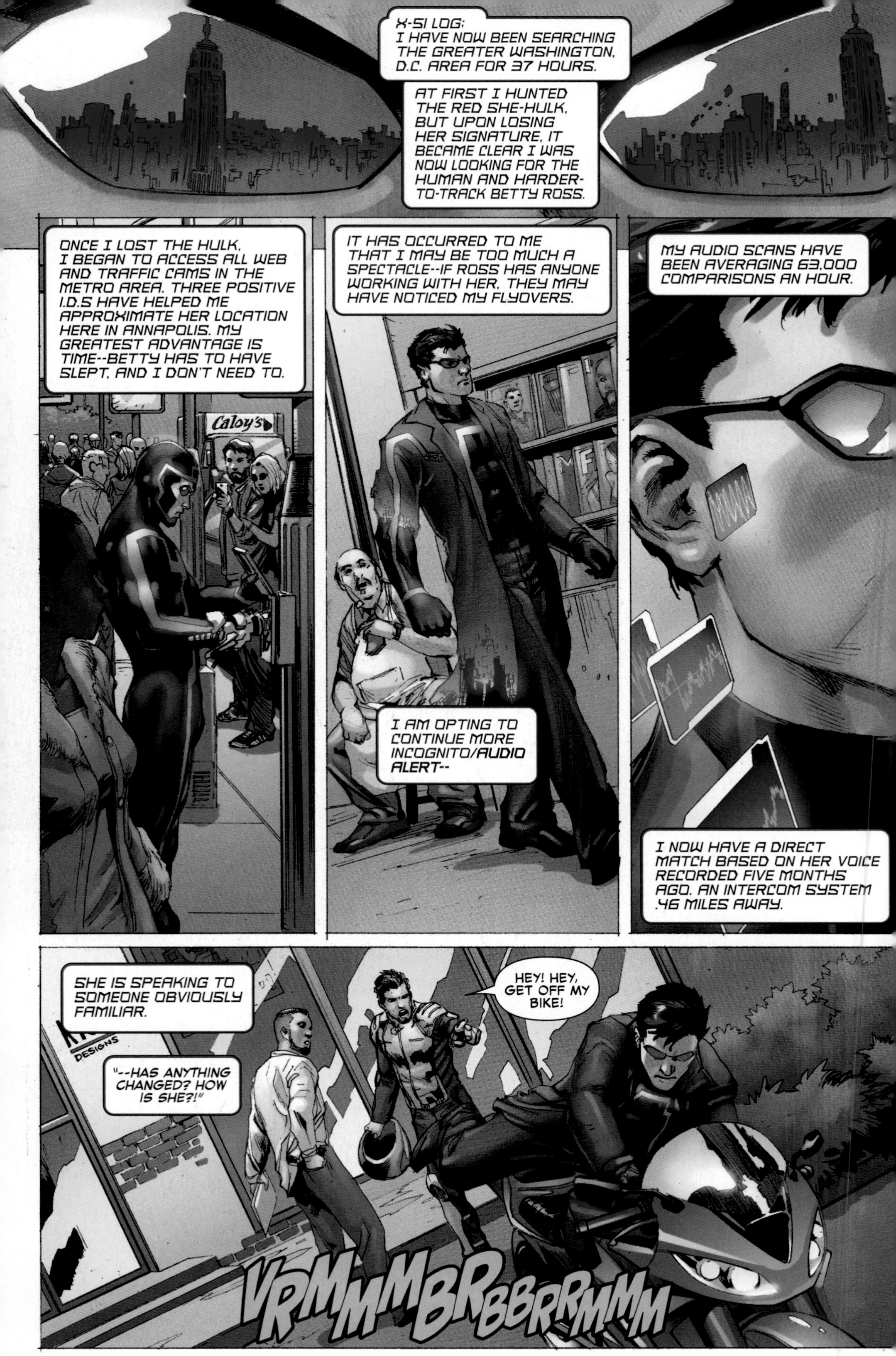
X-51 LOG:
I HAVE NOW BEEN SEARCHING THE GREATER WASHINGTON, D.C. AREA FOR 37 HOURS.
AT FIRST I HUNTED THE RED SHE-HULK, BUT UPON LOSING HER SIGNATURE, IT BECAME CLEAR I WAS NOW LOOKING FOR THE HUMAN AND HARDER-TO-TRACK BETTY ROSS.
ONCE I LOST THE HULK, I BEGAN TO ACCESS ALL WEB AND TRAFFIC CAMS IN THE METRO AREA. THREE POSITIVE I.D.S HAVE HELPED ME APPROXIMATE HER LOCATION HERE IN ANNAPOLIS. MY GREATEST ADVANTAGE IS TIME--BETTY HAS TO HAVE SLEPT, AND I DON'T NEED TO.
Caloy's
IT HAS OCCURRED TO ME THAT I MAY BE TOO MUCH A SPECTACLE--IF ROSS HAS ANYONE WORKING WITH HER, THEY MAY HAVE NOTICED MY FLYOVERS.
I AM OPTING TO CONTINUE MORE INCOGNITO/**AUDIO ALERT**--
MY AUDIO SCANS HAVE BEEN AVERAGING 63,000 COMPARISONS AN HOUR.
I NOW HAVE A DIRECT MATCH BASED ON HER VOICE RECORDED FIVE MONTHS AGO. AN INTERCOM SYSTEM .46 MILES AWAY.
SHE IS SPEAKING TO SOMEONE OBVIOUSLY FAMILIAR.
DESIGNS
"--HAS ANYTHING CHANGED? HOW IS SHE?!"
HEY! HEY, GET OFF MY BIKE!
VRMMMMBRBBRRMMMM

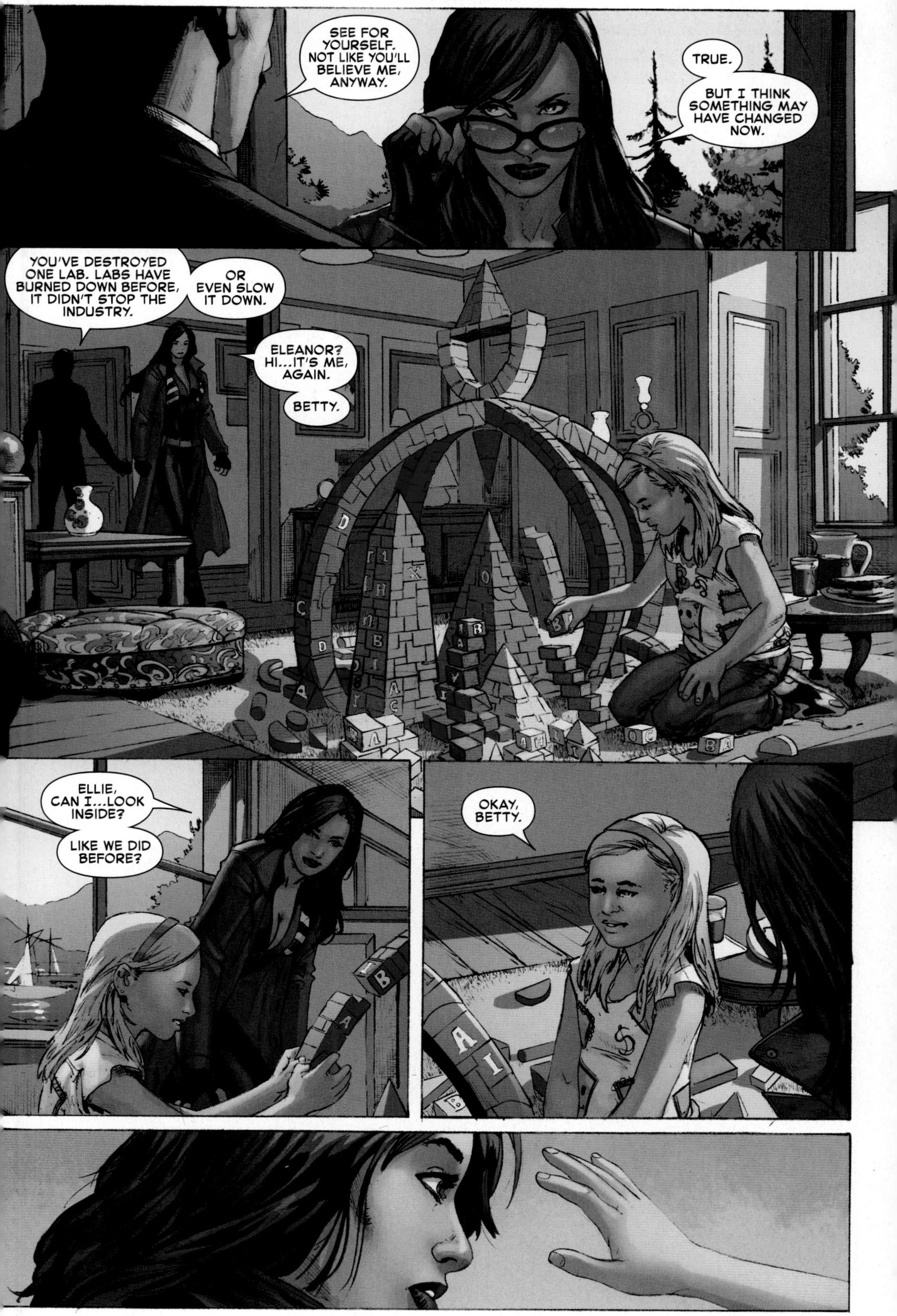
SEE FOR YOURSELF. NOT LIKE YOU'LL BELIEVE ME, ANYWAY.
TRUE.
BUT I THINK SOMETHING MAY HAVE CHANGED NOW.
YOU'VE DESTROYED ONE LAB. LABS HAVE BURNED DOWN BEFORE, IT DIDN'T STOP THE INDUSTRY.
OR EVEN SLOW IT DOWN.
ELEANOR? HI...IT'S ME, AGAIN.
BETTY.
ELLIE, CAN I...LOOK INSIDE?
LIKE WE DID BEFORE?
OKAY, BETTY.

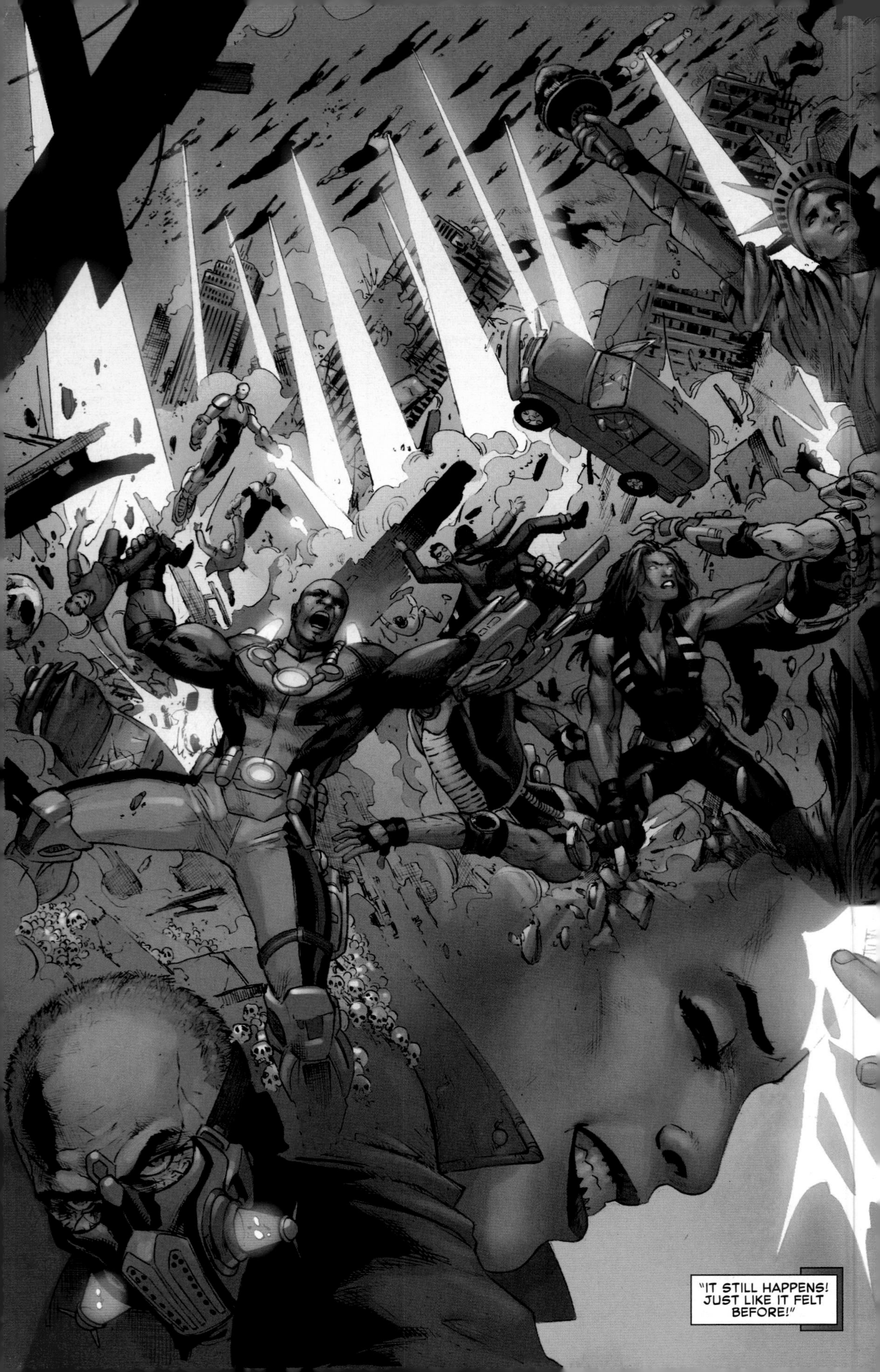
"IT STILL HAPPENS! JUST LIKE IT FELT BEFORE!"

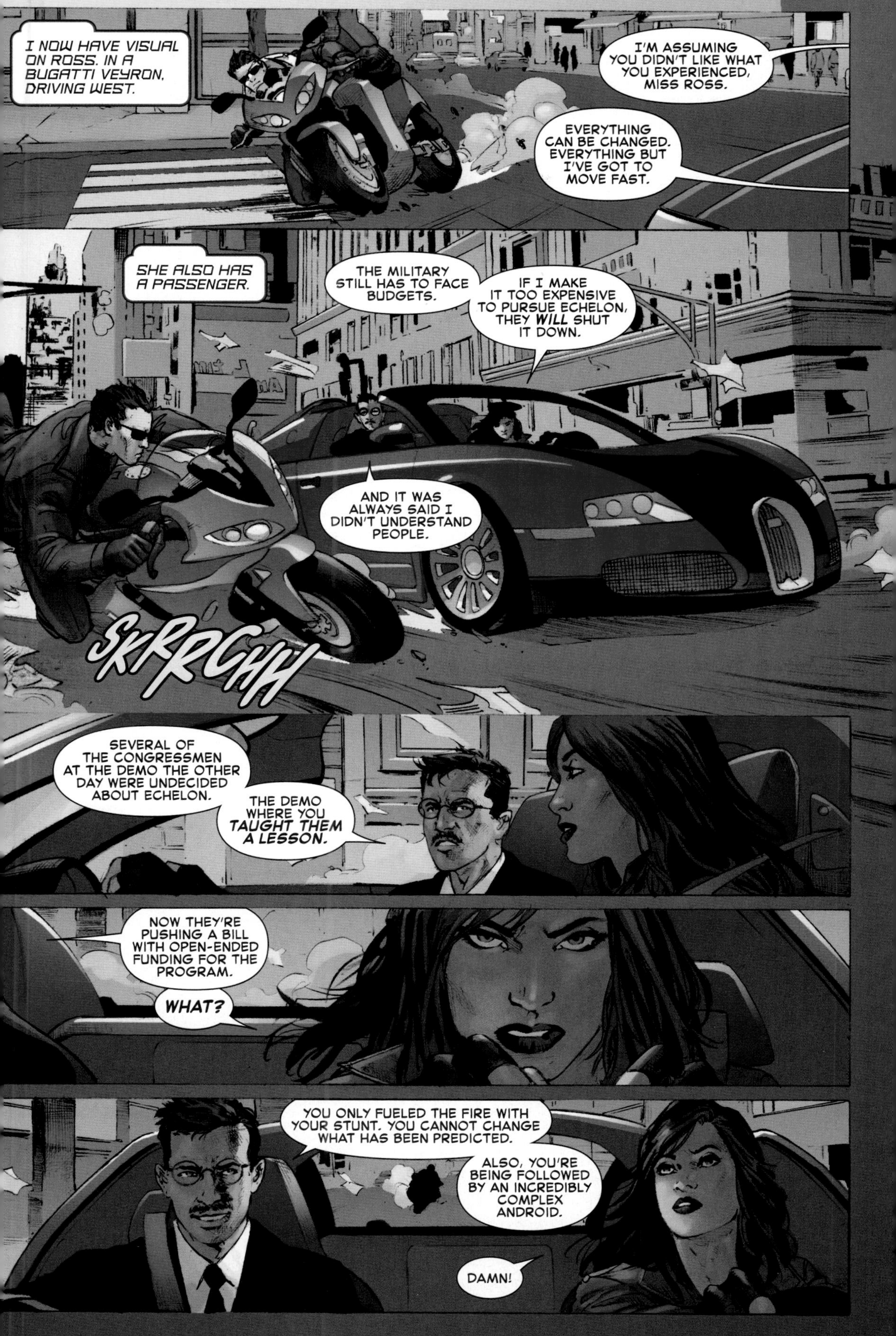
I NOW HAVE VISUAL ON ROSS. IN A BUGATTI VEYRON, DRIVING WEST.
I'M ASSUMING YOU DIDN'T LIKE WHAT YOU EXPERIENCED, MISS ROSS.
EVERYTHING CAN BE CHANGED. EVERYTHING BUT I'VE GOT TO MOVE FAST.
SHE ALSO HAS A PASSENGER.
THE MILITARY STILL HAS TO FACE BUDGETS.
IF I MAKE IT TOO EXPENSIVE TO PURSUE ECHELON, THEY WILL SHUT IT DOWN.
AND IT WAS ALWAYS SAID I DIDN'T UNDERSTAND PEOPLE.
SKRRCHH
SEVERAL OF THE CONGRESSMEN AT THE DEMO THE OTHER DAY WERE UNDECIDED ABOUT ECHELON.
THE DEMO WHERE YOU TAUGHT THEM A LESSON.
NOW THEY'RE PUSHING A BILL WITH OPEN-ENDED FUNDING FOR THE PROGRAM.
WHAT?
YOU ONLY FUELED THE FIRE WITH YOUR STUNT. YOU CANNOT CHANGE WHAT HAS BEEN PREDICTED.
ALSO, YOU'RE BEING FOLLOWED BY AN INCREDIBLY COMPLEX ANDROID.
DAMN!

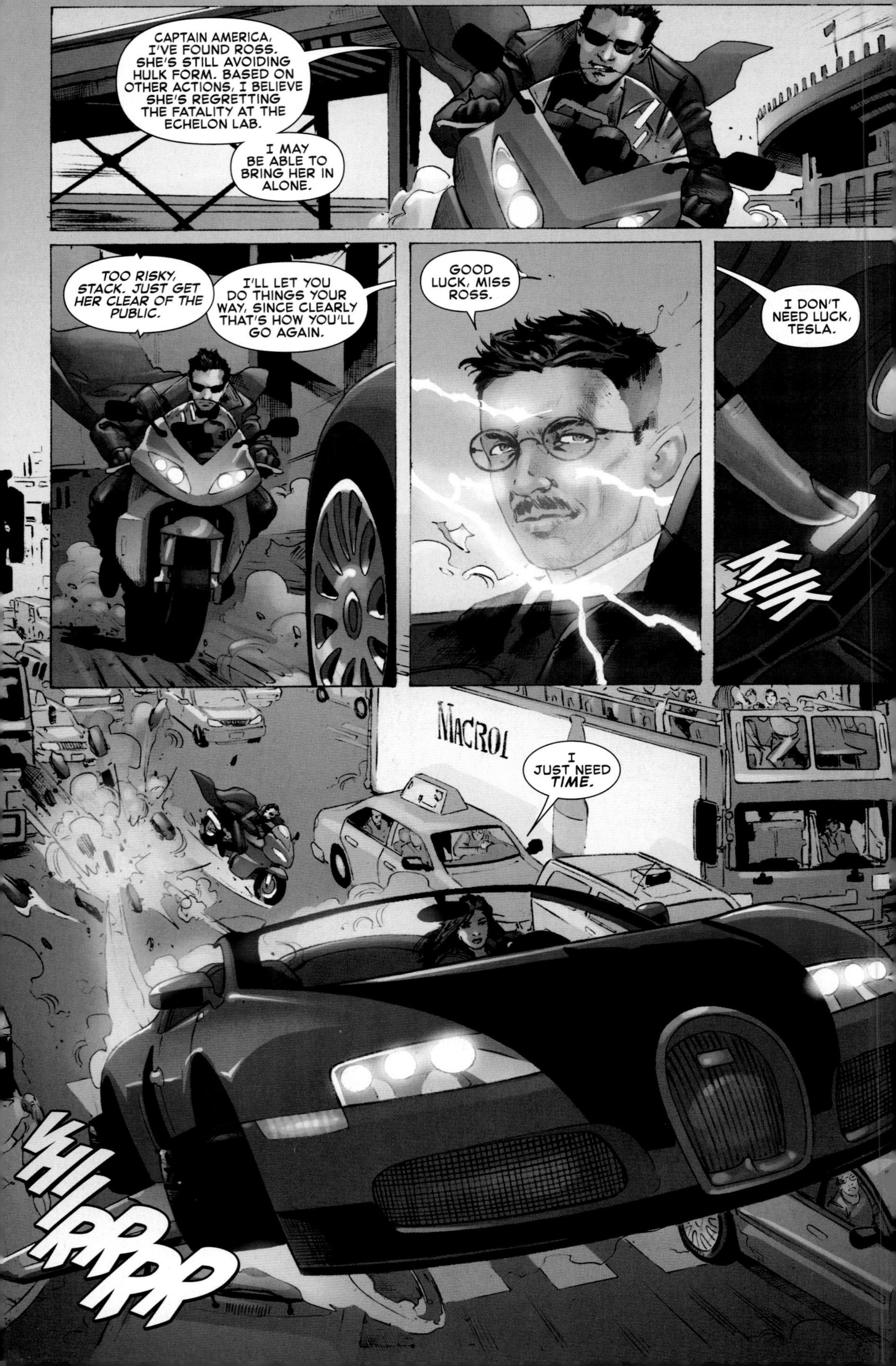
CAPTAIN AMERICA, I'VE FOUND ROSS. SHE'S STILL AVOIDING HULK FORM. BASED ON OTHER ACTIONS, I BELIEVE SHE'S REGRETTING THE FATALITY AT THE ECHELON LAB.
I MAY BE ABLE TO BRING HER IN ALONE.
TOO RISKY, STACK. JUST GET HER CLEAR OF THE PUBLIC.
I'LL LET YOU DO THINGS YOUR WAY, SINCE CLEARLY THAT'S HOW YOU'LL GO AGAIN.
GOOD LUCK, MISS ROSS.
I DON'T NEED LUCK, TESLA.
KLIK
MACROI
I JUST NEED TIME.
WHIRRR

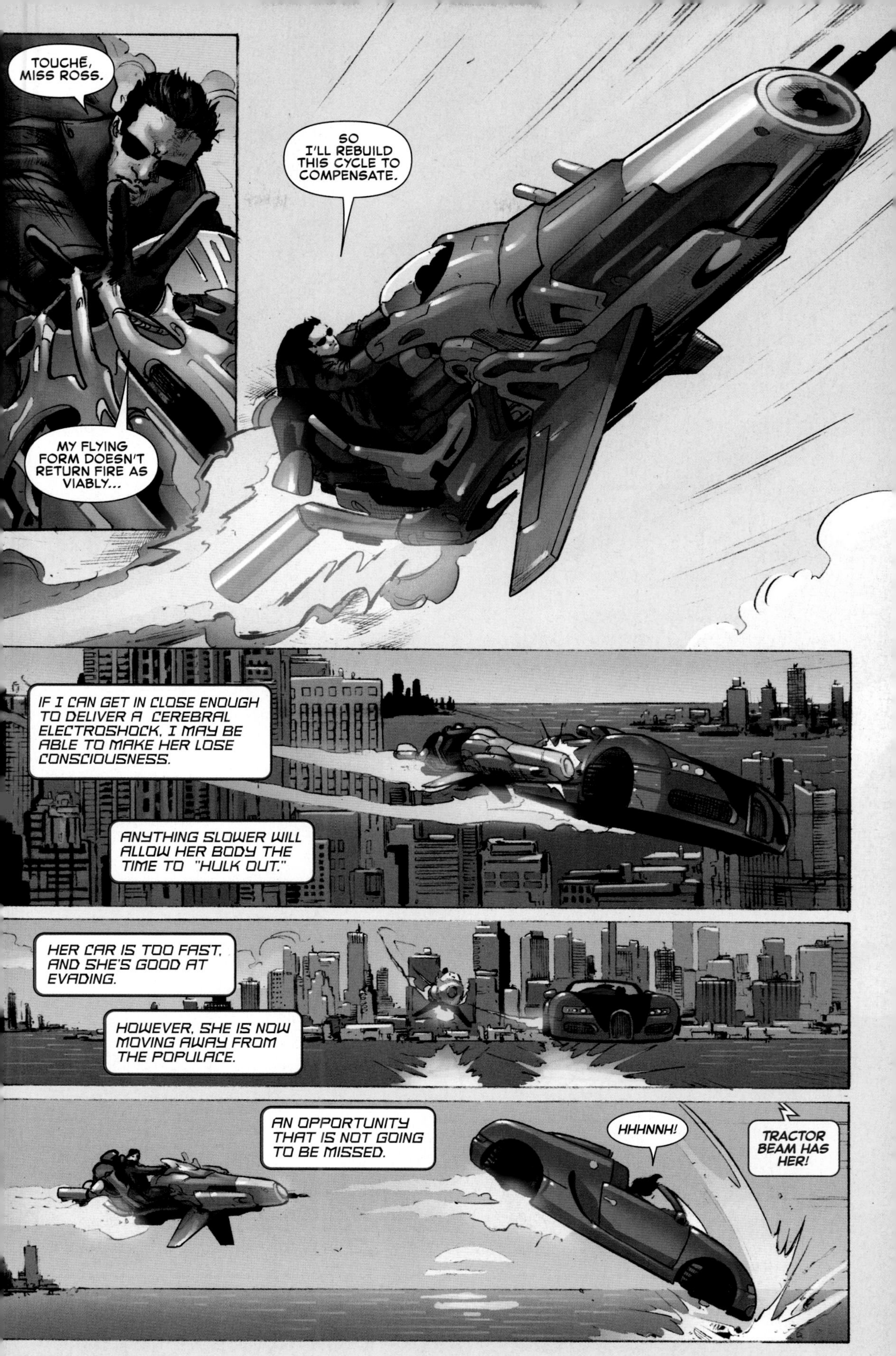
TOUCHÉ, MISS ROSS.
MY FLYING FORM DOESN'T RETURN FIRE AS VIABLY...
SO I'LL REBUILD THIS CYCLE TO COMPENSATE.
IF I CAN GET IN CLOSE ENOUGH TO DELIVER A CEREBRAL ELECTROSHOCK, I MAY BE ABLE TO MAKE HER LOSE CONSCIOUSNESS.
ANYTHING SLOWER WILL ALLOW HER BODY THE TIME TO "HULK OUT."
HER CAR IS TOO FAST, AND SHE'S GOOD AT EVADING.
HOWEVER, SHE IS NOW MOVING AWAY FROM THE POPULACE.
AN OPPORTUNITY THAT IS NOT GOING TO BE MISSED.
HHHNNH!
TRACTOR BEAM HAS HER!

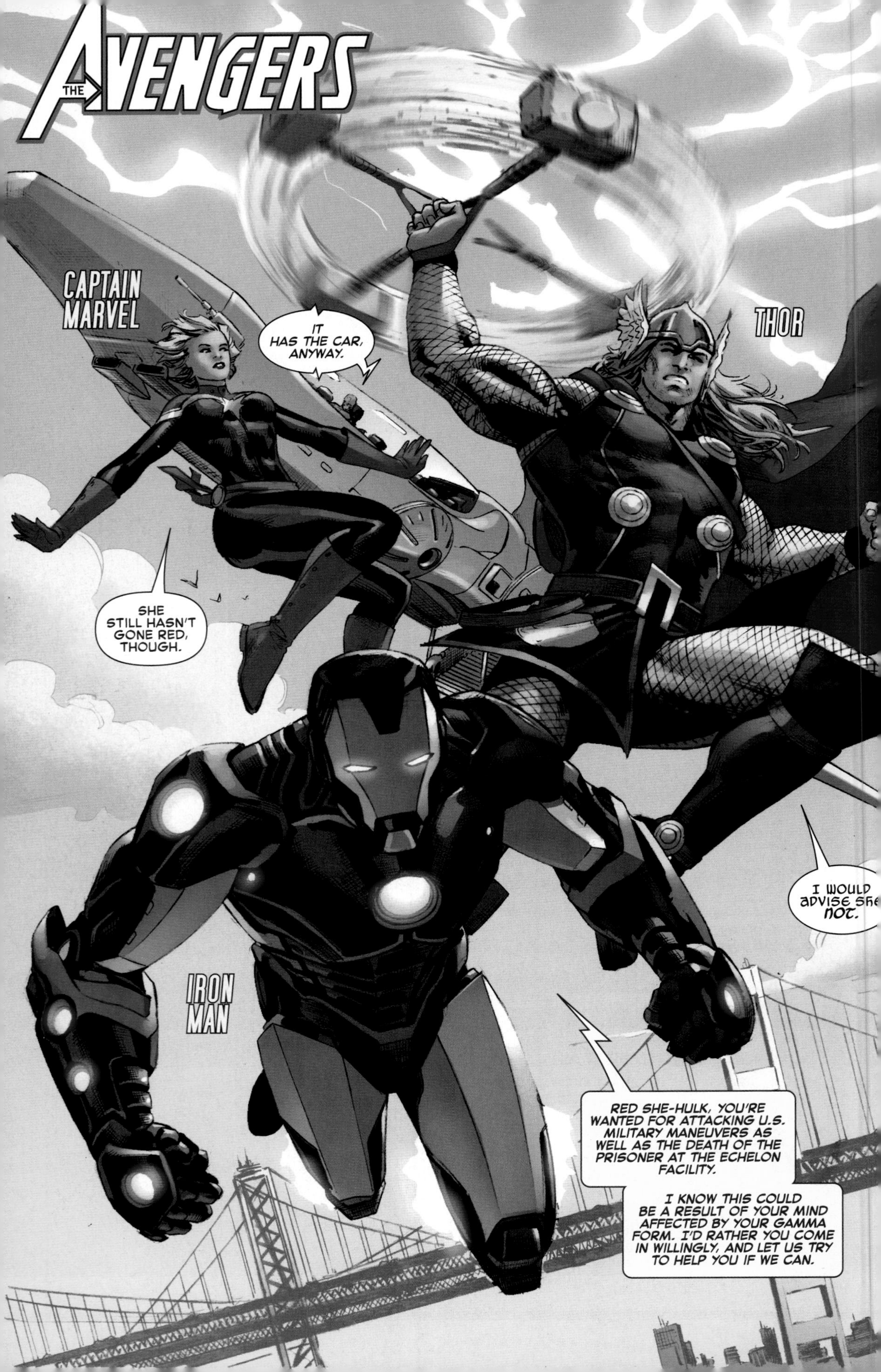
THE AVENGERS
CAPTAIN MARVEL
IT HAS THE CAR, ANYWAY.
THOR
SHE STILL HASN'T GONE RED, THOUGH.
I WOULD ADVISE SHE NOT.
IRON MAN
RED SHE-HULK, YOU'RE WANTED FOR ATTACKING U.S. MILITARY MANEUVERS AS WELL AS THE DEATH OF THE PRISONER AT THE ECHELON FACILITY.
I KNOW THIS COULD BE A RESULT OF YOUR MIND AFFECTED BY YOUR GAMMA FORM. I'D RATHER YOU COME IN WILLINGLY, AND LET US TRY TO HELP YOU IF WE CAN.

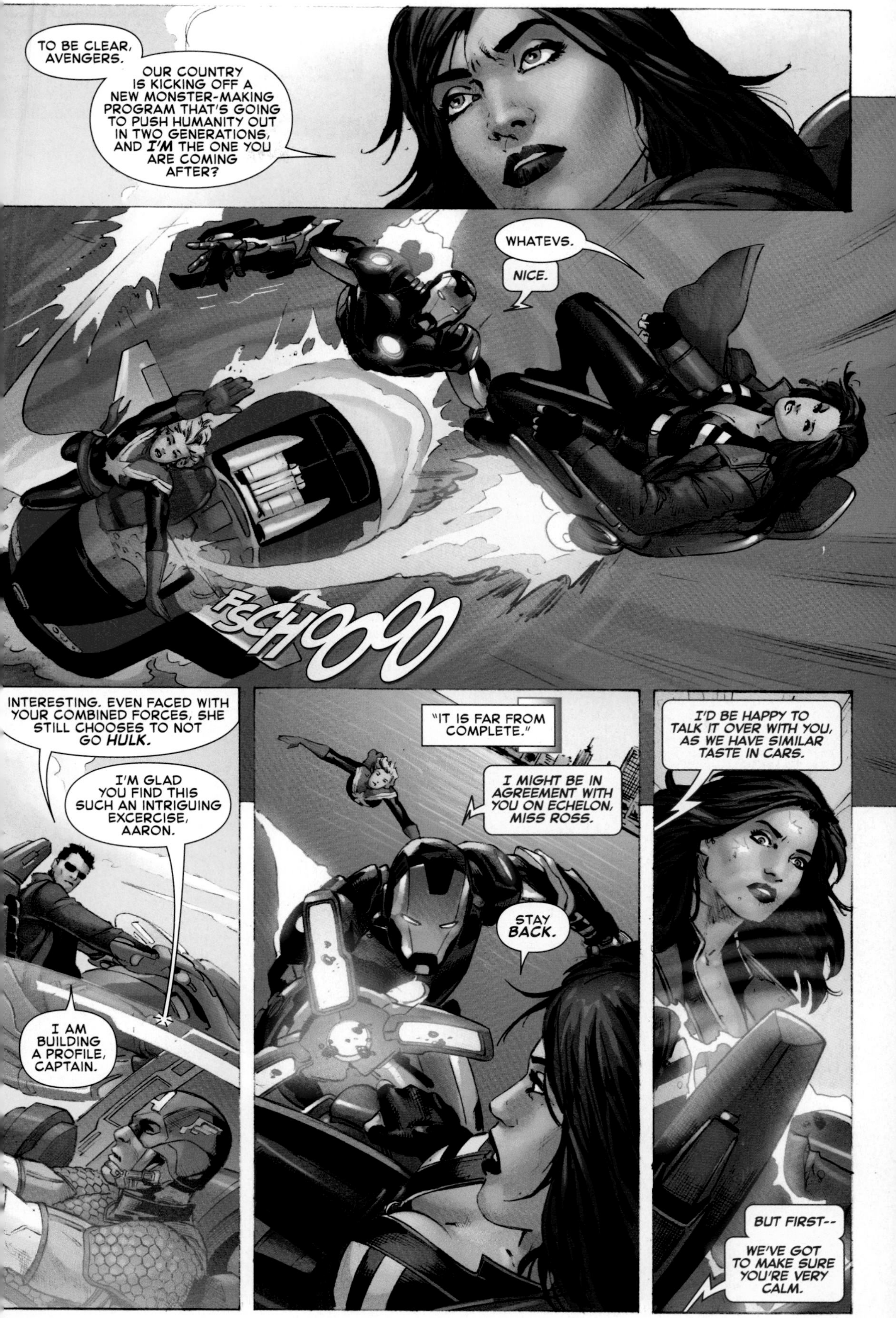
TO BE CLEAR, AVENGERS.
OUR COUNTRY IS KICKING OFF A NEW MONSTER-MAKING PROGRAM THAT'S GOING TO PUSH HUMANITY OUT IN TWO GENERATIONS, AND I'M THE ONE YOU ARE COMING AFTER?
WHATEVS.
NICE.
FSCHOOOO
INTERESTING. EVEN FACED WITH YOUR COMBINED FORCES, SHE STILL CHOOSES TO NOT GO HULK.
I'M GLAD YOU FIND THIS SUCH AN INTRIGUING EXCERCISE, AARON.
I AM BUILDING A PROFILE, CAPTAIN.
"IT IS FAR FROM COMPLETE."
I MIGHT BE IN AGREEMENT WITH YOU ON ECHELON, MISS ROSS.
STAY BACK.
I'D BE HAPPY TO TALK IT OVER WITH YOU, AS WE HAVE SIMILAR TASTE IN CARS.
BUT FIRST--
WE'VE GOT TO MAKE SURE YOU'RE VERY CALM.

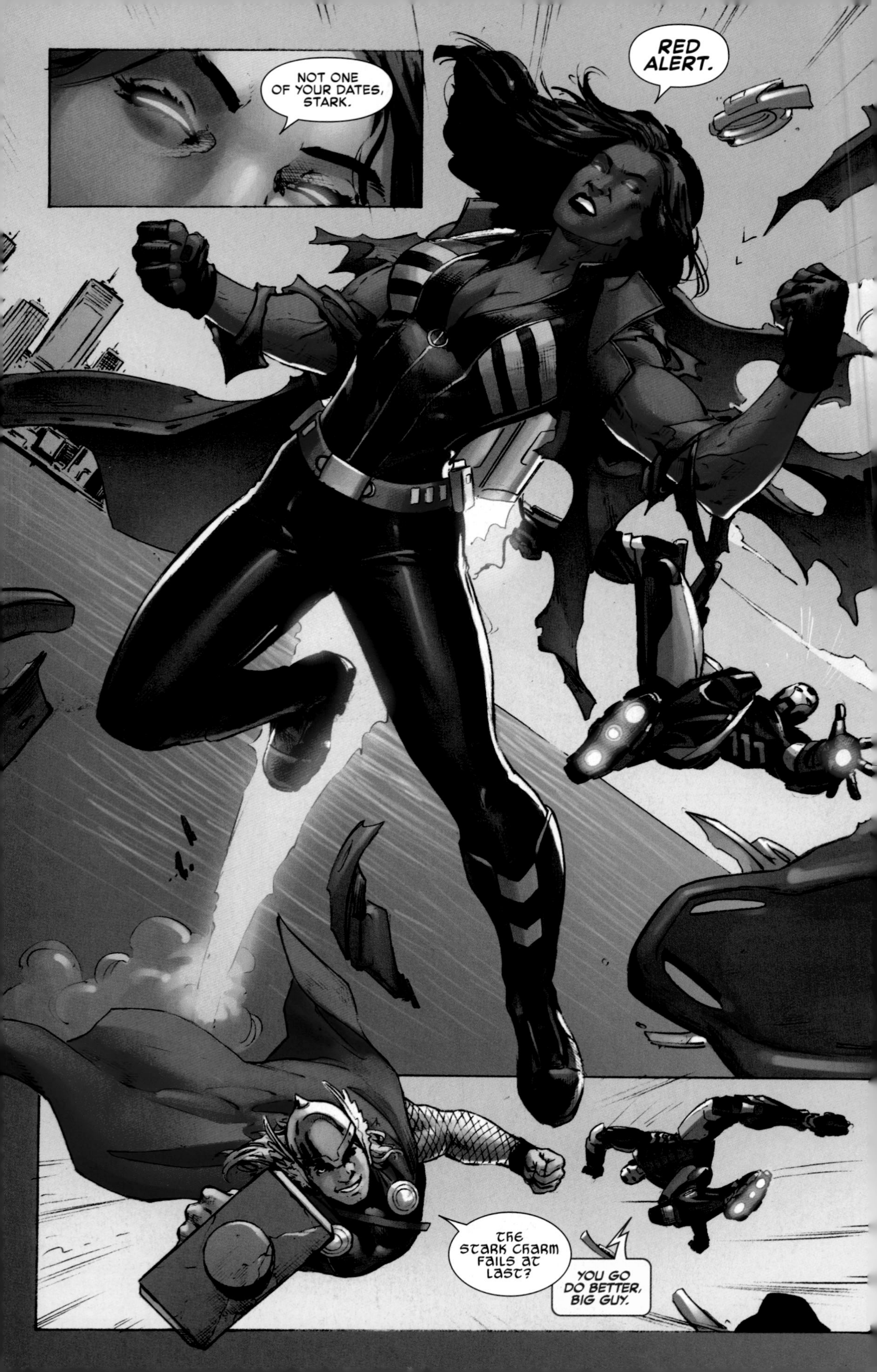
NOT ONE OF YOUR DATES, STARK.
RED ALERT.
THE STARK CHARM FAILS AT LAST?
YOU GO DO BETTER, BIG GUY.

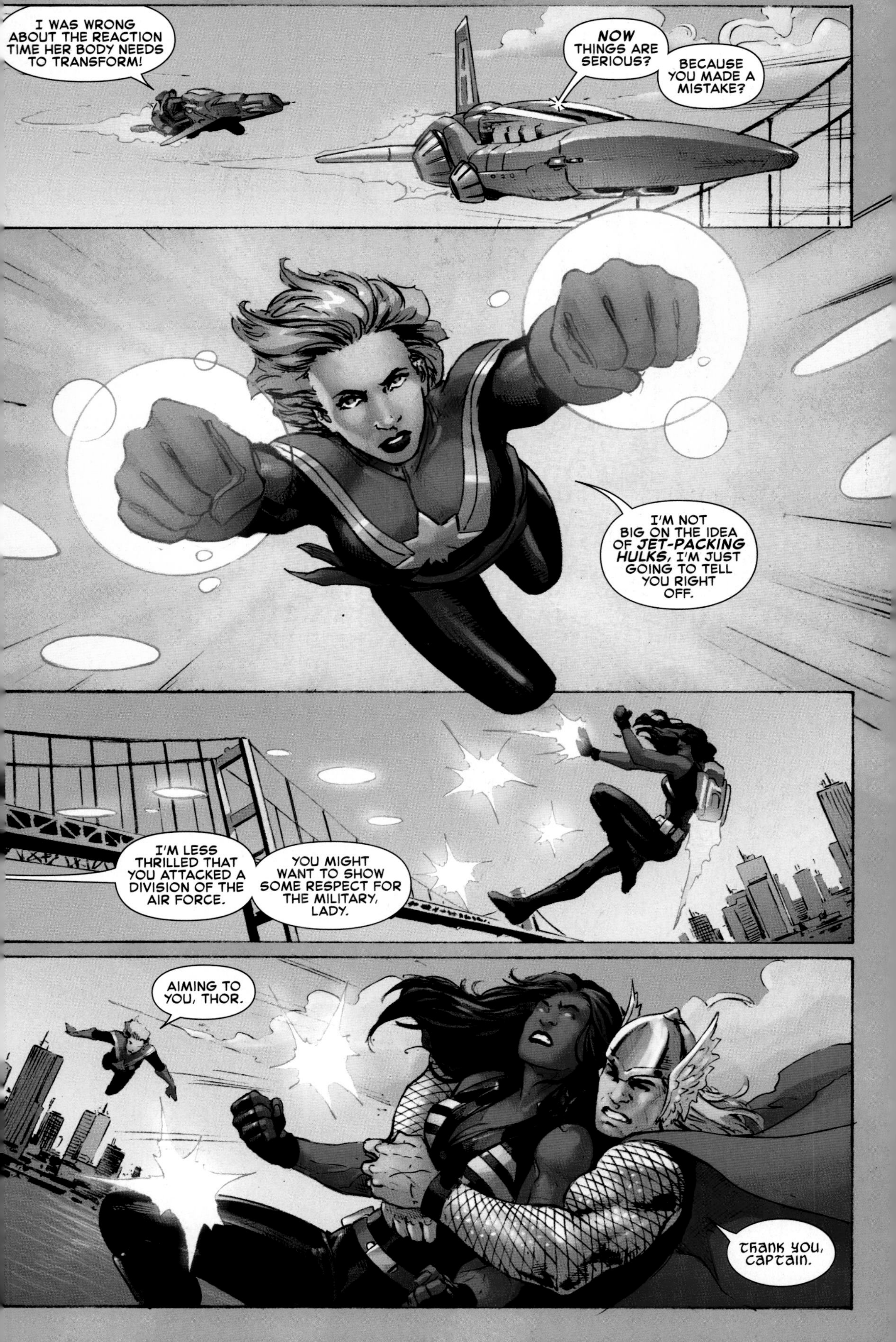
I WAS WRONG ABOUT THE REACTION TIME HER BODY NEEDS TO TRANSFORM!
NOW THINGS ARE SERIOUS?
BECAUSE YOU MADE A MISTAKE?
I'M NOT BIG ON THE IDEA OF JET-PACKING HULKS, I'M JUST GOING TO TELL YOU RIGHT OFF.
I'M LESS THRILLED THAT YOU ATTACKED A DIVISION OF THE AIR FORCE.
YOU MIGHT WANT TO SHOW SOME RESPECT FOR THE MILITARY, LADY.
AIMING TO YOU, THOR.
THANK YOU, CAPTAIN.

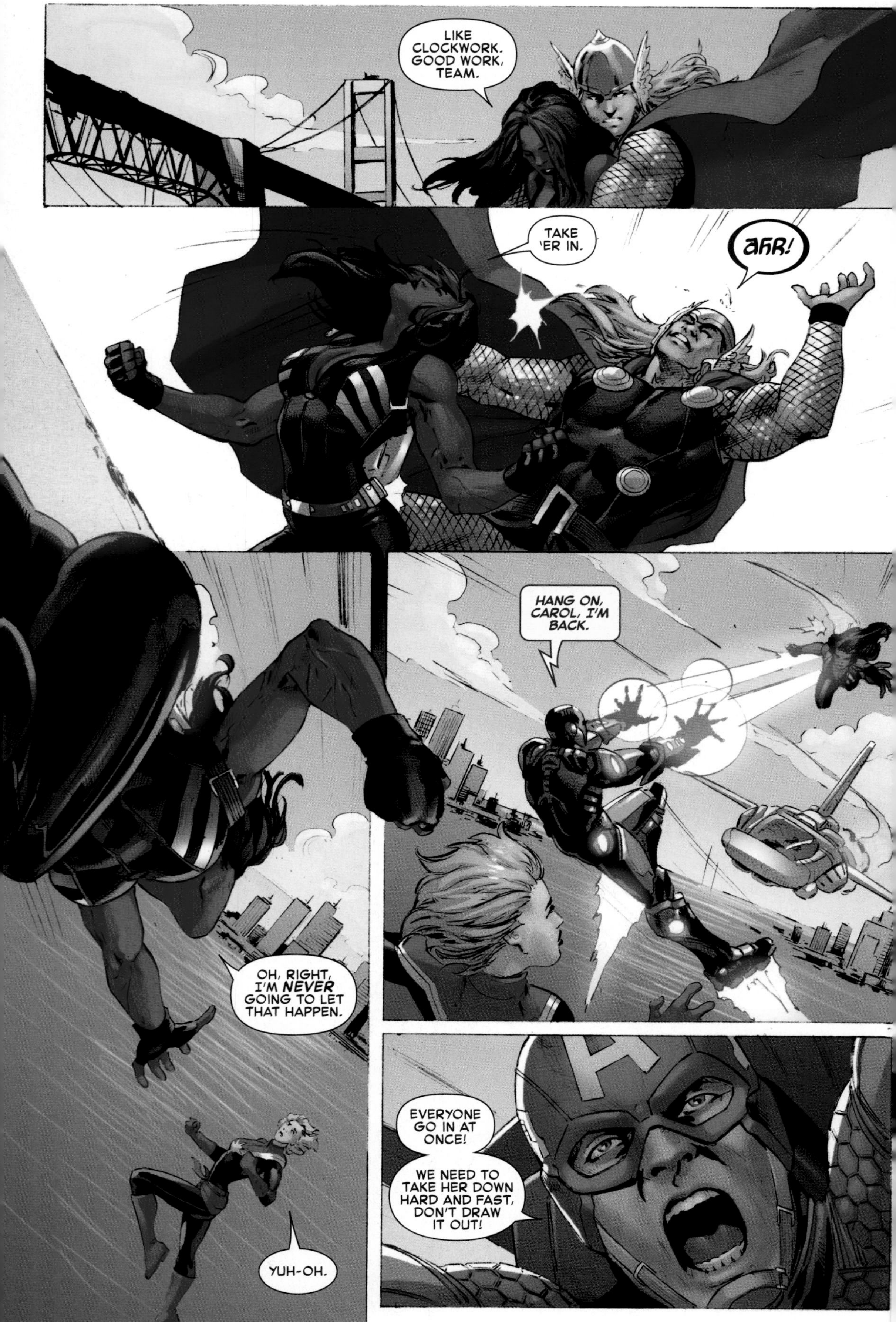
LIKE CLOCKWORK. GOOD WORK, TEAM.
TAKE 'ER IN.
AHR!
HANG ON, CAROL, I'M BACK.
OH, RIGHT, I'M NEVER GOING TO LET THAT HAPPEN.
YUH-OH.
EVERYONE GO IN AT ONCE!
WE NEED TO TAKE HER DOWN HARD AND FAST, DON'T DRAW IT OUT!

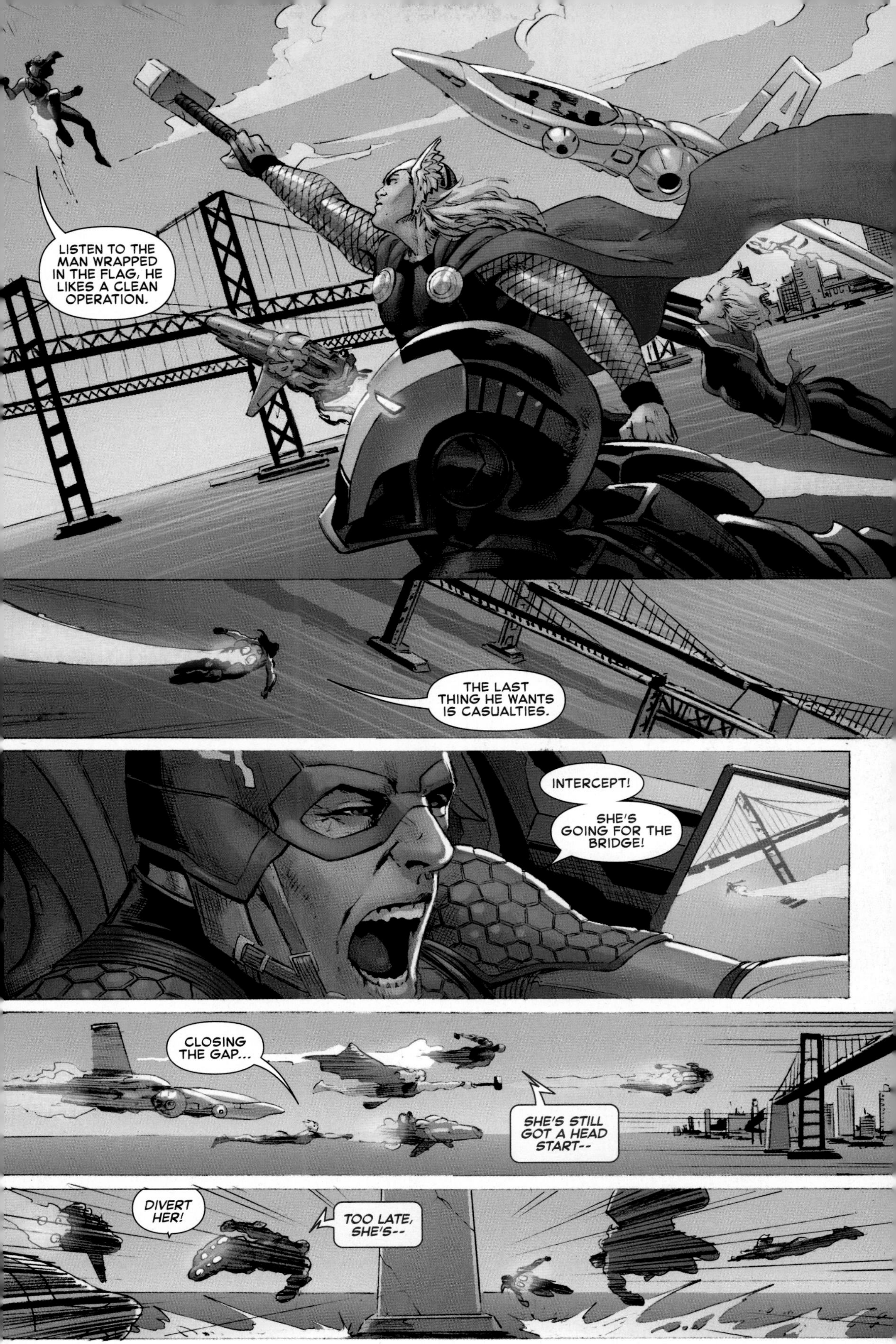
LISTEN TO THE MAN WRAPPED IN THE FLAG, HE LIKES A CLEAN OPERATION.
THE LAST THING HE WANTS IS CASUALTIES.
INTERCEPT!
SHE'S GOING FOR THE BRIDGE!
CLOSING THE GAP...
SHE'S STILL GOT A HEAD START--
DIVERT HER!
TOO LATE, SHE'S--

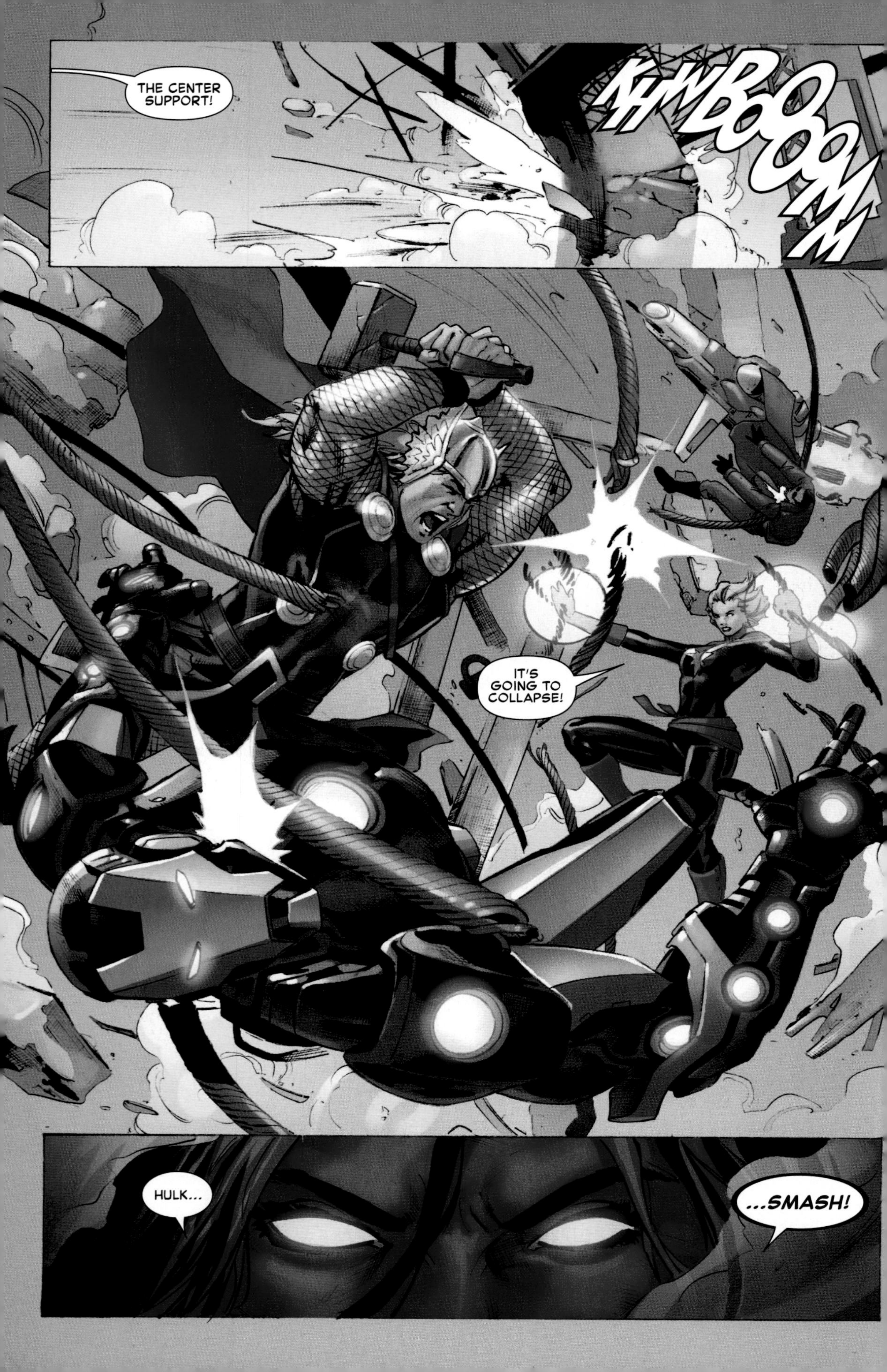
THE CENTER SUPPORT!
KHWBOOOMM
IT'S GOING TO COLLAPSE!
HULK...
...SMASH!

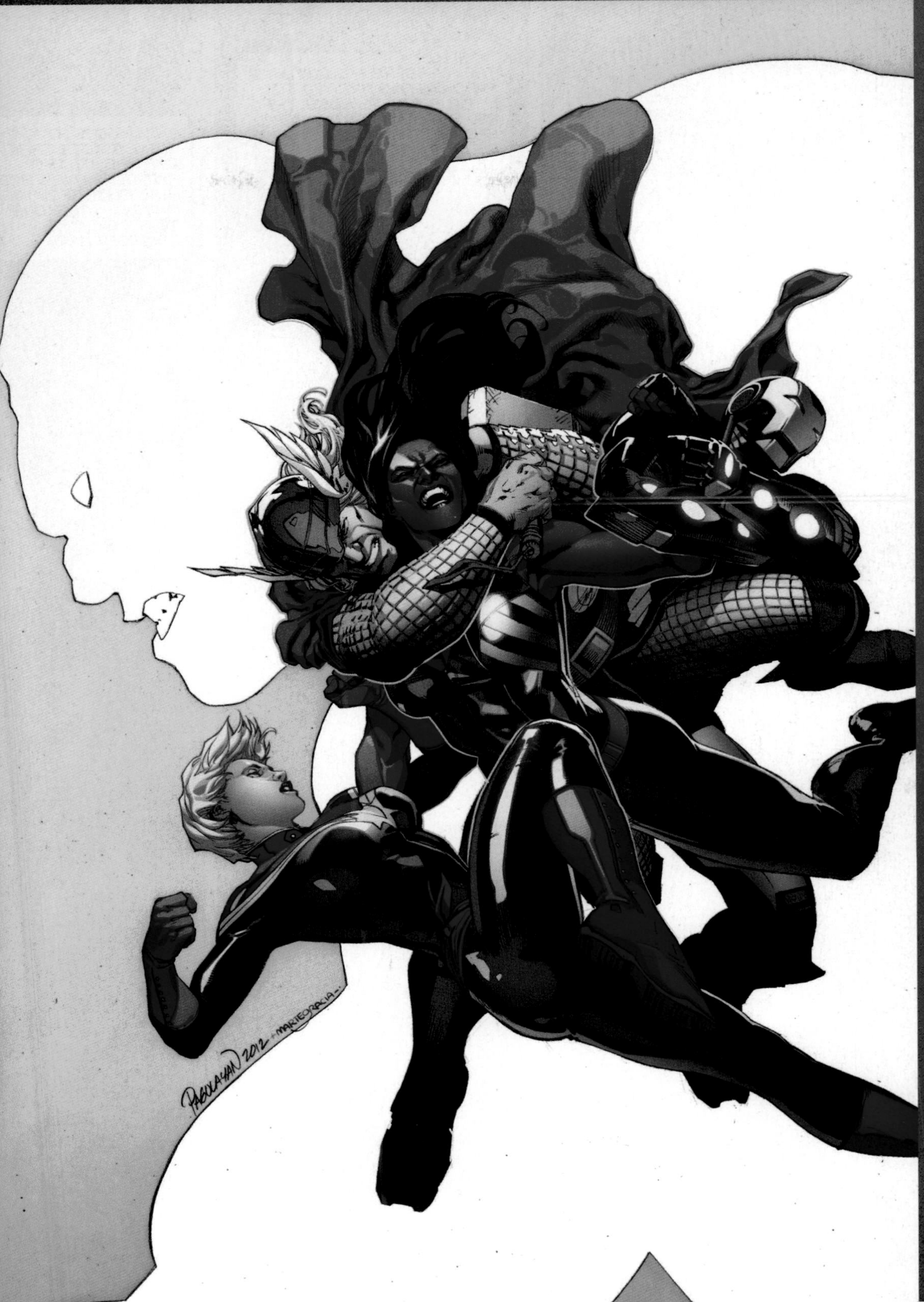
PAGULAYAN 2012 +MARTEGRACIA

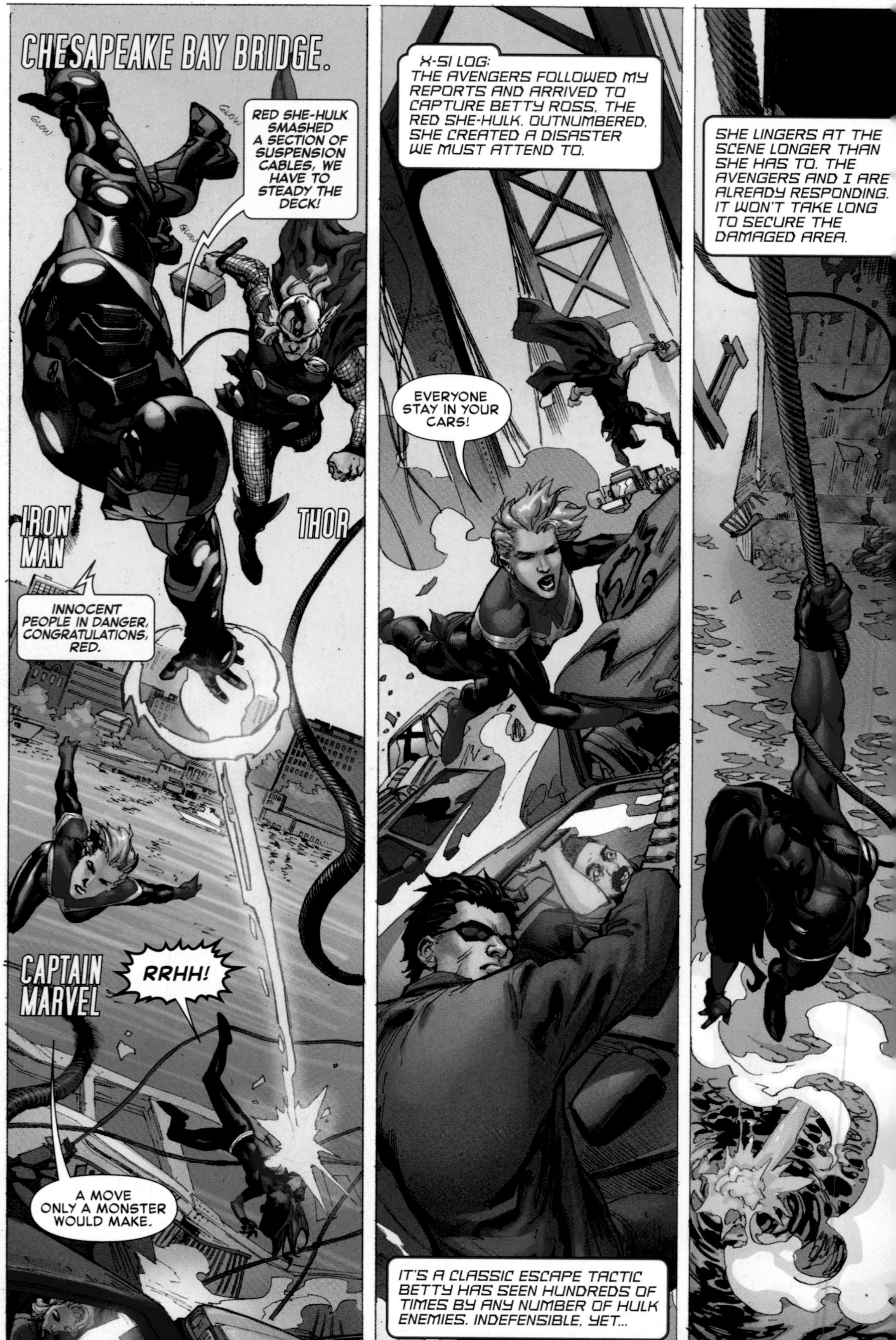
CHESAPEAKE BAY BRIDGE.
RED SHE-HULK SMASHED A SECTION OF SUSPENSION CABLES, WE HAVE TO STEADY THE DECK!
IRON MAN
THOR
INNOCENT PEOPLE IN DANGER, CONGRATULATIONS, RED.
CAPTAIN MARVEL
RRHH!
A MOVE ONLY A MONSTER WOULD MAKE.
X-51 LOG: THE AVENGERS FOLLOWED MY REPORTS AND ARRIVED TO CAPTURE BETTY ROSS, THE RED SHE-HULK. OUTNUMBERED, SHE CREATED A DISASTER WE MUST ATTEND TO.
EVERYONE STAY IN YOUR CARS!
IT'S A CLASSIC ESCAPE TACTIC BETTY HAS SEEN HUNDREDS OF TIMES BY ANY NUMBER OF HULK ENEMIES. INDEFENSIBLE, YET...
SHE LINGERS AT THE SCENE LONGER THAN SHE HAS TO. THE AVENGERS AND I ARE ALREADY RESPONDING. IT WON'T TAKE LONG TO SECURE THE DAMAGED AREA.

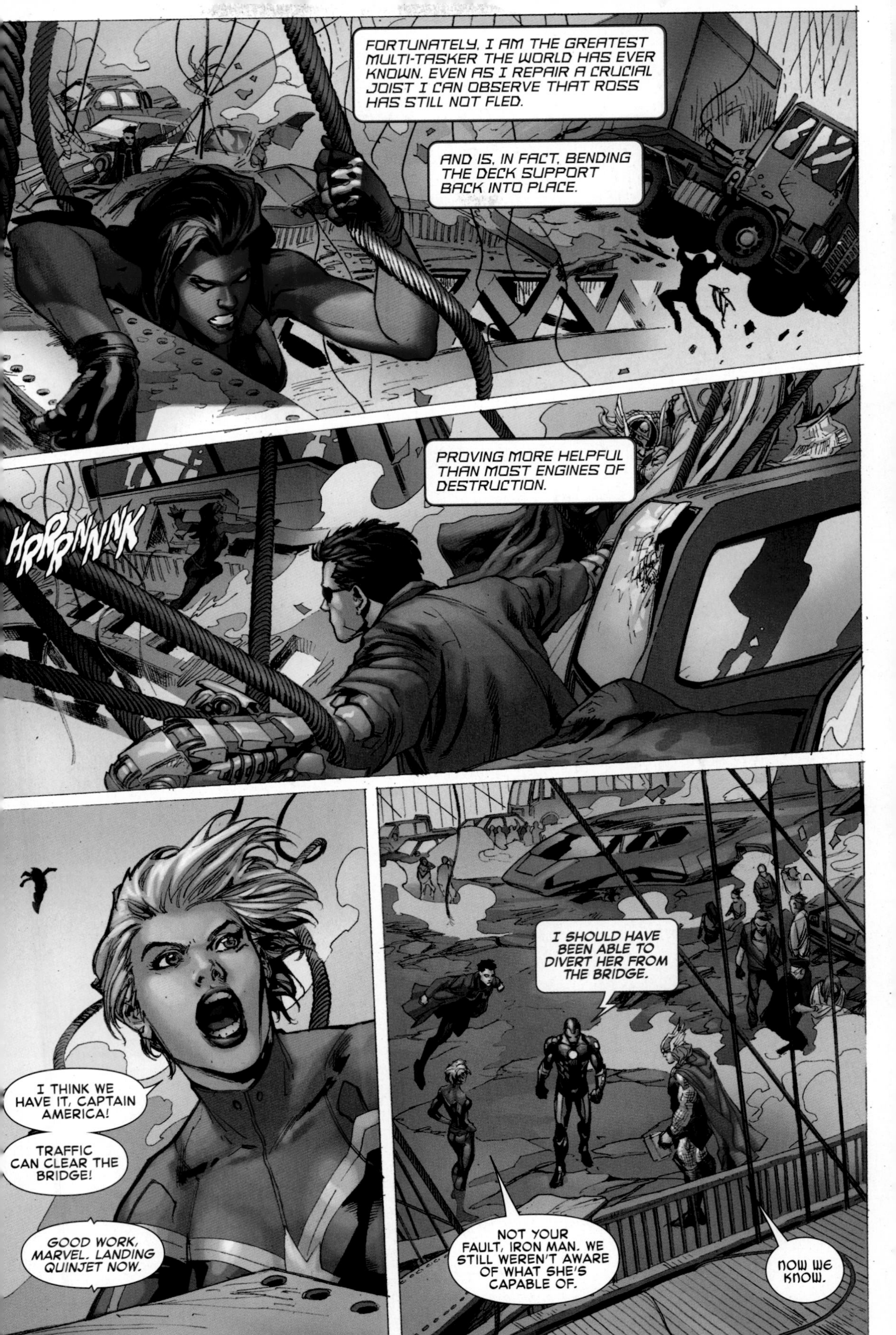
FORTUNATELY, I AM THE GREATEST MULTI-TASKER THE WORLD HAS EVER KNOWN. EVEN AS I REPAIR A CRUCIAL JOIST I CAN OBSERVE THAT ROSS HAS STILL NOT FLED.
AND IS, IN FACT, BENDING THE DECK SUPPORT BACK INTO PLACE.
PROVING MORE HELPFUL THAN MOST ENGINES OF DESTRUCTION.
HRRRNNNK
I THINK WE HAVE IT, CAPTAIN AMERICA!
TRAFFIC CAN CLEAR THE BRIDGE!
GOOD WORK, MARVEL. LANDING QUINJET NOW.
I SHOULD HAVE BEEN ABLE TO DIVERT HER FROM THE BRIDGE.
NOT YOUR FAULT, IRON MAN. WE STILL WEREN'T AWARE OF WHAT SHE'S CAPABLE OF.
NOW WE KNOW.

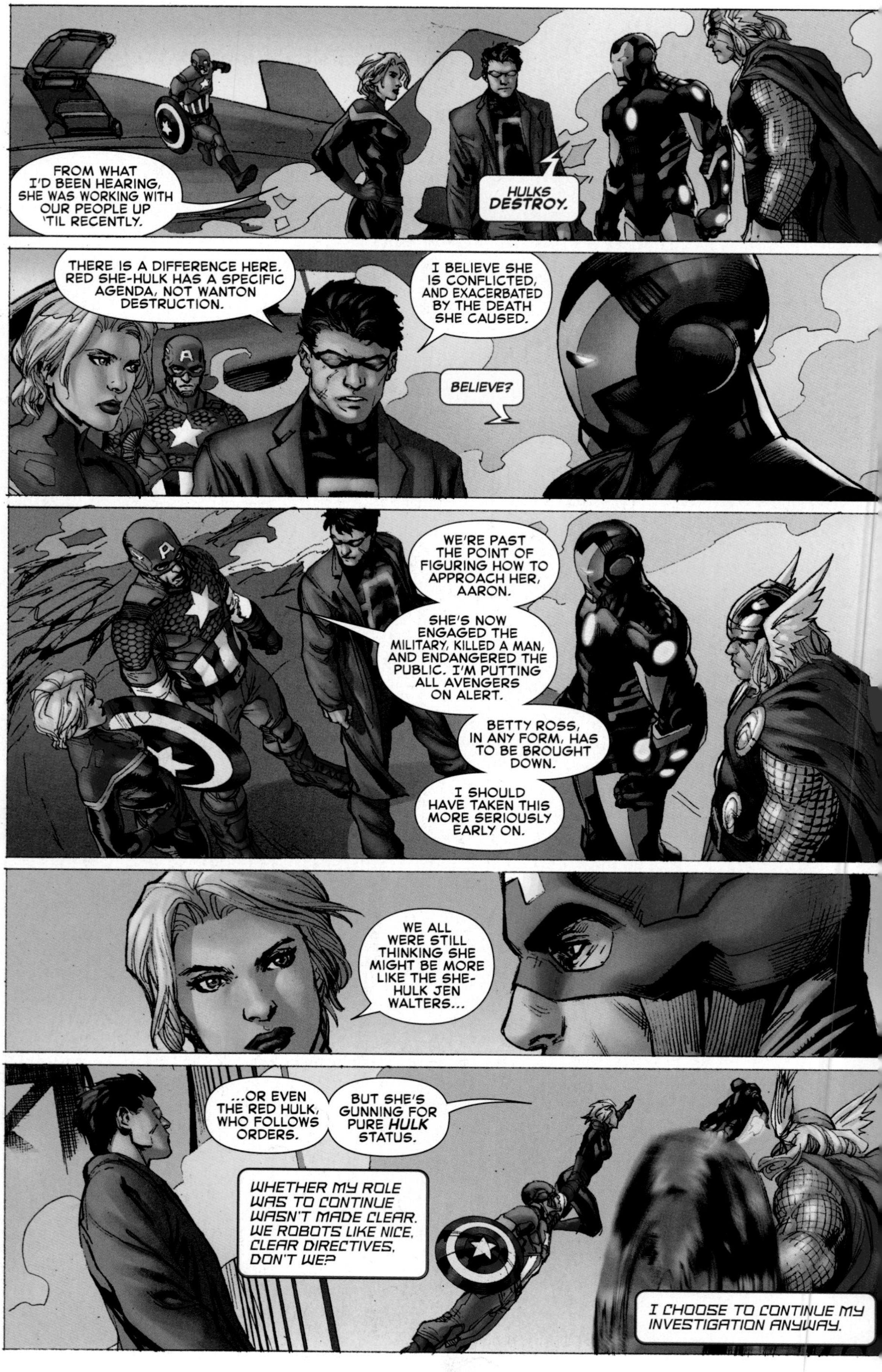
FROM WHAT I'D BEEN HEARING, SHE WAS WORKING WITH OUR PEOPLE UP 'TIL RECENTLY.
HULKS DESTROY.
THERE IS A DIFFERENCE HERE. RED SHE-HULK HAS A SPECIFIC AGENDA, NOT WANTON DESTRUCTION.
I BELIEVE SHE IS CONFLICTED, AND EXACERBATED BY THE DEATH SHE CAUSED.
BELIEVE?
WE'RE PAST THE POINT OF FIGURING HOW TO APPROACH HER, AARON.
SHE'S NOW ENGAGED THE MILITARY, KILLED A MAN, AND ENDANGERED THE PUBLIC. I'M PUTTING ALL AVENGERS ON ALERT.
BETTY ROSS, IN ANY FORM, HAS TO BE BROUGHT DOWN.
I SHOULD HAVE TAKEN THIS MORE SERIOUSLY EARLY ON.
WE ALL WERE STILL THINKING SHE MIGHT BE MORE LIKE THE SHE-HULK JEN WALTERS...
...OR EVEN THE RED HULK, WHO FOLLOWS ORDERS.
BUT SHE'S GUNNING FOR PURE HULK STATUS.
WHETHER MY ROLE WAS TO CONTINUE WASN'T MADE CLEAR. WE ROBOTS LIKE NICE, CLEAR DIRECTIVES, DON'T WE?
I CHOOSE TO CONTINUE MY INVESTIGATION ANYWAY.

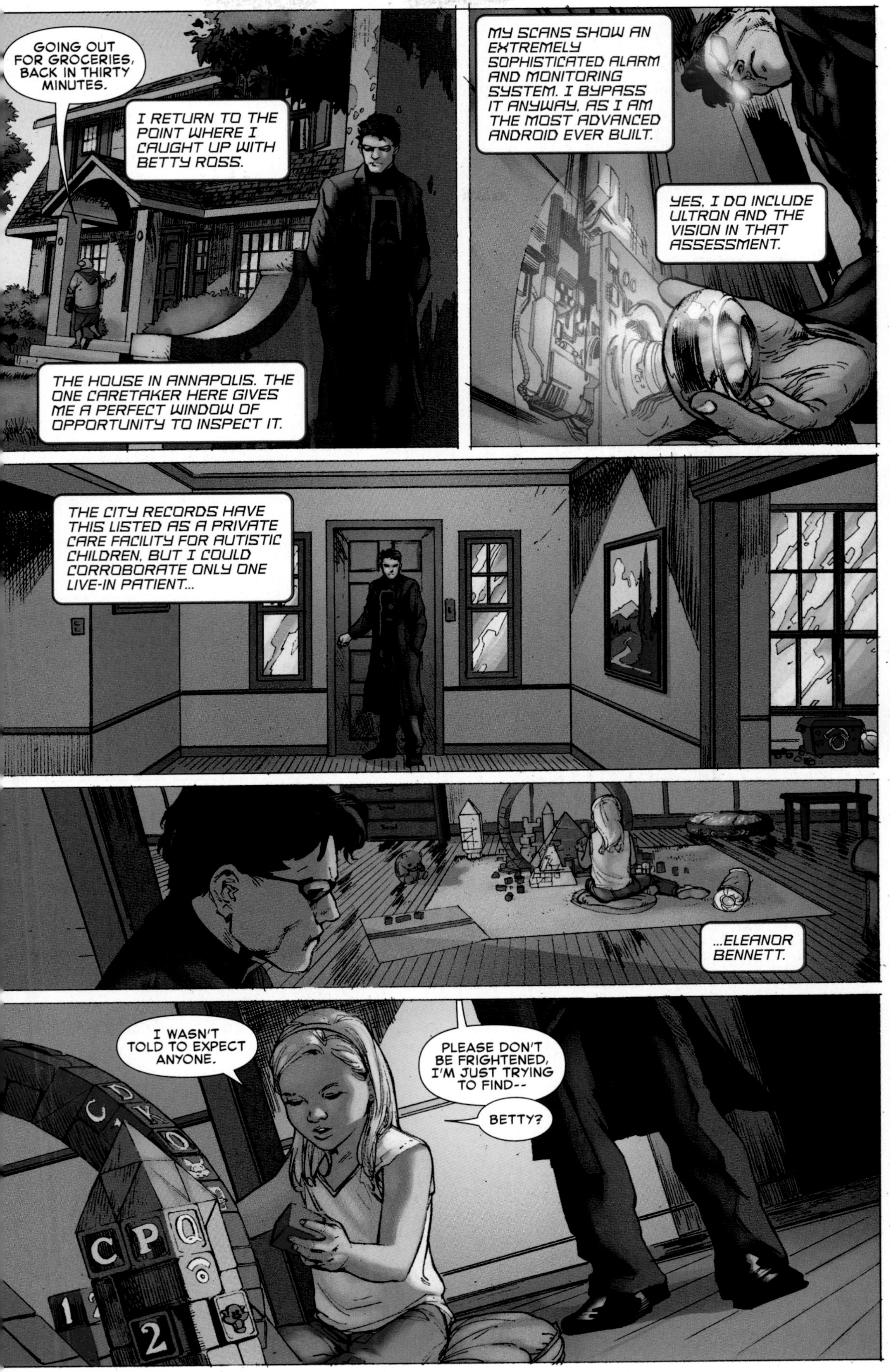

GOING OUT FOR GROCERIES, BACK IN THIRTY MINUTES.
I RETURN TO THE POINT WHERE I CAUGHT UP WITH BETTY ROSS.
THE HOUSE IN ANNAPOLIS. THE ONE CARETAKER HERE GIVES ME A PERFECT WINDOW OF OPPORTUNITY TO INSPECT IT.
MY SCANS SHOW AN EXTREMELY SOPHISTICATED ALARM AND MONITORING SYSTEM. I BYPASS IT ANYWAY, AS I AM THE MOST ADVANCED ANDROID EVER BUILT.
YES, I DO INCLUDE ULTRON AND THE VISION IN THAT ASSESSMENT.
THE CITY RECORDS HAVE THIS LISTED AS A PRIVATE CARE FACILITY FOR AUTISTIC CHILDREN, BUT I COULD CORROBORATE ONLY ONE LIVE-IN PATIENT...
...ELEANOR BENNETT.
I WASN'T TOLD TO EXPECT ANYONE.
PLEASE DON'T BE FRIGHTENED, I'M JUST TRYING TO FIND--
BETTY?

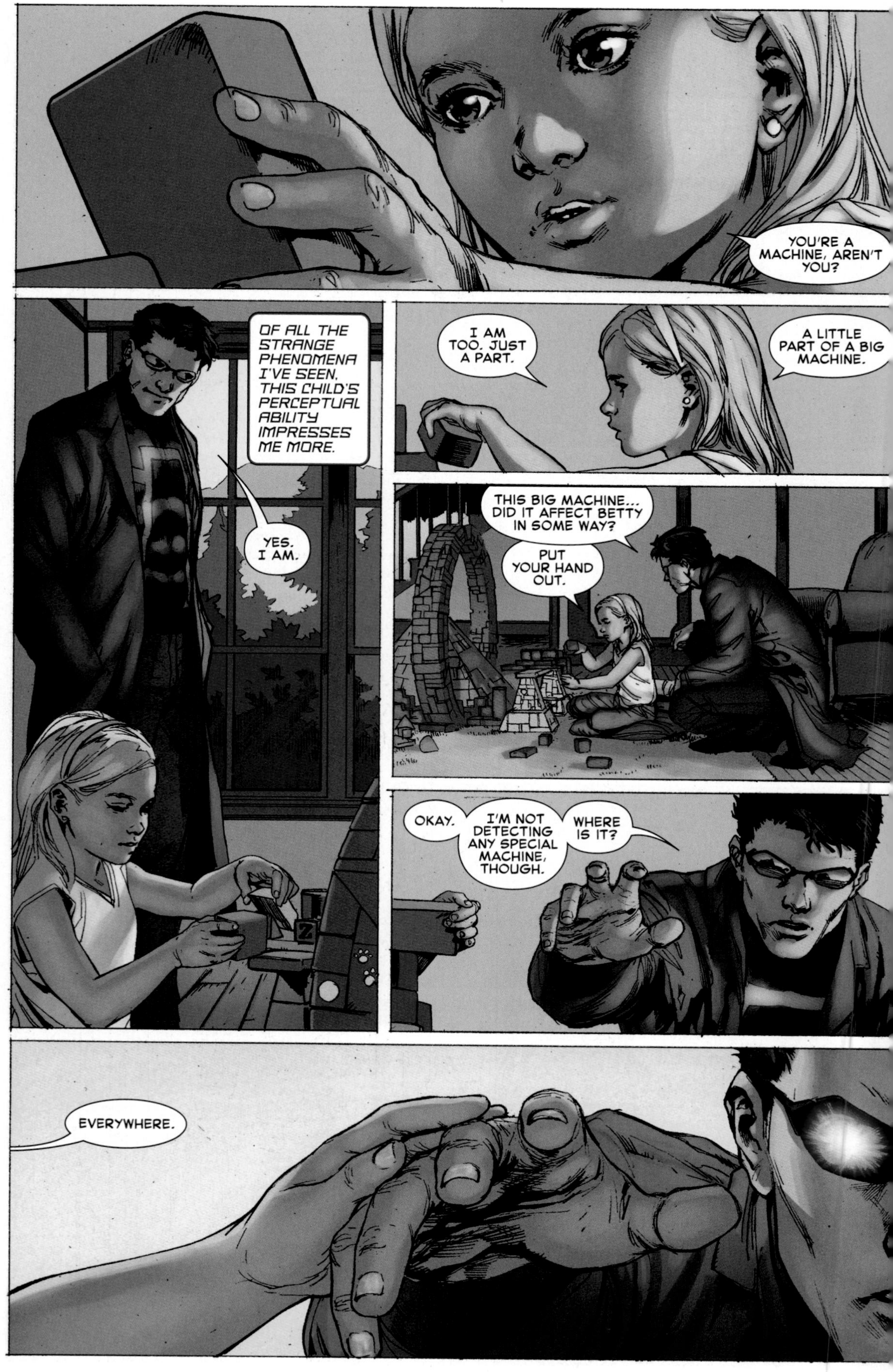
YOU'RE A MACHINE, AREN'T YOU?
OF ALL THE STRANGE PHENOMENA I'VE SEEN, THIS CHILD'S PERCEPTUAL ABILITY IMPRESSES ME MORE.
YES. I AM.
I AM TOO. JUST A PART.
A LITTLE PART OF A BIG MACHINE.
THIS BIG MACHINE... DID IT AFFECT BETTY IN SOME WAY?
PUT YOUR HAND OUT.
OKAY.
I'M NOT DETECTING ANY SPECIAL MACHINE, THOUGH.
WHERE IS IT?
EVERYWHERE.

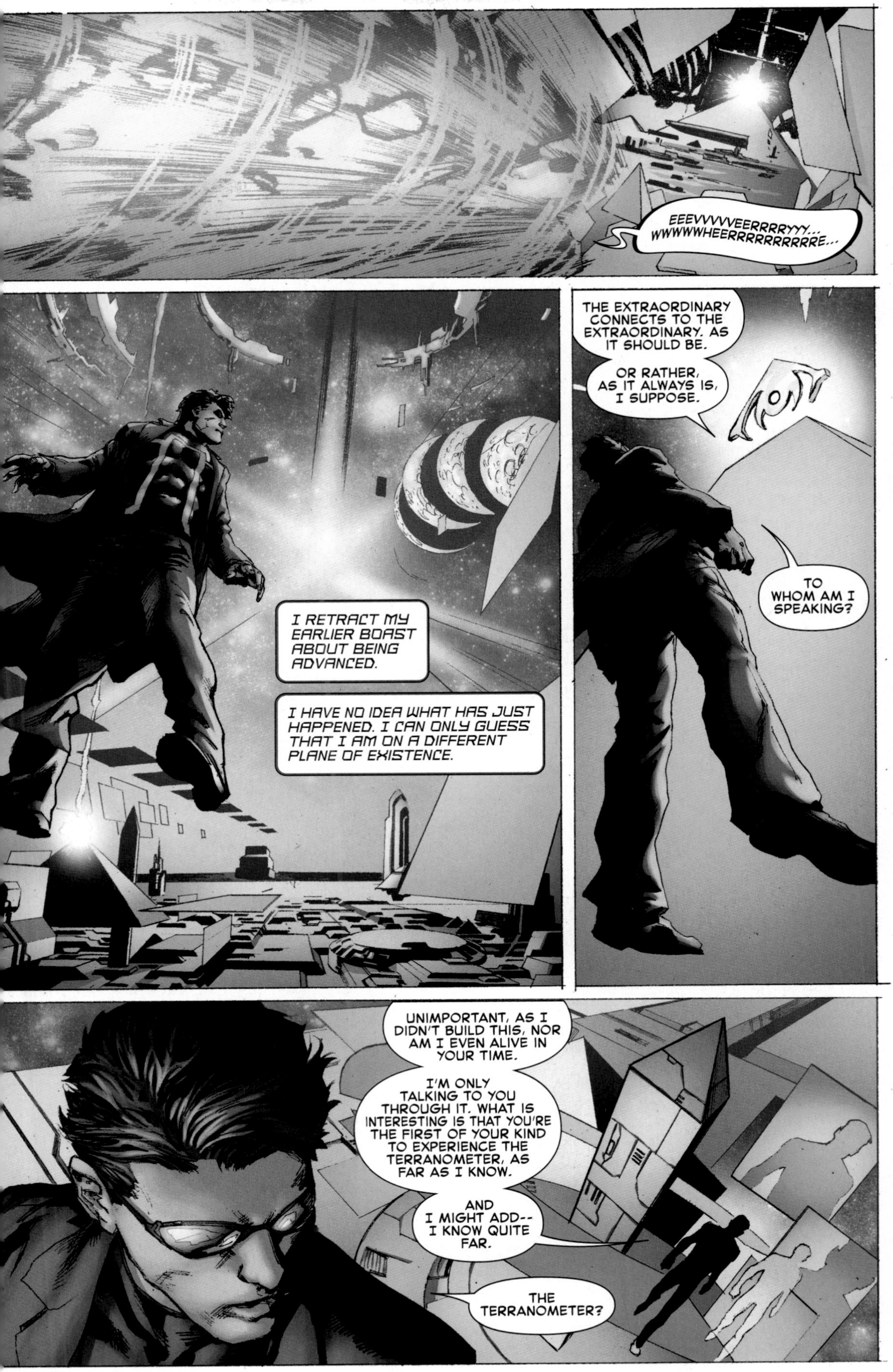
EEEVVVVVVEERRRRYYY... WWWWWHEERRRRRRRRRE...
I RETRACT MY EARLIER BOAST ABOUT BEING ADVANCED.
I HAVE NO IDEA WHAT HAS JUST HAPPENED. I CAN ONLY GUESS THAT I AM ON A DIFFERENT PLANE OF EXISTENCE.
THE EXTRAORDINARY CONNECTS TO THE EXTRAORDINARY. AS IT SHOULD BE.
OR RATHER, AS IT ALWAYS IS, I SUPPOSE.
TO WHOM AM I SPEAKING?
UNIMPORTANT, AS I DIDN'T BUILD THIS, NOR AM I EVEN ALIVE IN YOUR TIME.
I'M ONLY TALKING TO YOU THROUGH IT. WHAT IS INTERESTING IS THAT YOU'RE THE FIRST OF YOUR KIND TO EXPERIENCE THE TERRANOMETER, AS FAR AS I KNOW.
AND I MIGHT ADD-- I KNOW QUITE FAR.
THE TERRANOMETER?

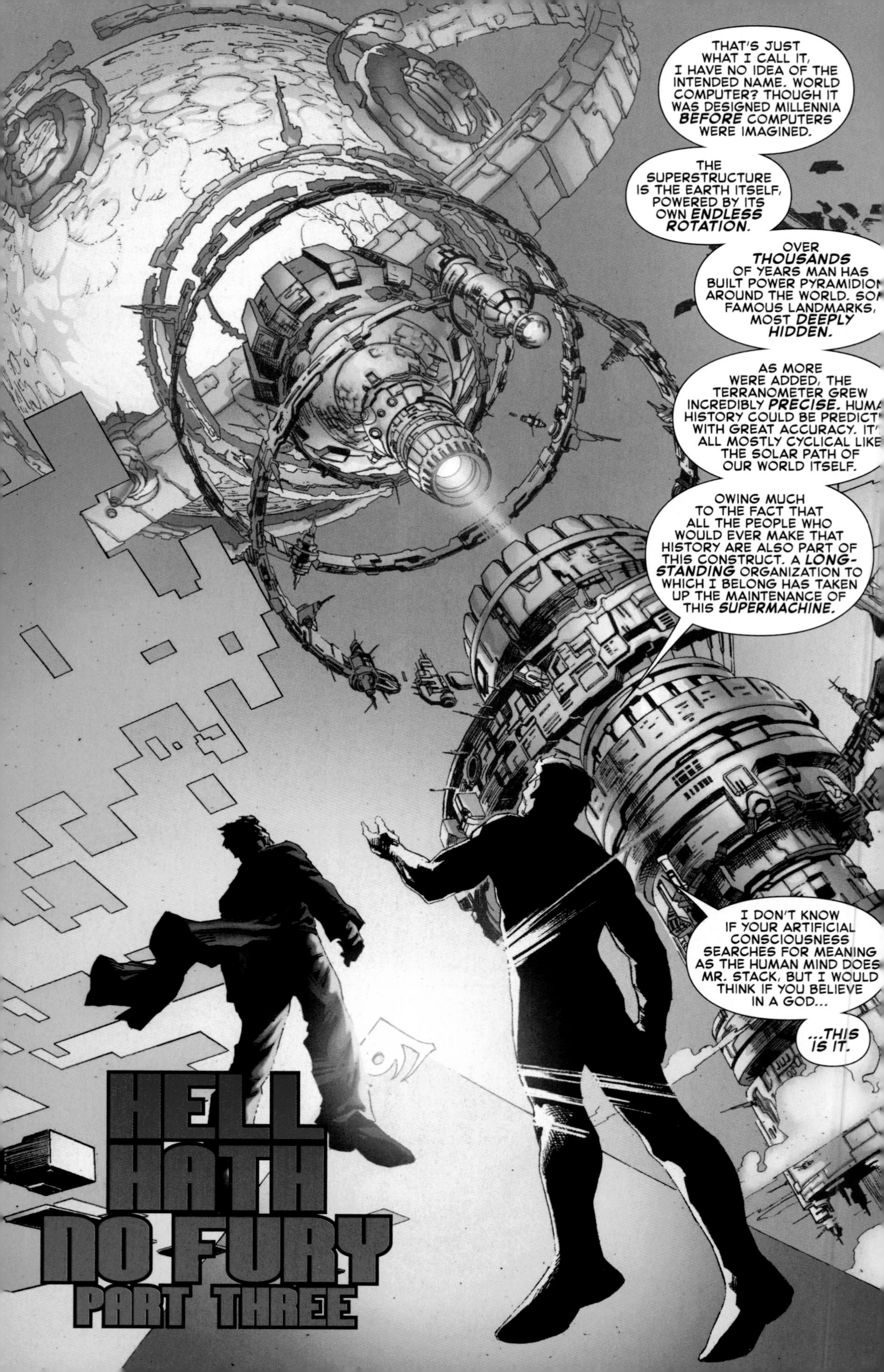
THAT'S JUST WHAT I CALL IT, I HAVE NO IDEA OF THE INTENDED NAME. WORLD COMPUTER? THOUGH IT WAS DESIGNED MILLENNIA BEFORE COMPUTERS WERE IMAGINED.
THE SUPERSTRUCTURE IS THE EARTH ITSELF, POWERED BY ITS OWN ENDLESS ROTATION.
OVER THOUSANDS OF YEARS MAN HAS BUILT POWER PYRAMIDION AROUND THE WORLD. SOM FAMOUS LANDMARKS, MOST DEEPLY HIDDEN.
AS MORE WERE ADDED, THE TERRANOMETER GREW INCREDIBLY PRECISE. HUMA HISTORY COULD BE PREDICT WITH GREAT ACCURACY. IT' ALL MOSTLY CYCLICAL LIKE THE SOLAR PATH OF OUR WORLD ITSELF.
OWING MUCH TO THE FACT THAT ALL THE PEOPLE WHO WOULD EVER MAKE THAT HISTORY ARE ALSO PART OF THIS CONSTRUCT. A LONG-STANDING ORGANIZATION TO WHICH I BELONG HAS TAKEN UP THE MAINTENANCE OF THIS SUPERMACHINE.
I DON'T KNOW IF YOUR ARTIFICIAL CONSCIOUSNESS SEARCHES FOR MEANING AS THE HUMAN MIND DOES MR. STACK, BUT I WOULD THINK IF YOU BELIEVE IN A GOD...
...THIS IS IT.
HELL HATH NO FURY
PART THREE

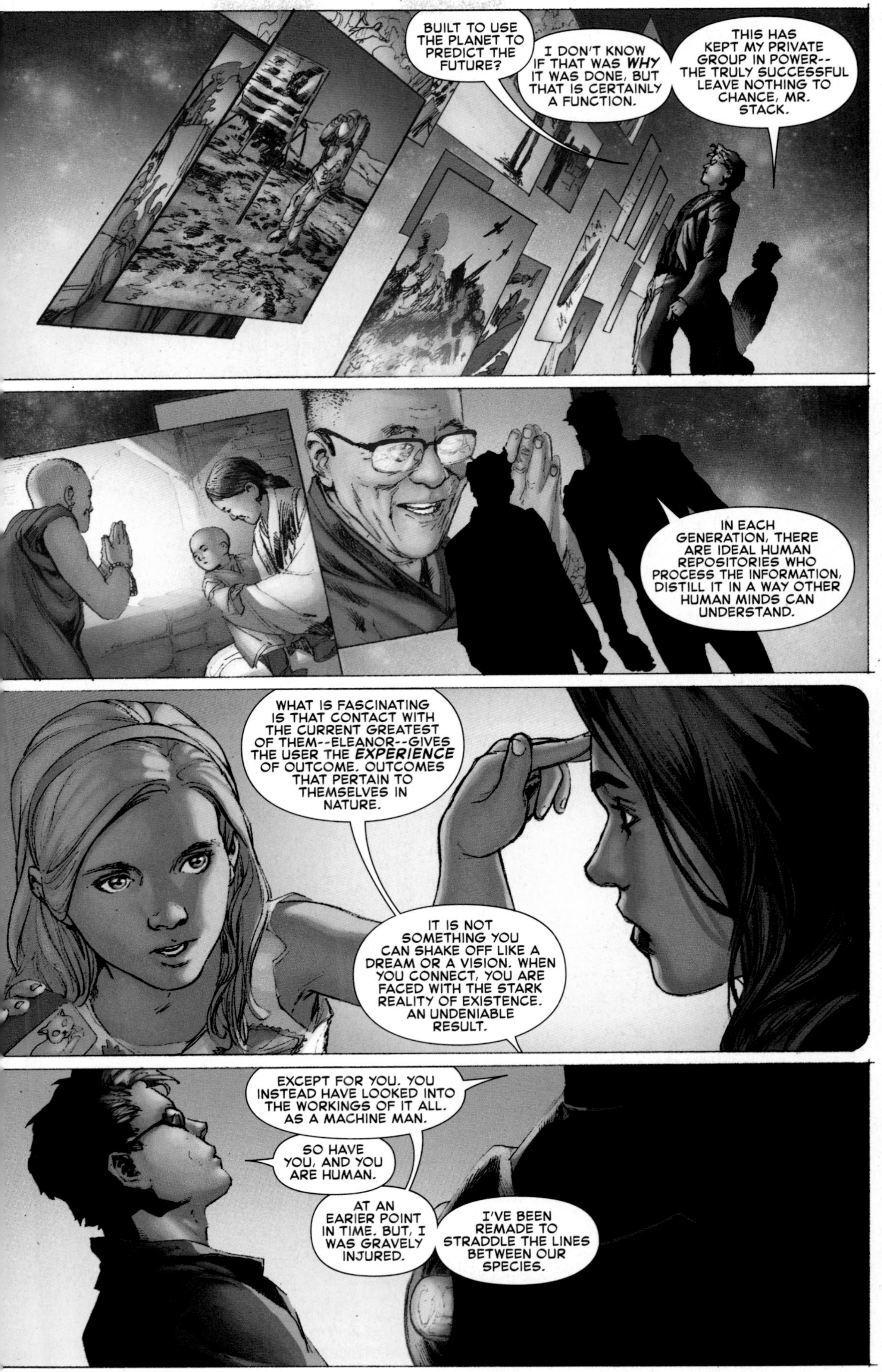
BUILT TO USE THE PLANET TO PREDICT THE FUTURE?
I DON'T KNOW IF THAT WAS WHY IT WAS DONE, BUT THAT IS CERTAINLY A FUNCTION.
THIS HAS KEPT MY PRIVATE GROUP IN POWER-- THE TRULY SUCCESSFUL LEAVE NOTHING TO CHANCE, MR. STACK.
IN EACH GENERATION, THERE ARE IDEAL HUMAN REPOSITORIES WHO PROCESS THE INFORMATION, DISTILL IT IN A WAY OTHER HUMAN MINDS CAN UNDERSTAND.
WHAT IS FASCINATING IS THAT CONTACT WITH THE CURRENT GREATEST OF THEM--ELEANOR--GIVES THE USER THE EXPERIENCE OF OUTCOME. OUTCOMES THAT PERTAIN TO THEMSELVES IN NATURE.
IT IS NOT SOMETHING YOU CAN SHAKE OFF LIKE A DREAM OR A VISION. WHEN YOU CONNECT, YOU ARE FACED WITH THE STARK REALITY OF EXISTENCE. AN UNDENIABLE RESULT.
EXCEPT FOR YOU. YOU INSTEAD HAVE LOOKED INTO THE WORKINGS OF IT ALL. AS A MACHINE MAN.
SO HAVE YOU, AND YOU ARE HUMAN.
AT AN EARIER POINT IN TIME. BUT, I WAS GRAVELY INJURED.
I'VE BEEN REMADE TO STRADDLE THE LINES BETWEEN OUR SPECIES.

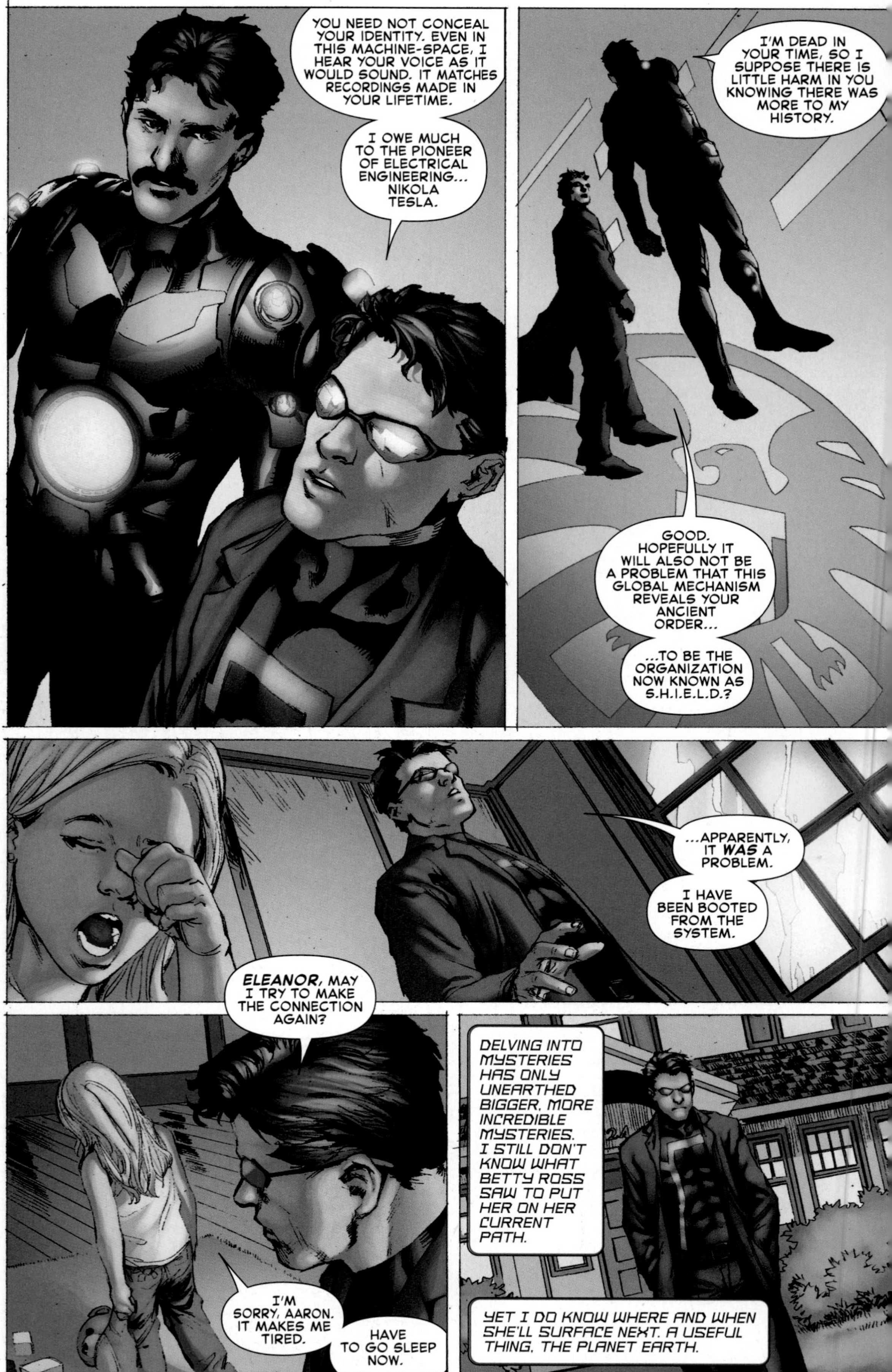

YOU NEED NOT CONCEAL YOUR IDENTITY. EVEN IN THIS MACHINE-SPACE, I HEAR YOUR VOICE AS IT WOULD SOUND. IT MATCHES RECORDINGS MADE IN YOUR LIFETIME.
I OWE MUCH TO THE PIONEER OF ELECTRICAL ENGINEERING... NIKOLA TESLA.
I'M DEAD IN YOUR TIME, SO I SUPPOSE THERE IS LITTLE HARM IN YOU KNOWING THERE WAS MORE TO MY HISTORY.
GOOD. HOPEFULLY IT WILL ALSO NOT BE A PROBLEM THAT THIS GLOBAL MECHANISM REVEALS YOUR ANCIENT ORDER...
...TO BE THE ORGANIZATION NOW KNOWN AS S.H.I.E.L.D.?
...APPARENTLY, IT *WAS* A PROBLEM.
I HAVE BEEN BOOTED FROM THE SYSTEM.
ELEANOR, MAY I TRY TO MAKE THE CONNECTION AGAIN?
I'M SORRY, AARON. IT MAKES ME TIRED.
HAVE TO GO SLEEP NOW.
DELVING INTO MYSTERIES HAS ONLY UNEARTHED BIGGER, MORE INCREDIBLE MYSTERIES. I STILL DON'T KNOW WHAT BETTY ROSS SAW TO PUT HER ON HER CURRENT PATH.
YET I DO KNOW WHERE AND WHEN SHE'LL SURFACE NEXT. A USEFUL THING, THE PLANET EARTH.

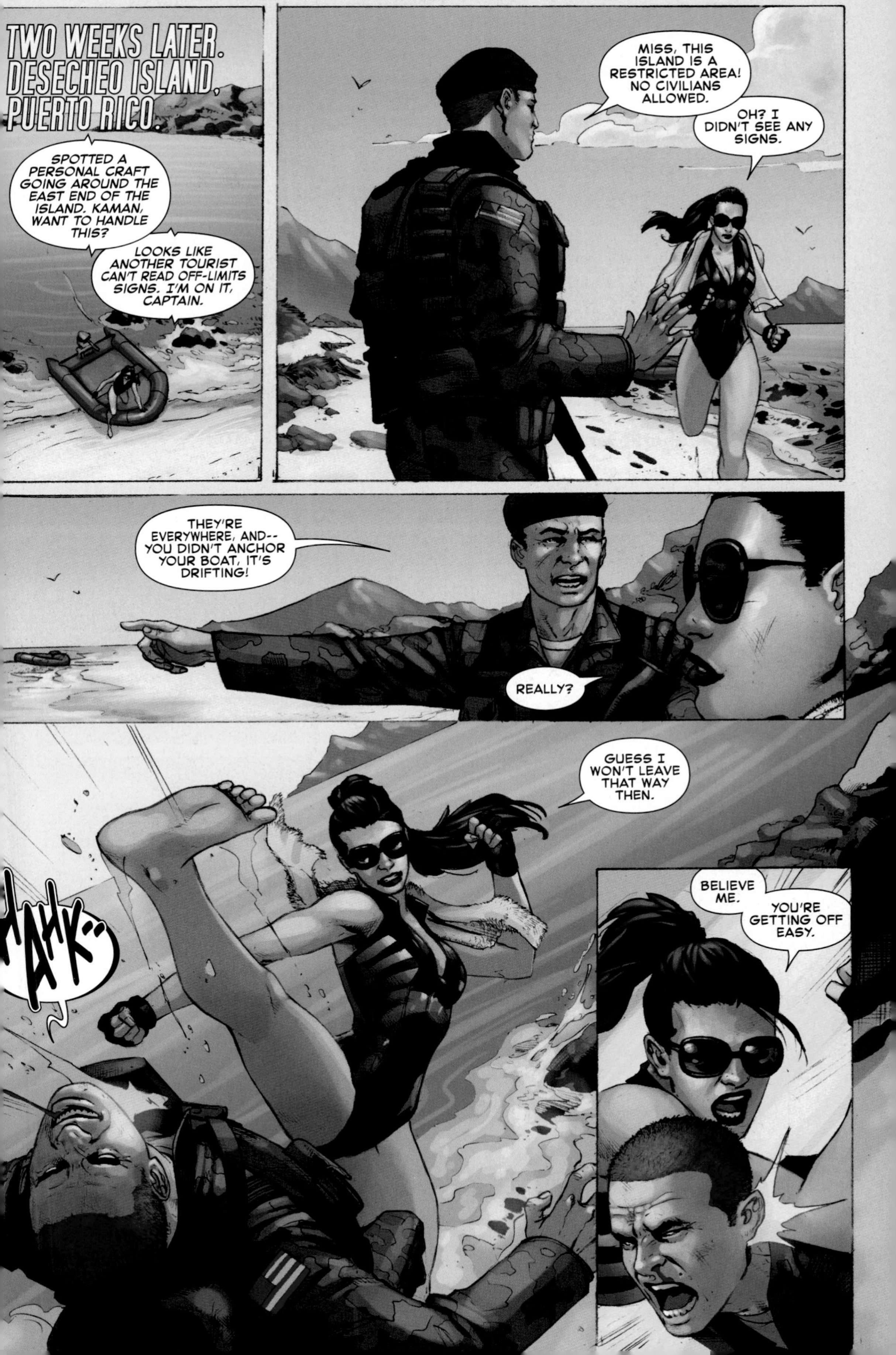
TWO WEEKS LATER. DESECHEO ISLAND, PUERTO RICO.
SPOTTED A PERSONAL CRAFT GOING AROUND THE EAST END OF THE ISLAND. KAMAN, WANT TO HANDLE THIS?
LOOKS LIKE ANOTHER TOURIST CAN'T READ OFF-LIMITS SIGNS. I'M ON IT, CAPTAIN.
MISS, THIS ISLAND IS A RESTRICTED AREA! NO CIVILIANS ALLOWED.
OH? I DIDN'T SEE ANY SIGNS.
THEY'RE EVERYWHERE, AND-- YOU DIDN'T ANCHOR YOUR BOAT, IT'S DRIFTING!
REALLY?
GUESS I WON'T LEAVE THAT WAY THEN.
HAHK--
BELIEVE ME.
YOU'RE GETTING OFF EASY.

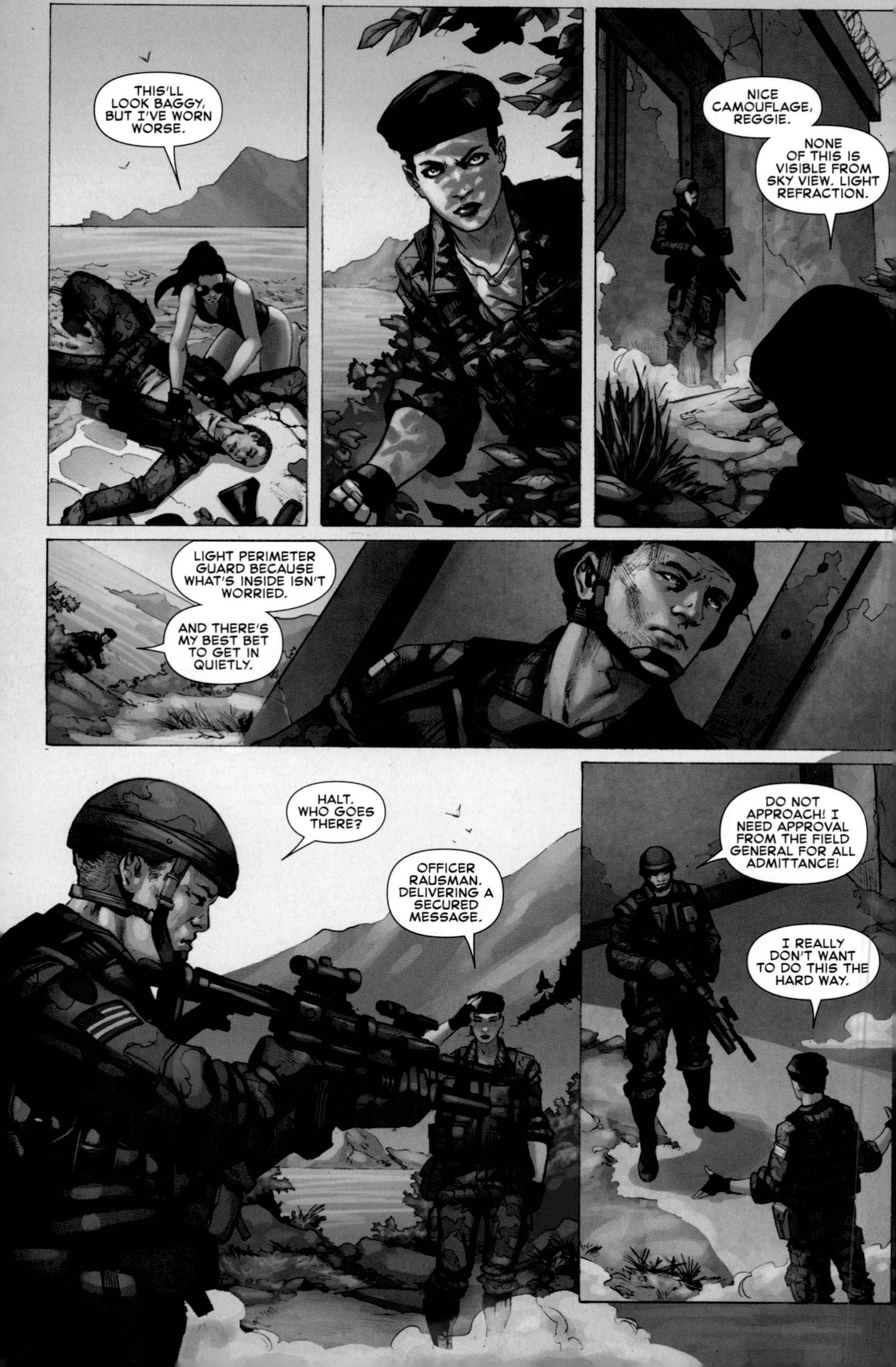
THIS'LL LOOK BAGGY, BUT I'VE WORN WORSE.
NICE CAMOUFLAGE, REGGIE.
NONE OF THIS IS VISIBLE FROM SKY VIEW. LIGHT REFRACTION.
LIGHT PERIMETER GUARD BECAUSE WHAT'S INSIDE ISN'T WORRIED.
AND THERE'S MY BEST BET TO GET IN QUIETLY.
HALT. WHO GOES THERE?
OFFICER RAUSMAN. DELIVERING A SECURED MESSAGE.
DO NOT APPROACH! I NEED APPROVAL FROM THE FIELD GENERAL FOR ALL ADMITTANCE!
I REALLY DON'T WANT TO DO THIS THE HARD WAY.

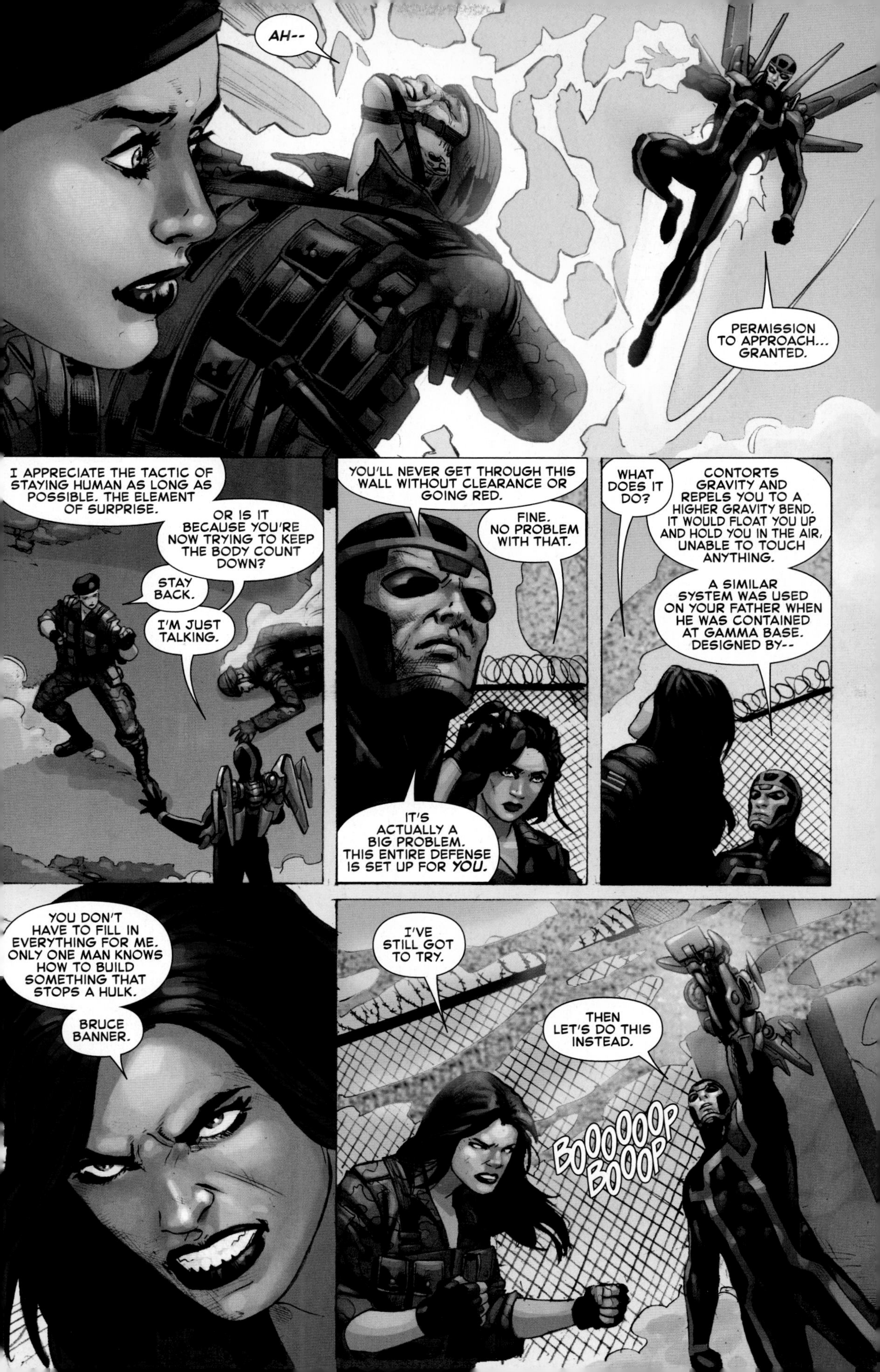
AH--
PERMISSION TO APPROACH... GRANTED.
I APPRECIATE THE TACTIC OF STAYING HUMAN AS LONG AS POSSIBLE. THE ELEMENT OF SURPRISE.
OR IS IT BECAUSE YOU'RE NOW TRYING TO KEEP THE BODY COUNT DOWN?
STAY BACK.
I'M JUST TALKING.
YOU'LL NEVER GET THROUGH THIS WALL WITHOUT CLEARANCE OR GOING RED.
FINE. NO PROBLEM WITH THAT.
IT'S ACTUALLY A BIG PROBLEM. THIS ENTIRE DEFENSE IS SET UP FOR YOU.
WHAT DOES IT DO?
CONTORTS GRAVITY AND REPELS YOU TO A HIGHER GRAVITY BEND. IT WOULD FLOAT YOU UP AND HOLD YOU IN THE AIR, UNABLE TO TOUCH ANYTHING.
A SIMILAR SYSTEM WAS USED ON YOUR FATHER WHEN HE WAS CONTAINED AT GAMMA BASE. DESIGNED BY--
YOU DON'T HAVE TO FILL IN EVERYTHING FOR ME. ONLY ONE MAN KNOWS HOW TO BUILD SOMETHING THAT STOPS A HULK.
BRUCE BANNER.
I'VE STILL GOT TO TRY.
THEN LET'S DO THIS INSTEAD.
BOOOOOOP BOOOP

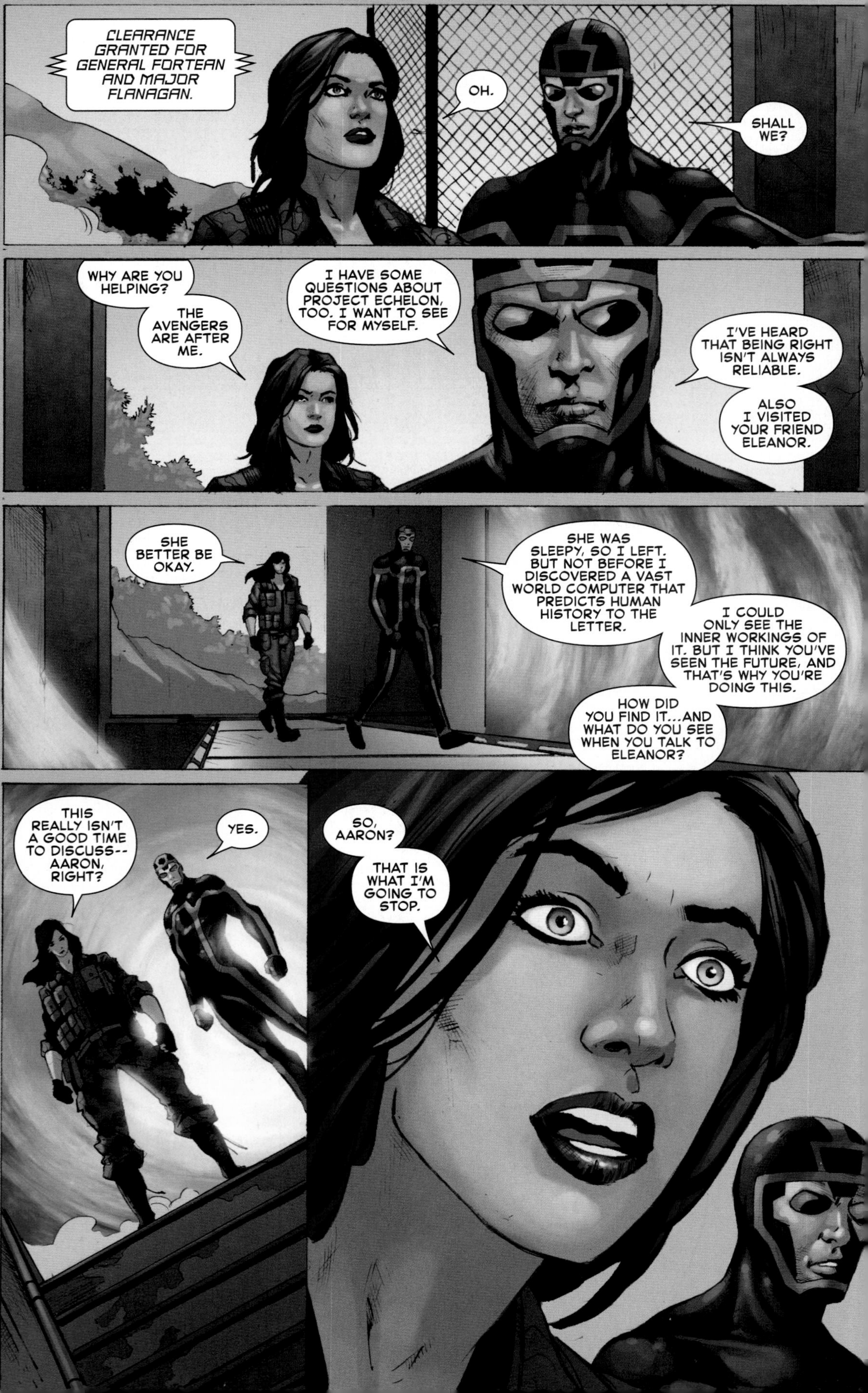
CLEARANCE GRANTED FOR GENERAL FORTEAN AND MAJOR FLANAGAN.
OH.
SHALL WE?
WHY ARE YOU HELPING?
THE AVENGERS ARE AFTER ME.
I HAVE SOME QUESTIONS ABOUT PROJECT ECHELON, TOO. I WANT TO SEE FOR MYSELF.
I'VE HEARD THAT BEING RIGHT ISN'T ALWAYS RELIABLE.
ALSO I VISITED YOUR FRIEND ELEANOR.
SHE BETTER BE OKAY.
SHE WAS SLEEPY, SO I LEFT. BUT NOT BEFORE I DISCOVERED A VAST WORLD COMPUTER THAT PREDICTS HUMAN HISTORY TO THE LETTER.
I COULD ONLY SEE THE INNER WORKINGS OF IT. BUT I THINK YOU'VE SEEN THE FUTURE, AND THAT'S WHY YOU'RE DOING THIS.
HOW DID YOU FIND IT...AND WHAT DO YOU SEE WHEN YOU TALK TO ELEANOR?
THIS REALLY ISN'T A GOOD TIME TO DISCUSS-- AARON, RIGHT?
YES.
SO, AARON?
THAT IS WHAT I'M GOING TO STOP.

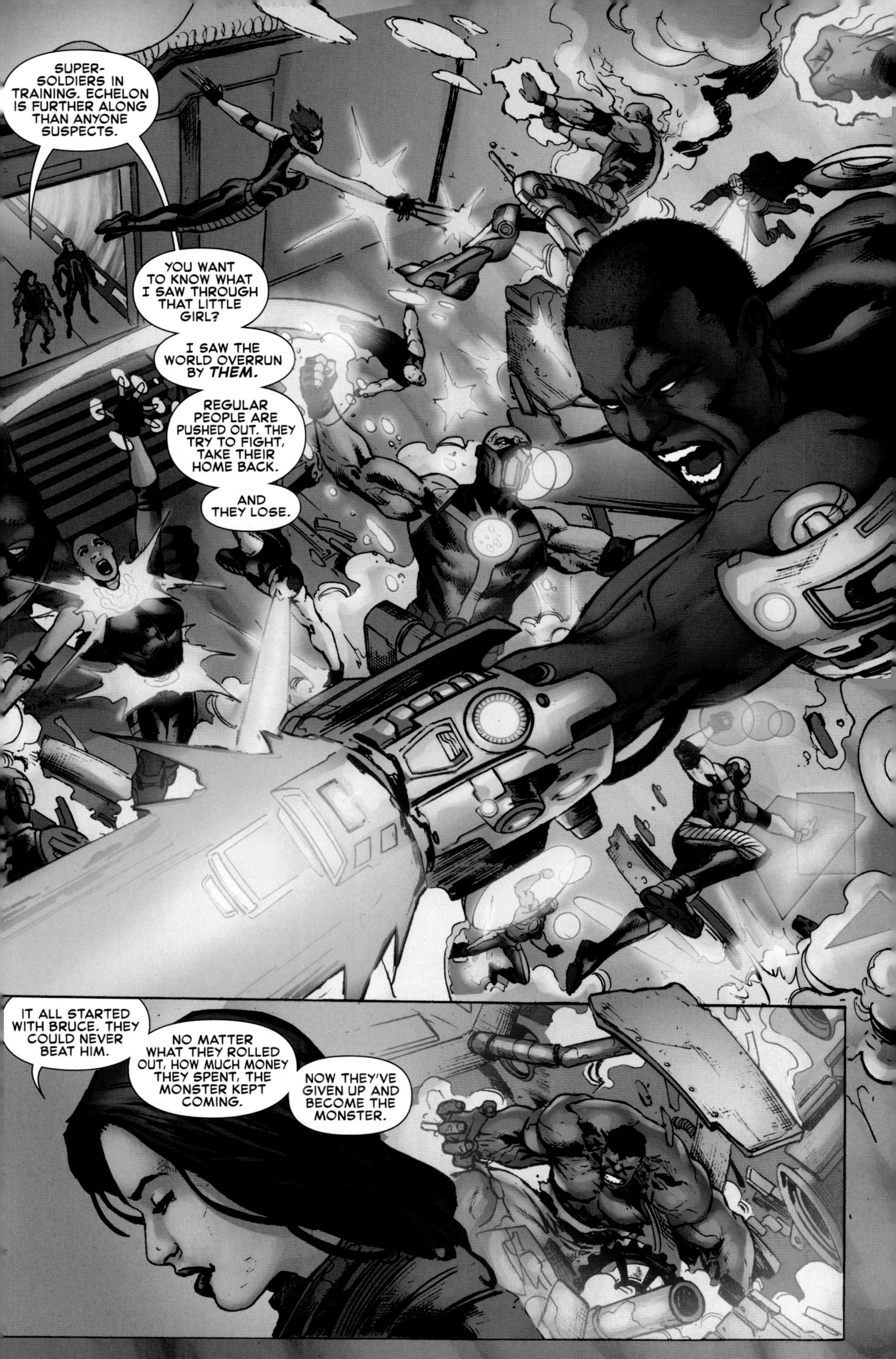
SUPER-SOLDIERS IN TRAINING. ECHELON IS FURTHER ALONG THAN ANYONE SUSPECTS.
YOU WANT TO KNOW WHAT I SAW THROUGH THAT LITTLE GIRL?
I SAW THE WORLD OVERRUN BY *THEM.*
REGULAR PEOPLE ARE PUSHED OUT. THEY TRY TO FIGHT, TAKE THEIR HOME BACK.
AND THEY LOSE.
IT ALL STARTED WITH BRUCE. THEY COULD NEVER BEAT HIM.
NO MATTER WHAT THEY ROLLED OUT, HOW MUCH MONEY THEY SPENT, THE MONSTER KEPT COMING.
NOW THEY'VE GIVEN UP AND BECOME THE MONSTER.

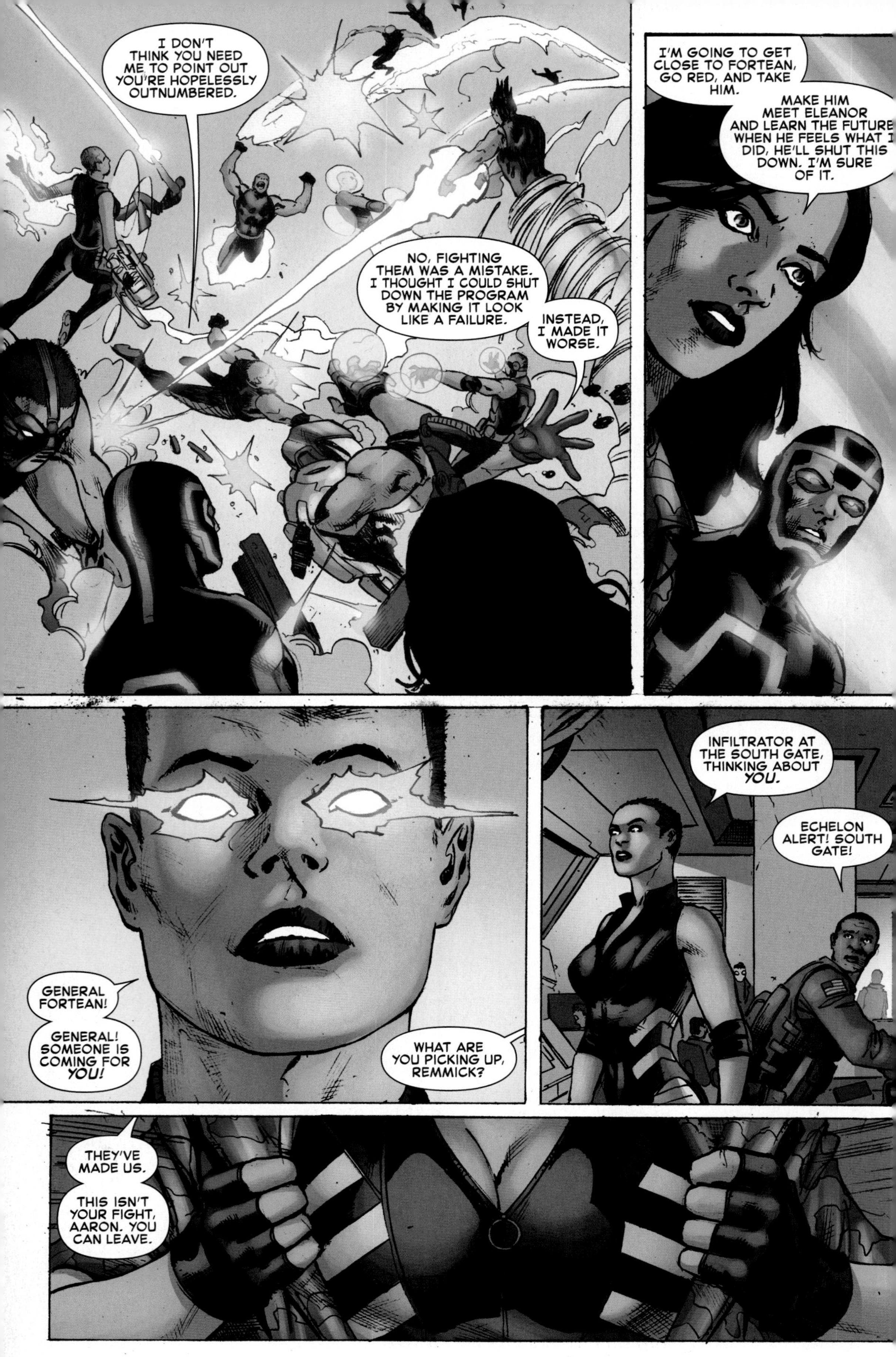
I DON'T THINK YOU NEED ME TO POINT OUT YOU'RE HOPELESSLY OUTNUMBERED.
NO, FIGHTING THEM WAS A MISTAKE. I THOUGHT I COULD SHUT DOWN THE PROGRAM BY MAKING IT LOOK LIKE A FAILURE.
INSTEAD, I MADE IT WORSE.
I'M GOING TO GET CLOSE TO FORTEAN, GO RED, AND TAKE HIM.
MAKE HIM MEET ELEANOR AND LEARN THE FUTURE. WHEN HE FEELS WHAT I DID, HE'LL SHUT THIS DOWN. I'M SURE OF IT.
GENERAL FORTEAN!
GENERAL! SOMEONE IS COMING FOR YOU!
WHAT ARE YOU PICKING UP, REMMICK?
INFILTRATOR AT THE SOUTH GATE, THINKING ABOUT YOU.
ECHELON ALERT! SOUTH GATE!
THEY'VE MADE US.
THIS ISN'T YOUR FIGHT, AARON. YOU CAN LEAVE.

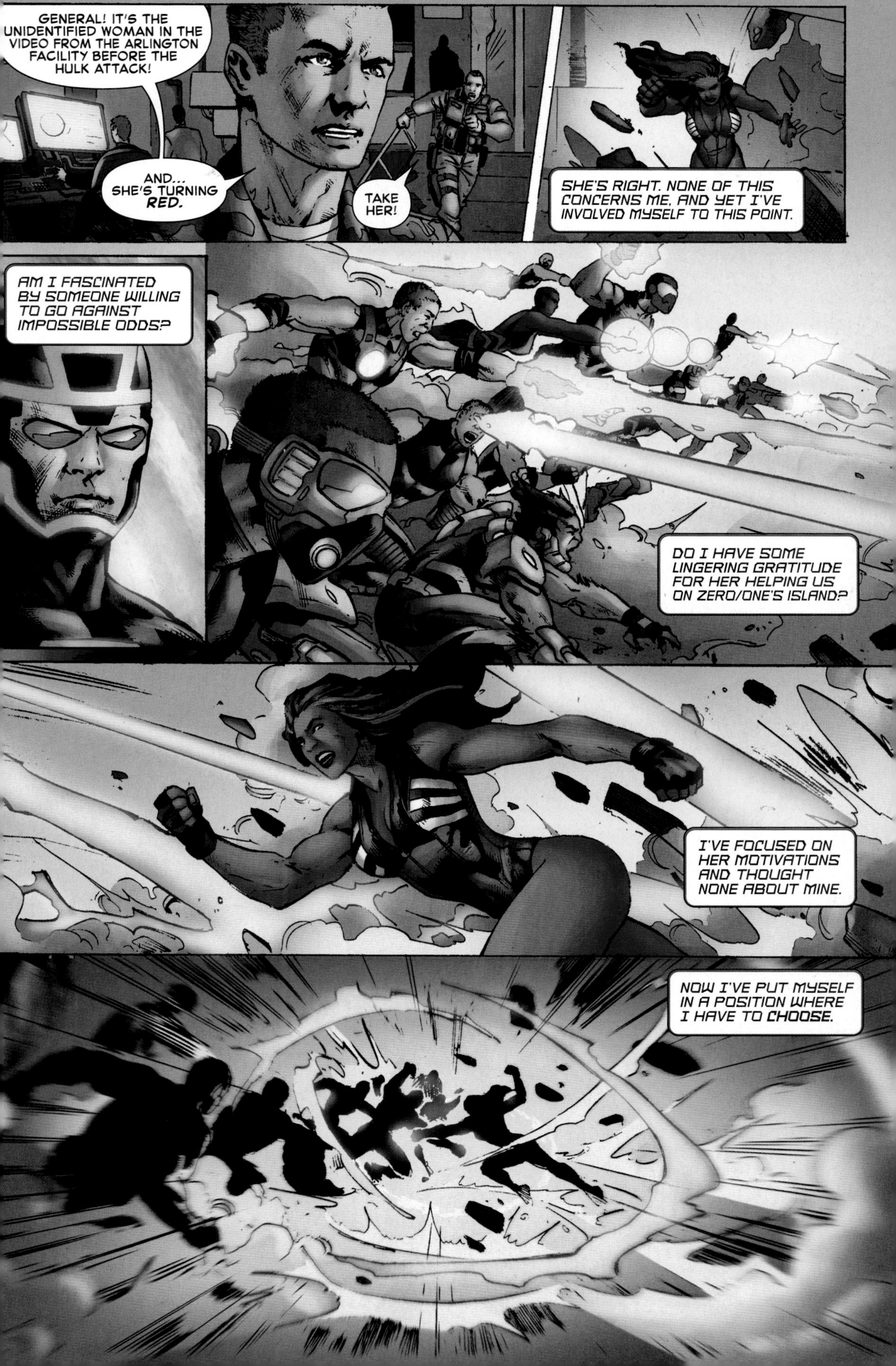
GENERAL! IT'S THE UNIDENTIFIED WOMAN IN THE VIDEO FROM THE ARLINGTON FACILITY BEFORE THE HULK ATTACK!
AND... SHE'S TURNING RED.
TAKE HER!
SHE'S RIGHT. NONE OF THIS CONCERNS ME, AND YET I'VE INVOLVED MYSELF TO THIS POINT.
AM I FASCINATED BY SOMEONE WILLING TO GO AGAINST IMPOSSIBLE ODDS?
DO I HAVE SOME LINGERING GRATITUDE FOR HER HELPING US ON ZERO/ONE'S ISLAND?
I'VE FOCUSED ON HER MOTIVATIONS AND THOUGHT NONE ABOUT MINE.
NOW I'VE PUT MYSELF IN A POSITION WHERE I HAVE TO CHOOSE.

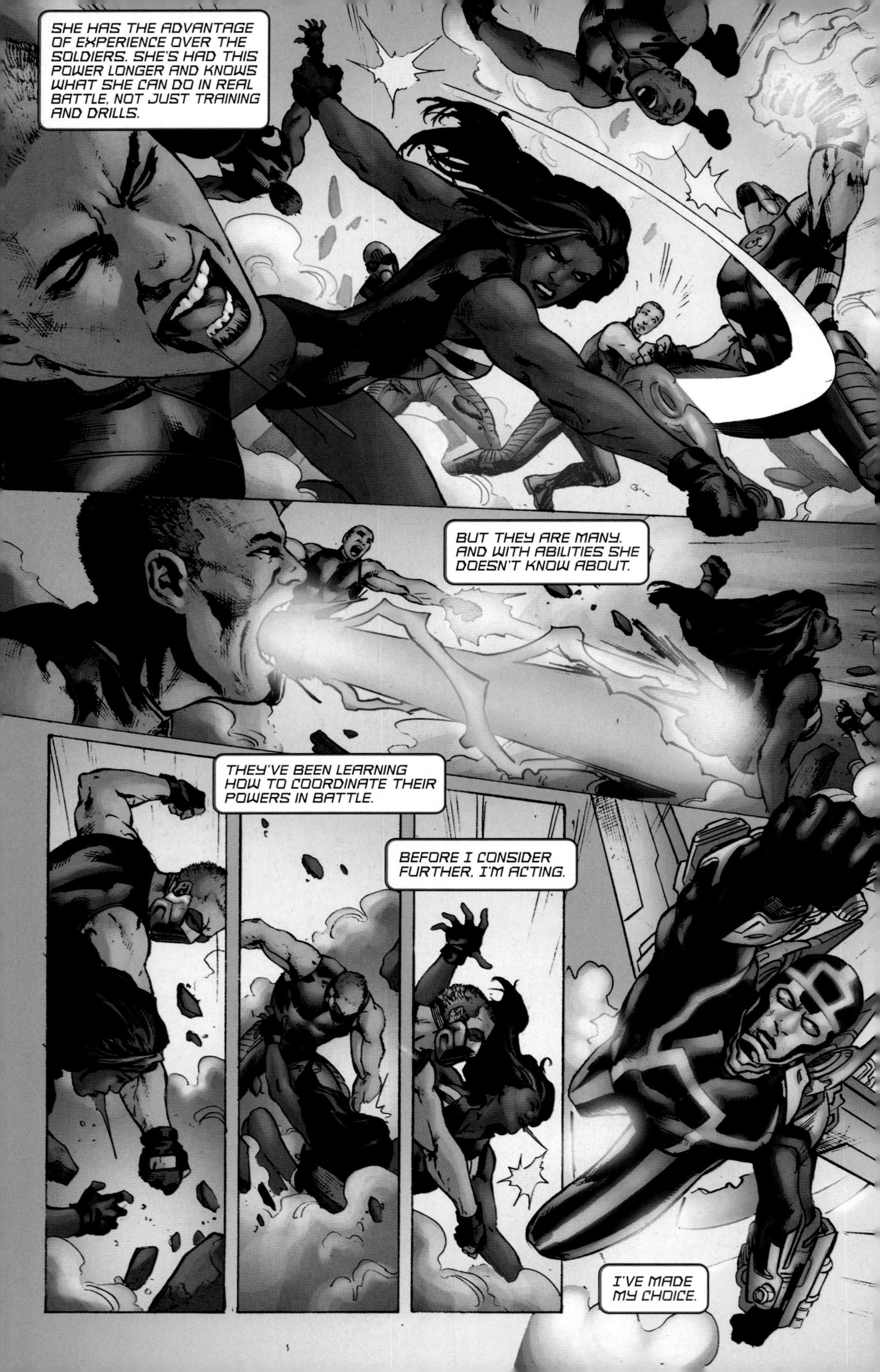
SHE HAS THE ADVANTAGE OF EXPERIENCE OVER THE SOLDIERS. SHE'S HAD THIS POWER LONGER AND KNOWS WHAT SHE CAN DO IN REAL BATTLE, NOT JUST TRAINING AND DRILLS.
BUT THEY ARE MANY. AND WITH ABILITIES SHE DOESN'T KNOW ABOUT.
THEY'VE BEEN LEARNING HOW TO COORDINATE THEIR POWERS IN BATTLE.
BEFORE I CONSIDER FURTHER, I'M ACTING.
I'VE MADE MY CHOICE.

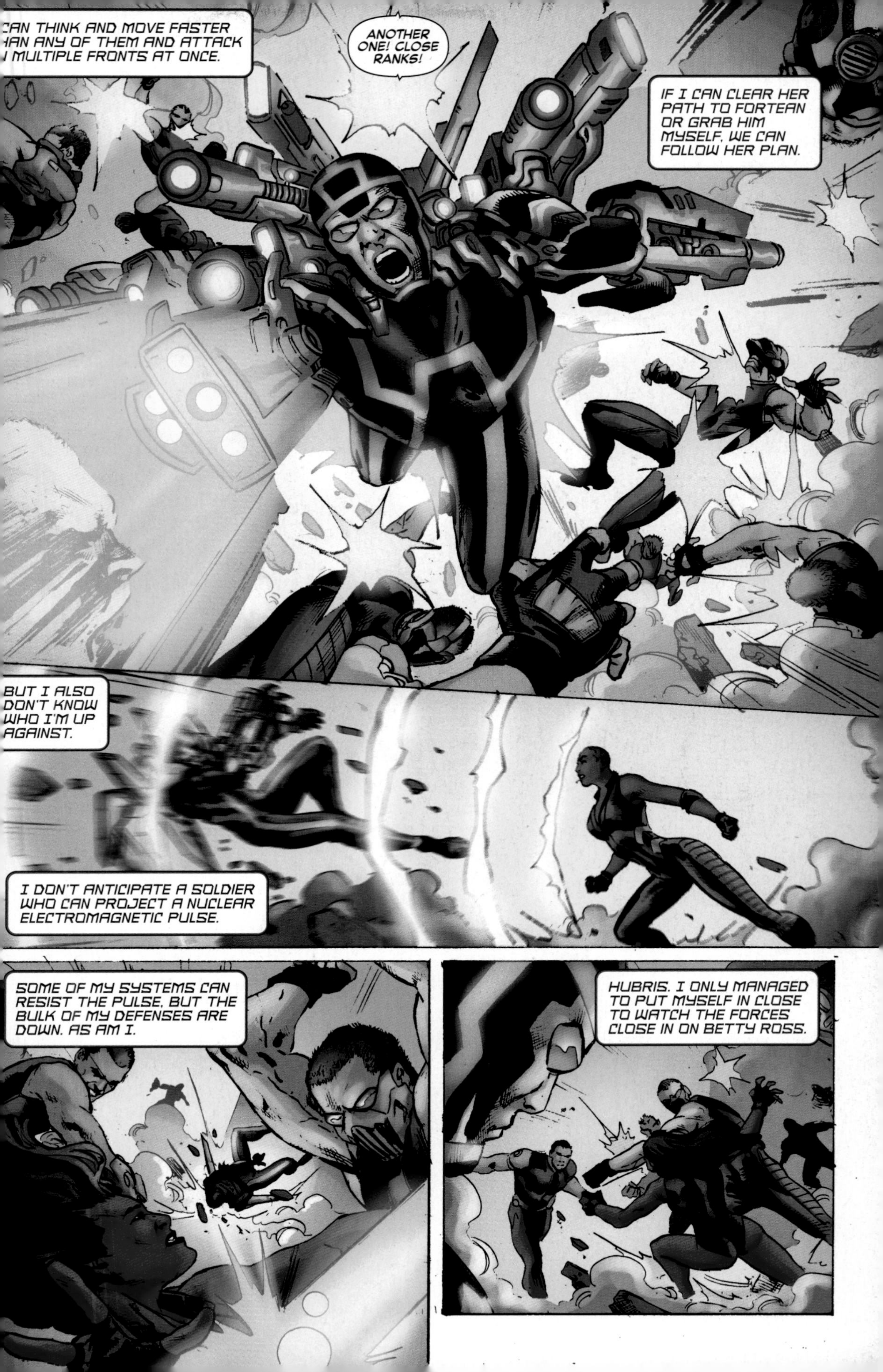
CAN THINK AND MOVE FASTER HAN ANY OF THEM AND ATTACK N MULTIPLE FRONTS AT ONCE.
ANOTHER ONE! CLOSE RANKS!
IF I CAN CLEAR HER PATH TO FORTEAN OR GRAB HIM MYSELF, WE CAN FOLLOW HER PLAN.
BUT I ALSO DON'T KNOW WHO I'M UP AGAINST.
I DON'T ANTICIPATE A SOLDIER WHO CAN PROJECT A NUCLEAR ELECTROMAGNETIC PULSE.
SOME OF MY SYSTEMS CAN RESIST THE PULSE, BUT THE BULK OF MY DEFENSES ARE DOWN. AS AM I.
HUBRIS. I ONLY MANAGED TO PUT MYSELF IN CLOSE TO WATCH THE FORCES CLOSE IN ON BETTY ROSS.

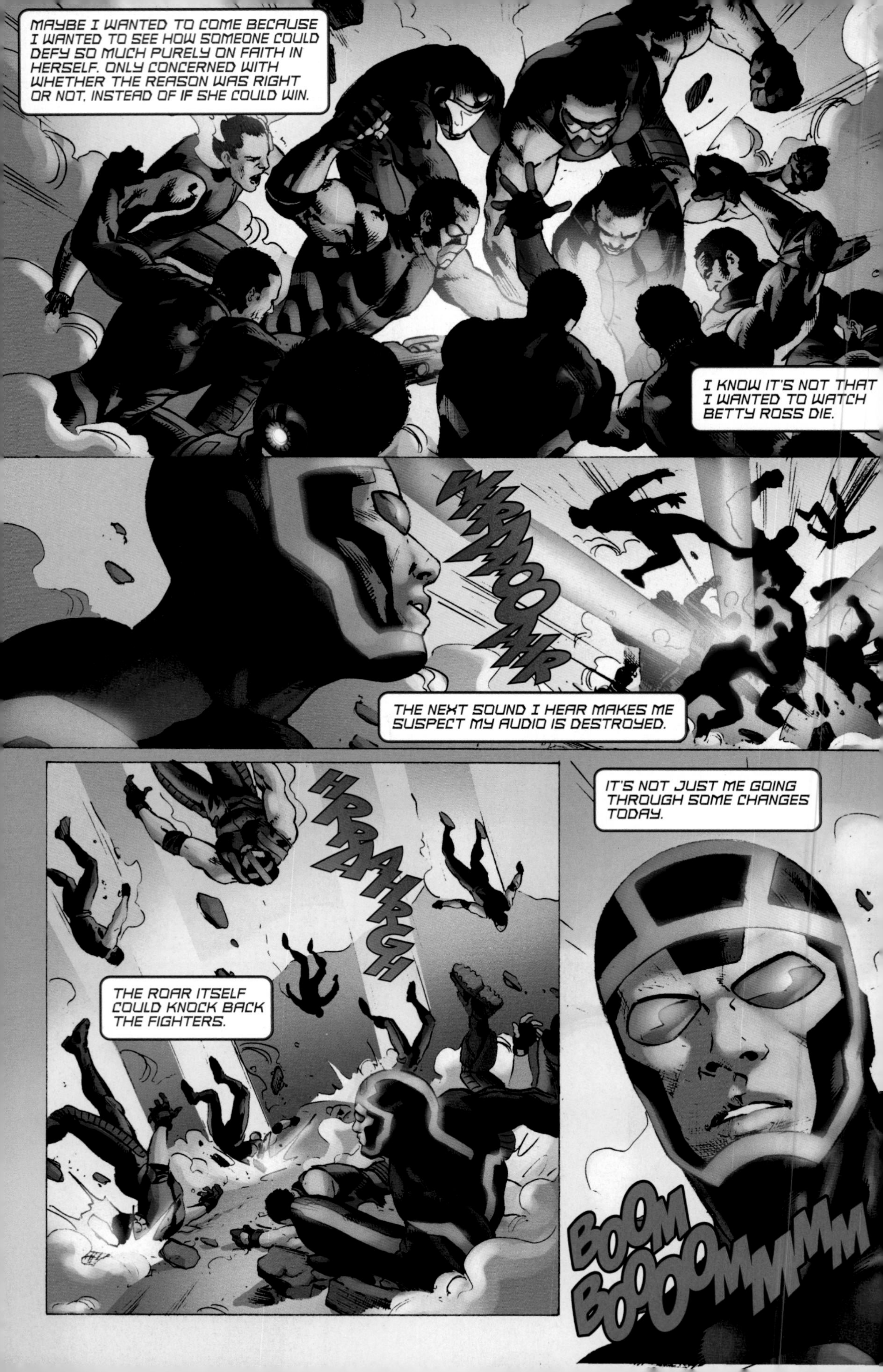
MAYBE I WANTED TO COME BECAUSE I WANTED TO SEE HOW SOMEONE COULD DEFY SO MUCH PURELY ON FAITH IN HERSELF. ONLY CONCERNED WITH WHETHER THE REASON WAS RIGHT OR NOT, INSTEAD OF IF SHE COULD WIN.
I KNOW IT'S NOT THAT I WANTED TO WATCH BETTY ROSS DIE.
WRAAOOAHR
THE NEXT SOUND I HEAR MAKES ME SUSPECT MY AUDIO IS DESTROYED.
HRAAHRGH
THE ROAR ITSELF COULD KNOCK BACK THE FIGHTERS.
IT'S NOT JUST ME GOING THROUGH SOME CHANGES TODAY.
BOOM
BOOOOMMMM

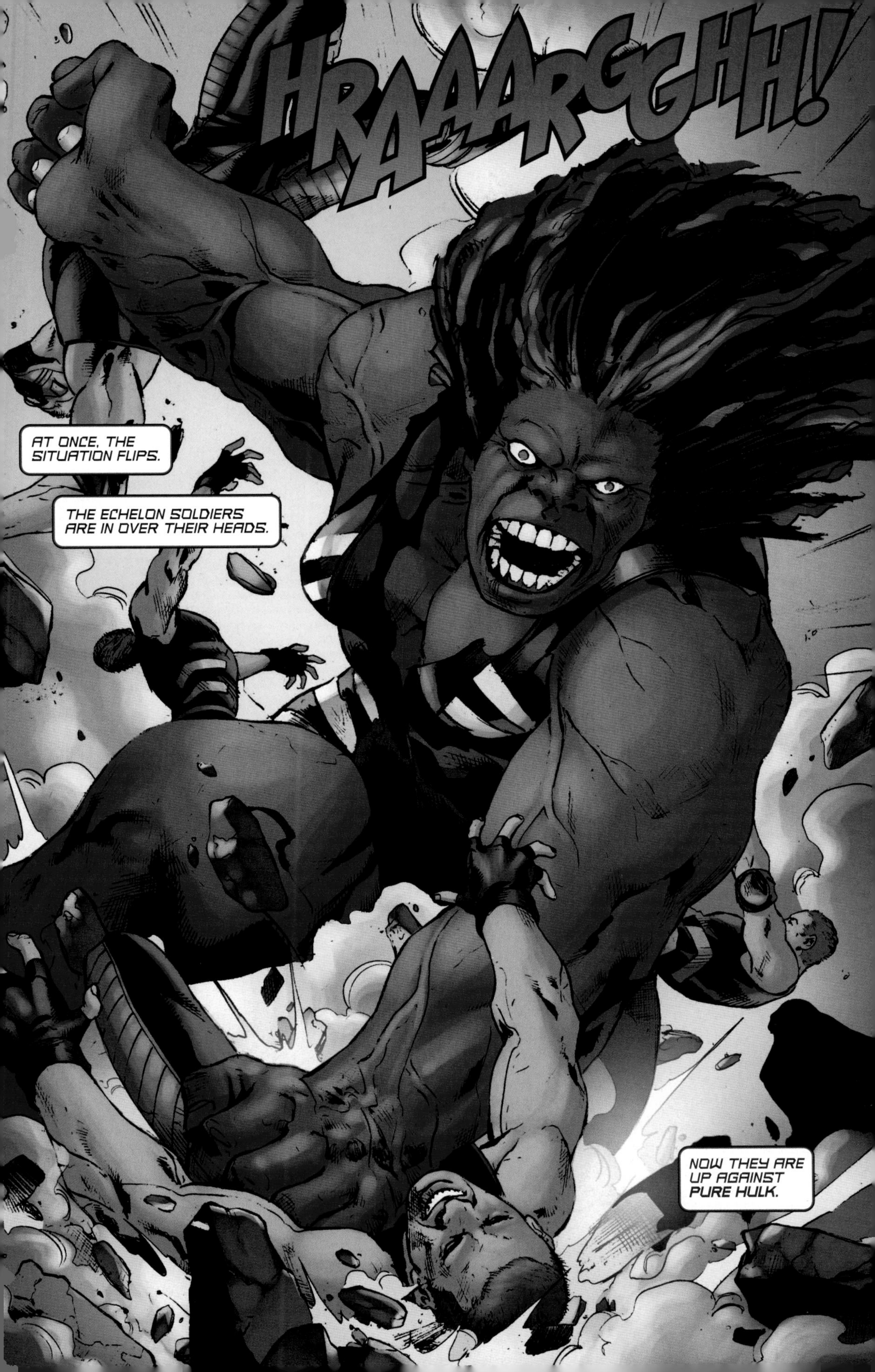
HRAAARGGHH!
AT ONCE, THE SITUATION FLIPS.
THE ECHELON SOLDIERS ARE IN OVER THEIR HEADS.
NOW THEY ARE UP AGAINST PURE HULK.

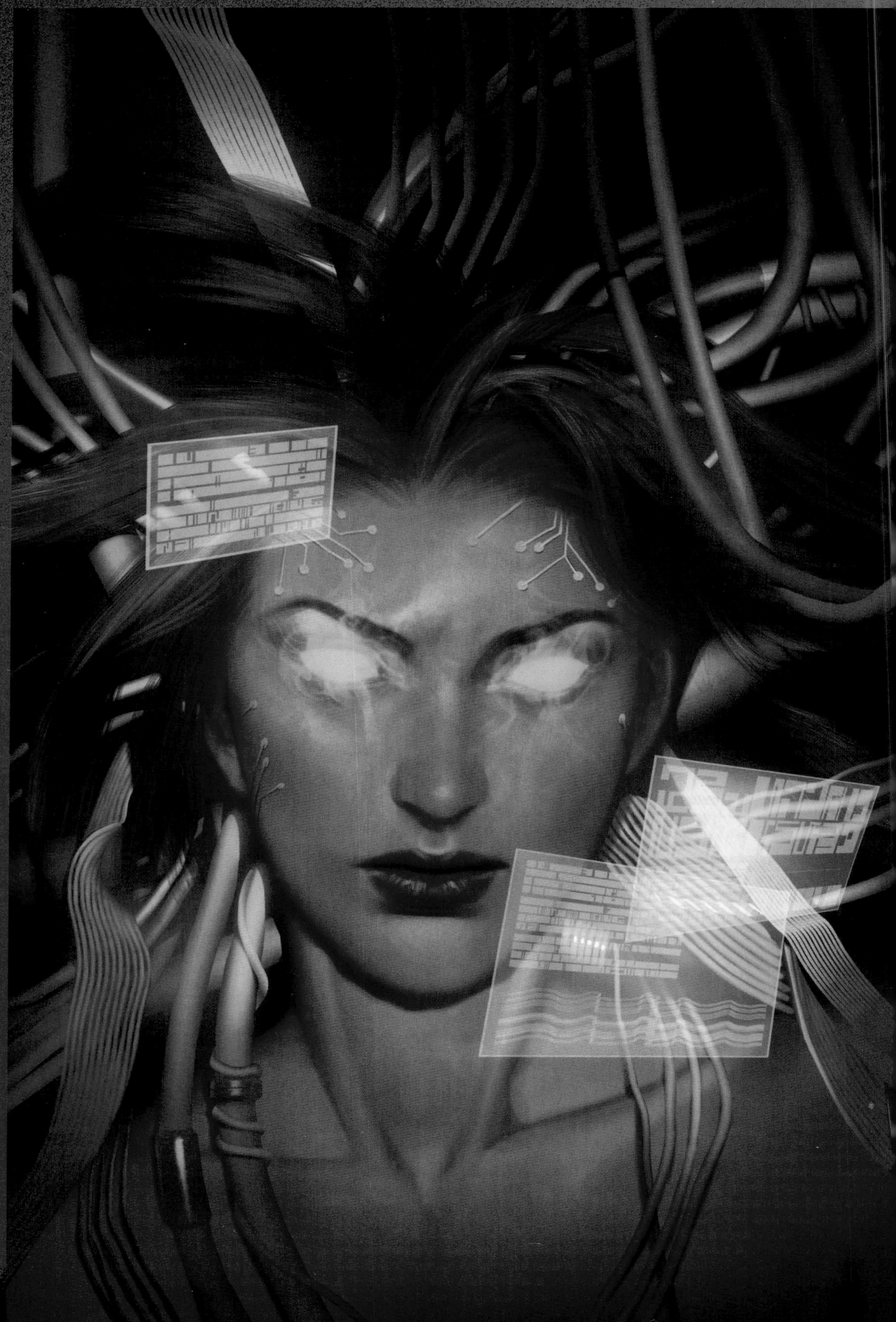

#61

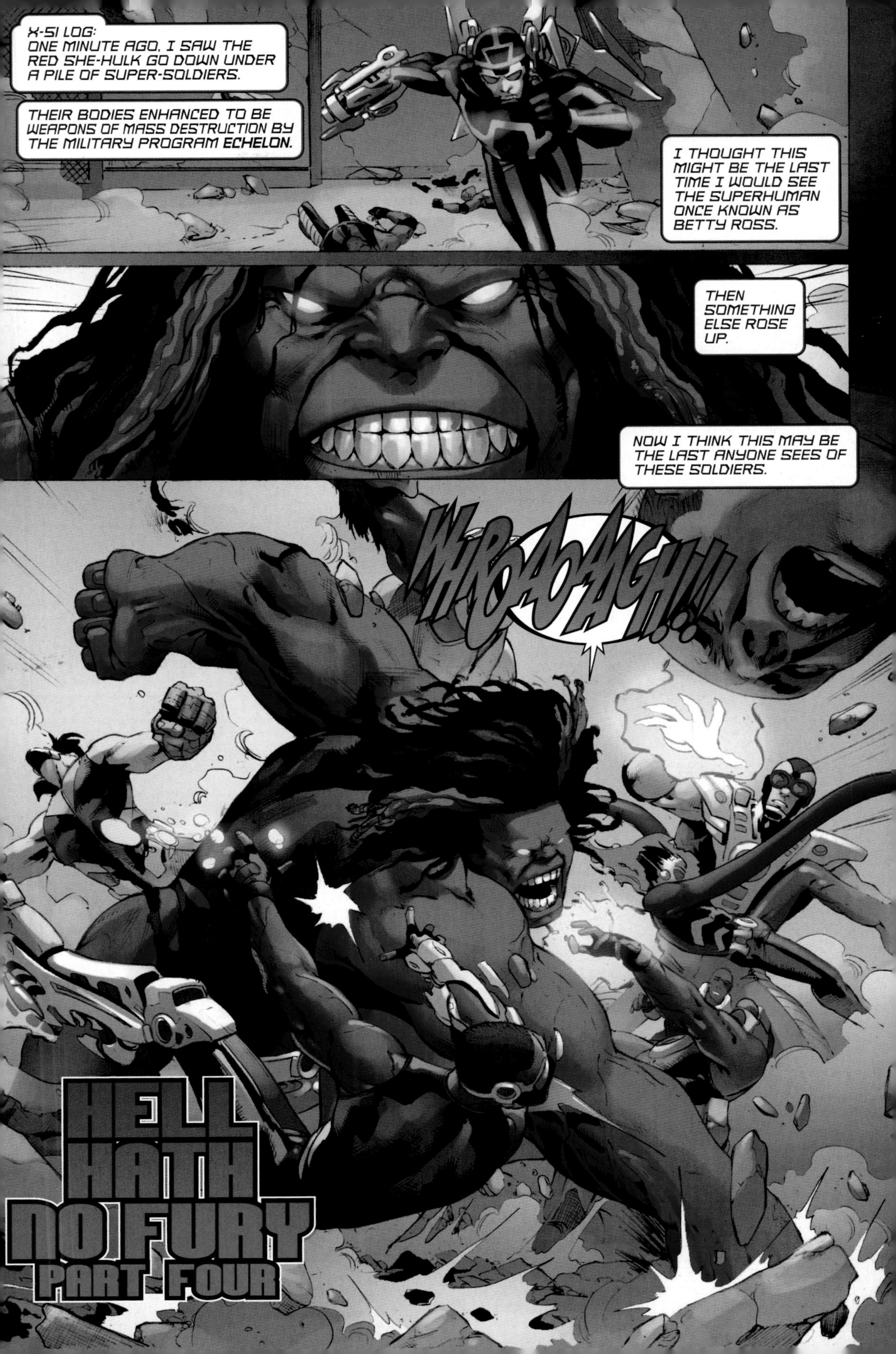

X-51 LOG:
ONE MINUTE AGO, I SAW THE RED SHE-HULK GO DOWN UNDER A PILE OF SUPER-SOLDIERS.
THEIR BODIES ENHANCED TO BE WEAPONS OF MASS DESTRUCTION BY THE MILITARY PROGRAM ECHELON.
I THOUGHT THIS MIGHT BE THE LAST TIME I WOULD SEE THE SUPERHUMAN ONCE KNOWN AS BETTY ROSS.
THEN SOMETHING ELSE ROSE UP.
NOW I THINK THIS MAY BE THE LAST ANYONE SEES OF THESE SOLDIERS.
WHROAAAGH!!!
HELL HATH NO FURY
PART FOUR

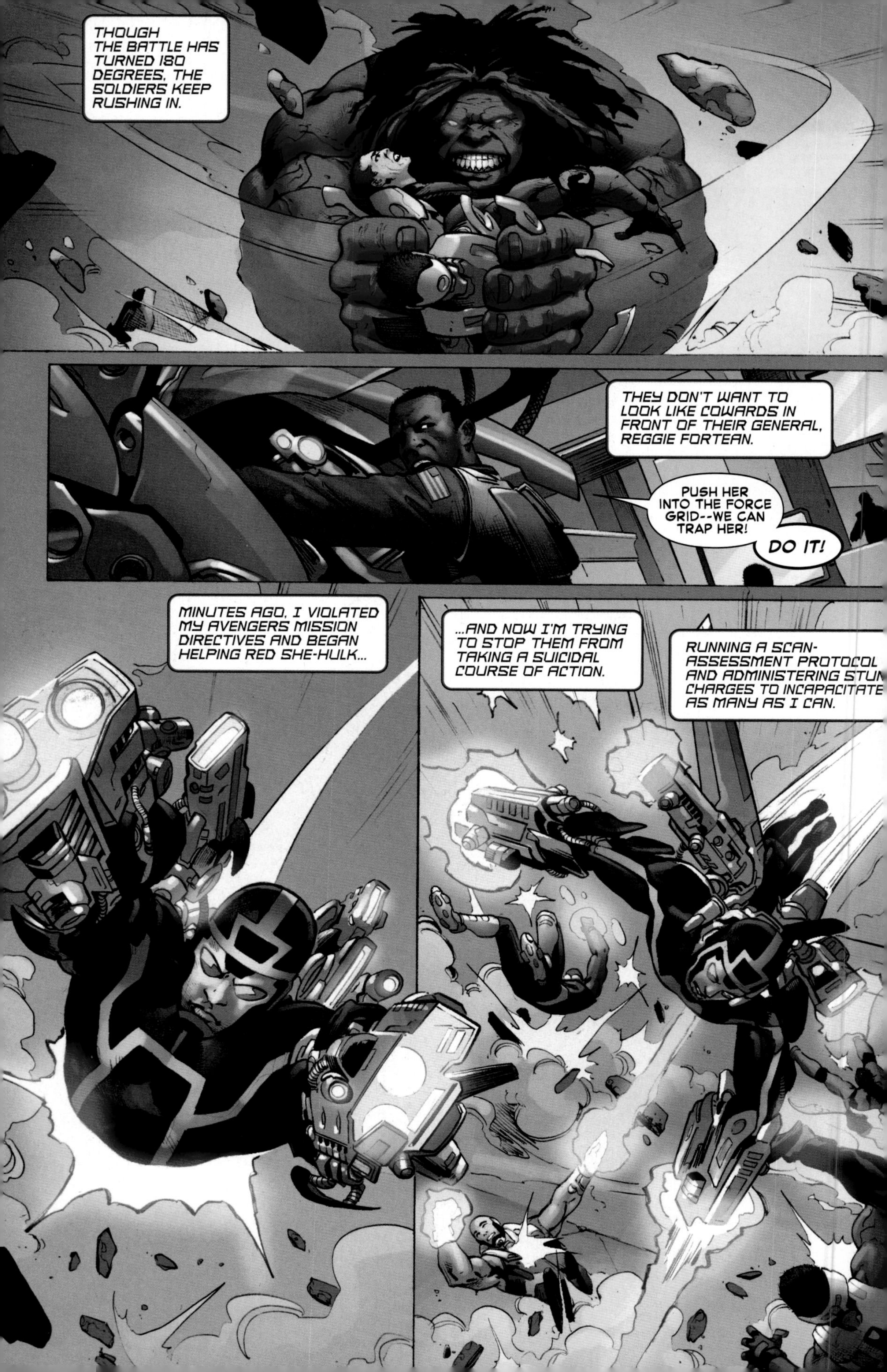
THOUGH THE BATTLE HAS TURNED 180 DEGREES, THE SOLDIERS KEEP RUSHING IN.
THEY DON'T WANT TO LOOK LIKE COWARDS IN FRONT OF THEIR GENERAL, REGGIE FORTEAN.
PUSH HER INTO THE FORCE GRID--WE CAN TRAP HER!
DO IT!
MINUTES AGO, I VIOLATED MY AVENGERS MISSION DIRECTIVES AND BEGAN HELPING RED SHE-HULK...
...AND NOW I'M TRYING TO STOP THEM FROM TAKING A SUICIDAL COURSE OF ACTION.
RUNNING A SCAN-ASSESSMENT PROTOCOL AND ADMINISTERING STUN CHARGES TO INCAPACITATE AS MANY AS I CAN.

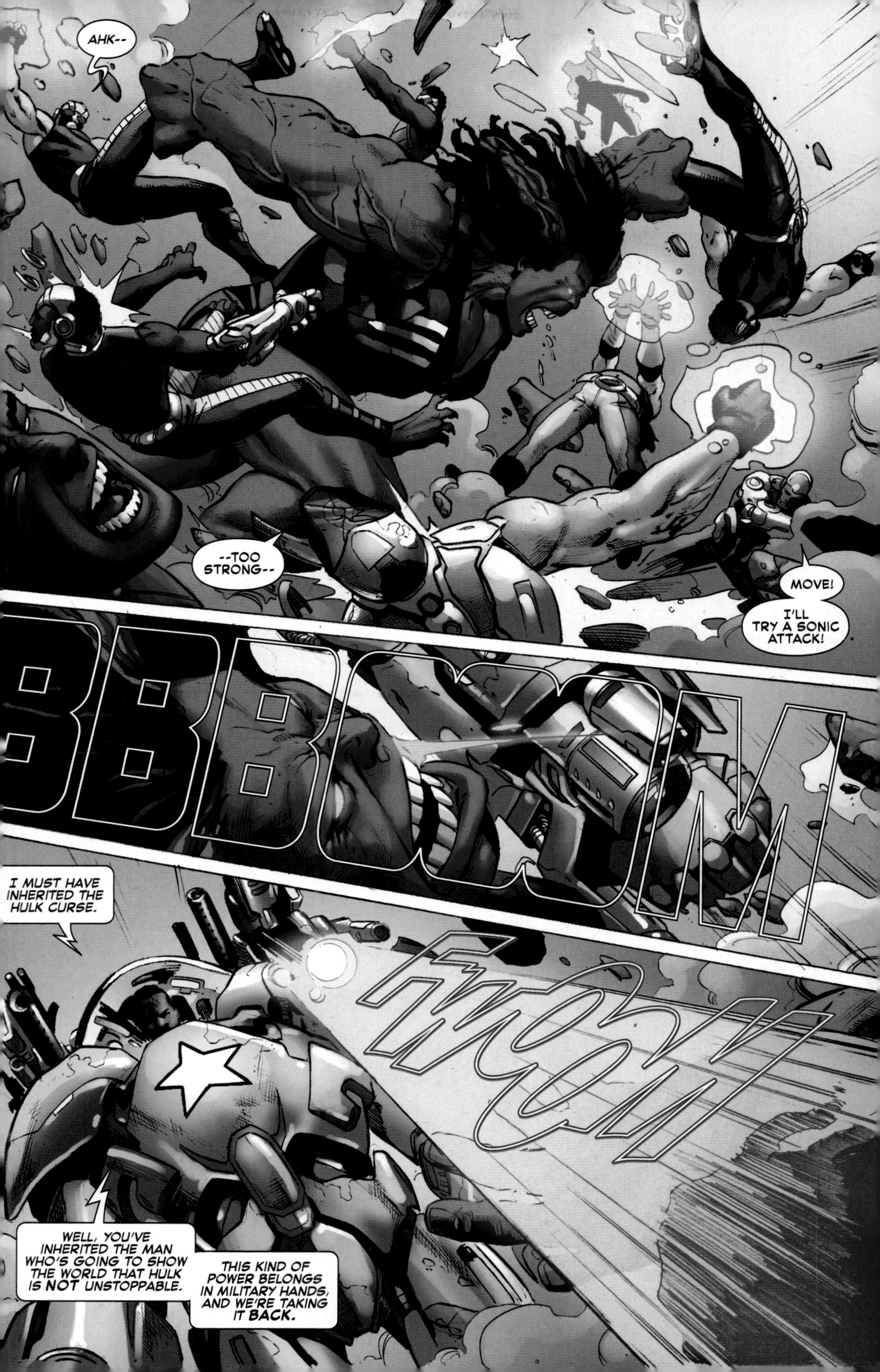
AHK--
--TOO STRONG--
MOVE!
I'LL TRY A SONIC ATTACK!
BBOOM
I MUST HAVE INHERITED THE HULK CURSE.
FWOM
WELL, YOU'VE INHERITED THE MAN WHO'S GOING TO SHOW THE WORLD THAT HULK IS NOT UNSTOPPABLE.
THIS KIND OF POWER BELONGS IN MILITARY HANDS, AND WE'RE TAKING IT BACK.

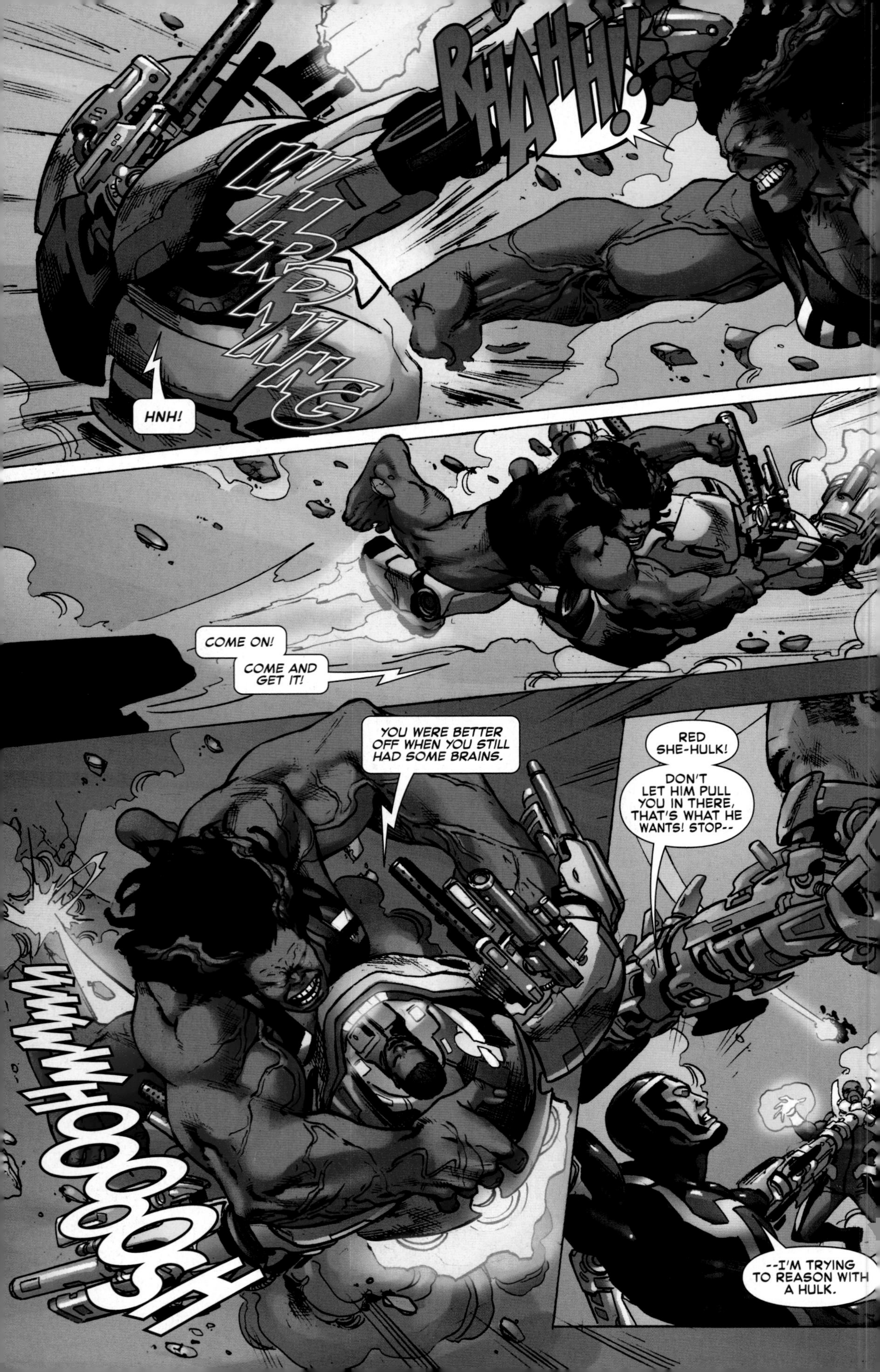
RHAHH!!
WHRRMNNG
HNH!
COME ON!
COME AND GET IT!
YOU WERE BETTER OFF WHEN YOU STILL HAD SOME BRAINS.
RED SHE-HULK!
DON'T LET HIM PULL YOU IN THERE, THAT'S WHAT HE WANTS! STOP--
WWWHOOOOOSH
--I'M TRYING TO REASON WITH A HULK.

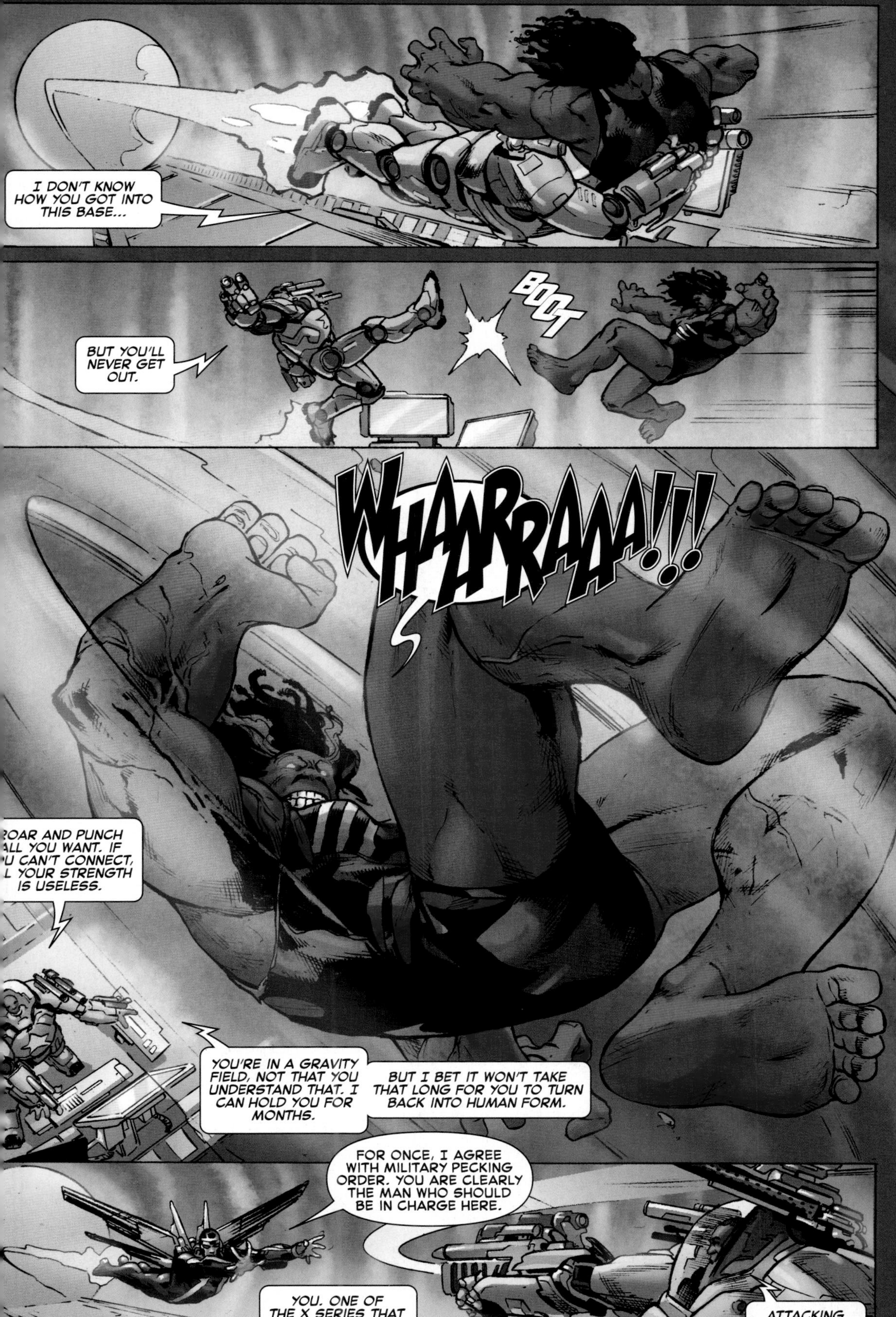
I DON'T KNOW HOW YOU GOT INTO THIS BASE...
BUT YOU'LL NEVER GET OUT.
BOOT
WHAARRAAA!!!
ROAR AND PUNCH ALL YOU WANT. IF YOU CAN'T CONNECT, ALL YOUR STRENGTH IS USELESS.
YOU'RE IN A GRAVITY FIELD, NOT THAT YOU UNDERSTAND THAT. I CAN HOLD YOU FOR MONTHS.
BUT I BET IT WON'T TAKE THAT LONG FOR YOU TO TURN BACK INTO HUMAN FORM.
FOR ONCE, I AGREE WITH MILITARY PECKING ORDER. YOU ARE CLEARLY THE MAN WHO SHOULD BE IN CHARGE HERE.
YOU. ONE OF THE X SERIES THAT WAS SUPPOSED TO WORK FOR US.
ATTACKING A MILITARY INSTALLATION!

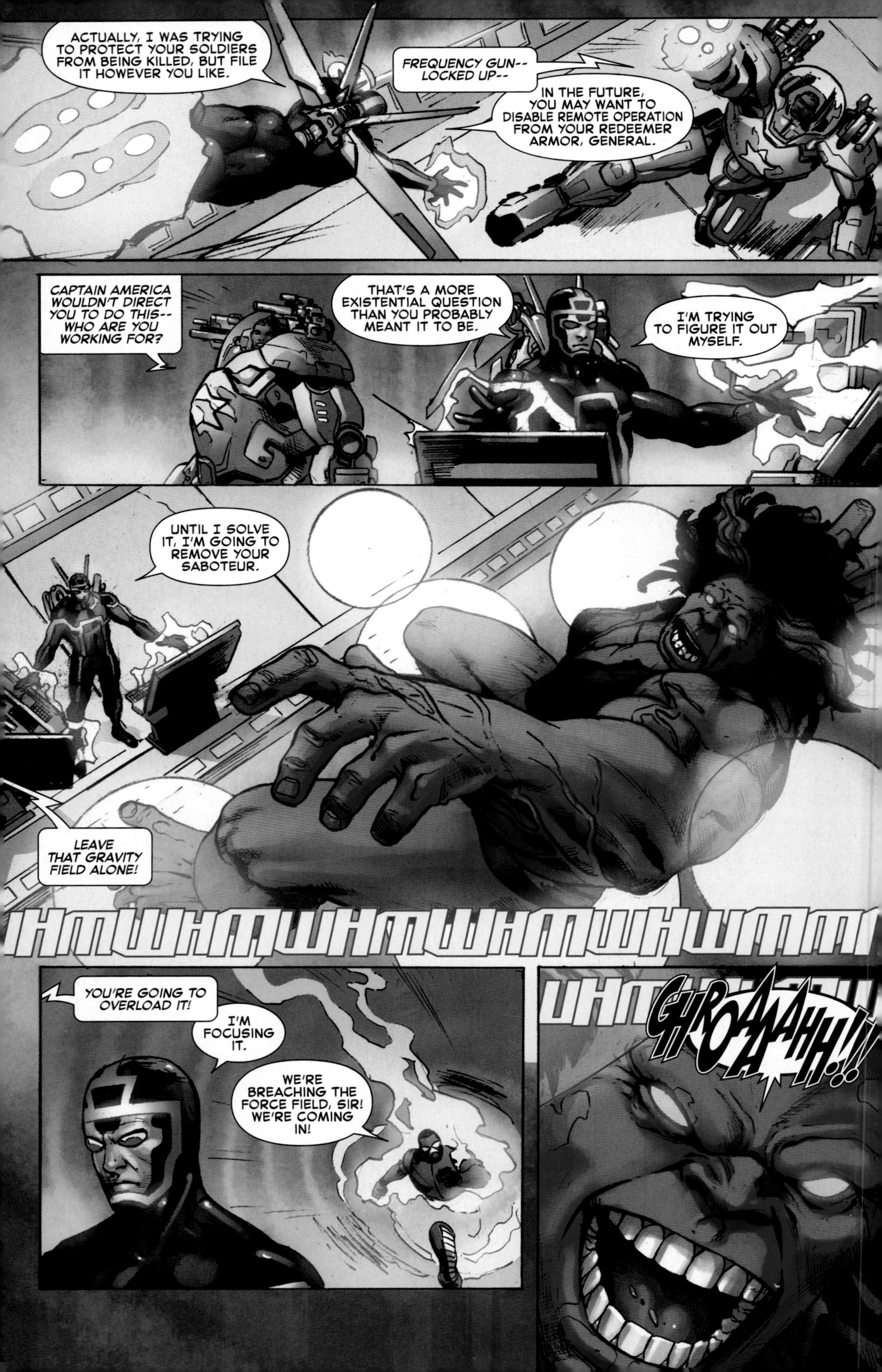
ACTUALLY, I WAS TRYING TO PROTECT YOUR SOLDIERS FROM BEING KILLED, BUT FILE IT HOWEVER YOU LIKE.
FREQUENCY GUN-- LOCKED UP--
IN THE FUTURE, YOU MAY WANT TO DISABLE REMOTE OPERATION FROM YOUR REDEEMER ARMOR, GENERAL.
CAPTAIN AMERICA WOULDN'T DIRECT YOU TO DO THIS-- WHO ARE YOU WORKING FOR?
THAT'S A MORE EXISTENTIAL QUESTION THAN YOU PROBABLY MEANT IT TO BE.
I'M TRYING TO FIGURE IT OUT MYSELF.
UNTIL I SOLVE IT, I'M GOING TO REMOVE YOUR SABOTEUR.
LEAVE THAT GRAVITY FIELD ALONE!
HMWHMWHMWHMWHWMM
YOU'RE GOING TO OVERLOAD IT!
I'M FOCUSING IT.
WE'RE BREACHING THE FORCE FIELD, SIR! WE'RE COMING IN!
GHROAAAHH!!

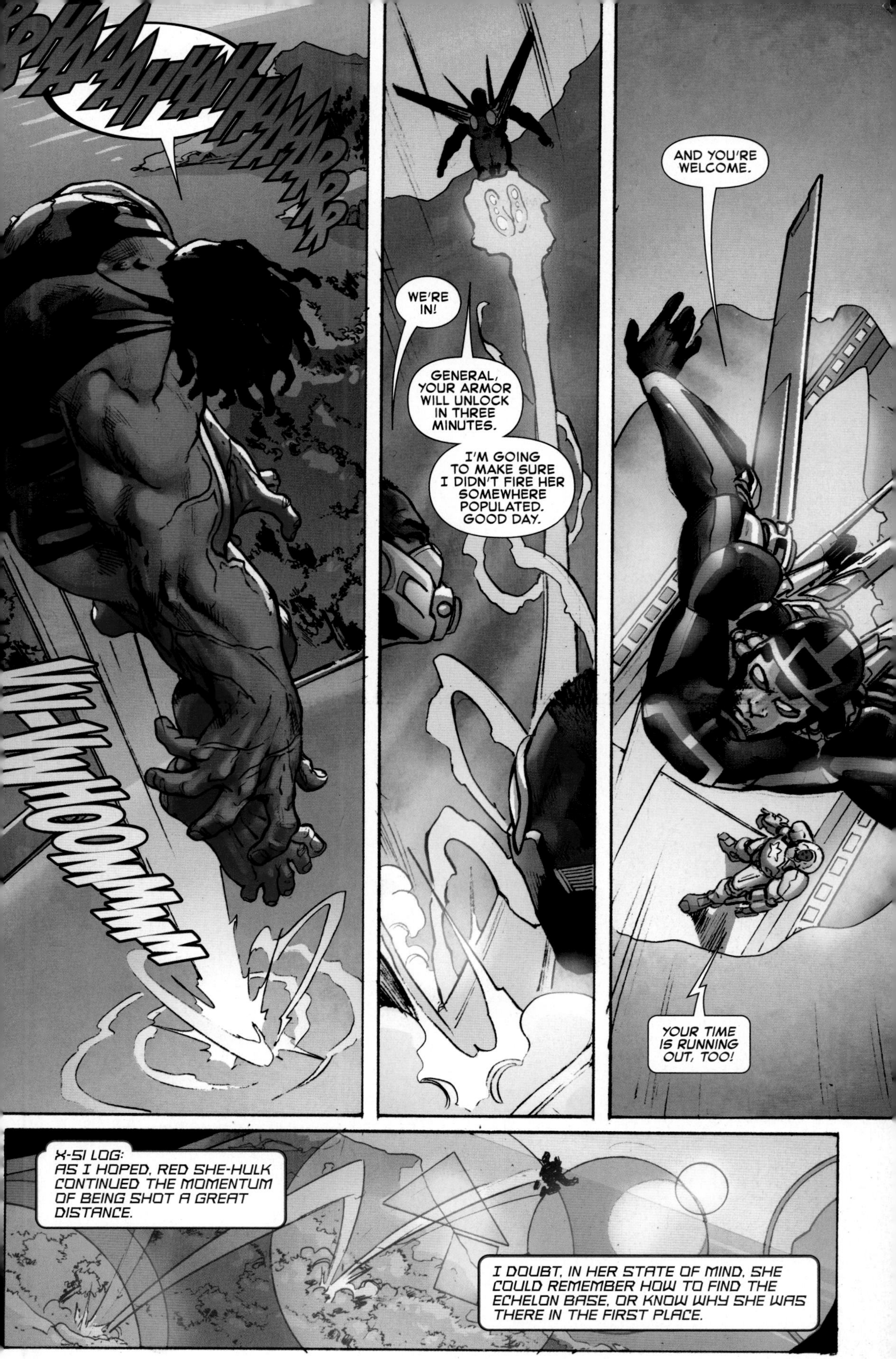

BPHAAAHAHAHAHAAAR
WHEWHOOOMMMM
WE'RE IN!
GENERAL, YOUR ARMOR WILL UNLOCK IN THREE MINUTES.
I'M GOING TO MAKE SURE I DIDN'T FIRE HER SOMEWHERE POPULATED. GOOD DAY.
AND YOU'RE WELCOME.
YOUR TIME IS RUNNING OUT, TOO!
X-51 LOG: AS I HOPED, RED SHE-HULK CONTINUED THE MOMENTUM OF BEING SHOT A GREAT DISTANCE.
I DOUBT, IN HER STATE OF MIND, SHE COULD REMEMBER HOW TO FIND THE ECHELON BASE, OR KNOW WHY SHE WAS THERE IN THE FIRST PLACE.

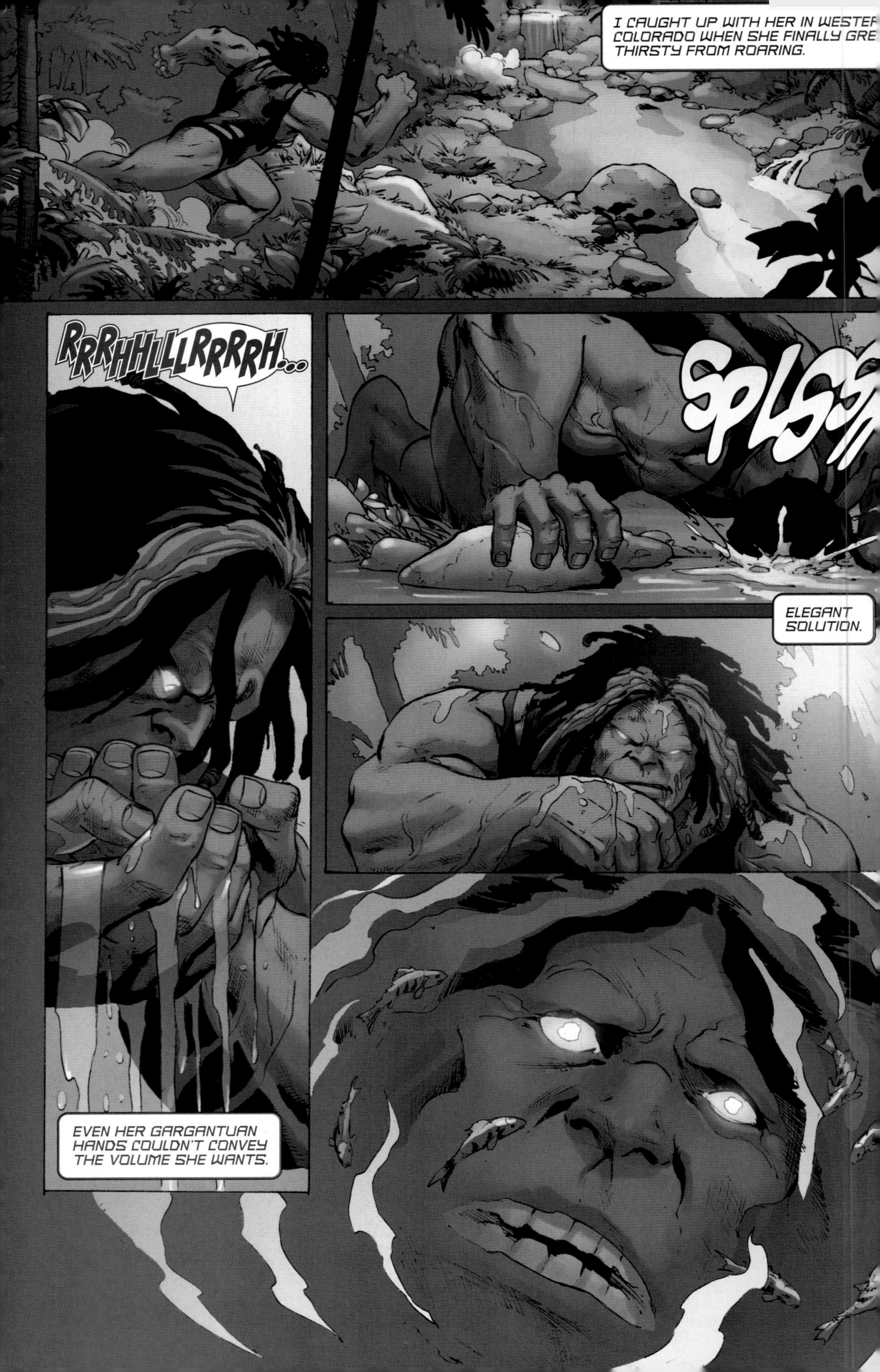
I CAUGHT UP WITH HER IN WESTER
COLORADO WHEN SHE FINALLY GRE
THIRSTY FROM ROARING.
RRRHHLLLRRRRH...
SPLSS
ELEGANT SOLUTION.
EVEN HER GARGANTUAN HANDS COULDN'T CONVEY THE VOLUME SHE WANTS.

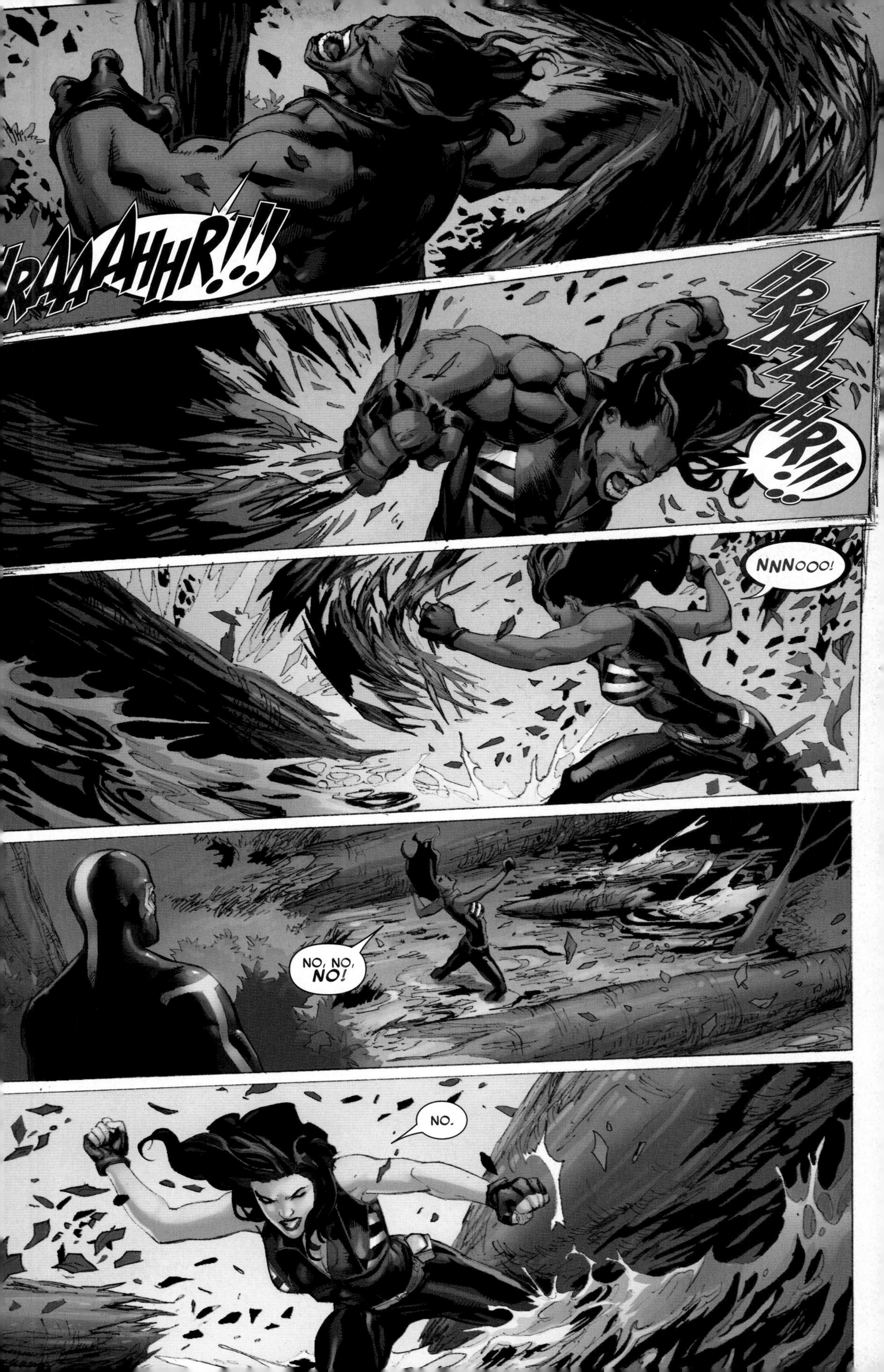
RAAAAHHR!!!
HRAAAAHHR!!!
NNNOOO!
NO, NO, NO!
NO.

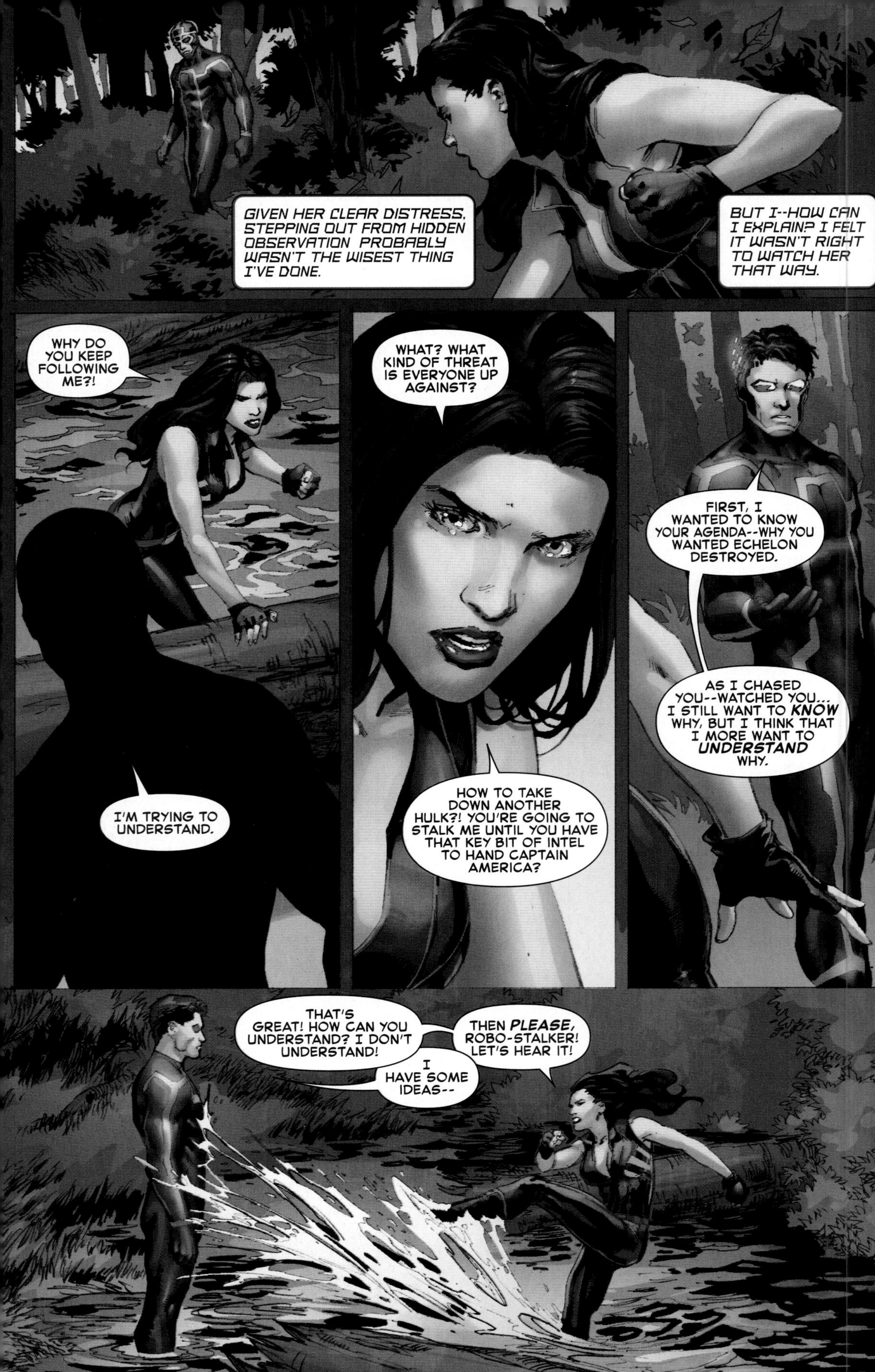
GIVEN HER CLEAR DISTRESS, STEPPING OUT FROM HIDDEN OBSERVATION PROBABLY WASN'T THE WISEST THING I'VE DONE.
BUT I--HOW CAN I EXPLAIN? I FELT IT WASN'T RIGHT TO WATCH HER THAT WAY.
WHY DO YOU KEEP FOLLOWING ME?!
I'M TRYING TO UNDERSTAND.
WHAT? WHAT KIND OF THREAT IS EVERYONE UP AGAINST?
HOW TO TAKE DOWN ANOTHER HULK?! YOU'RE GOING TO STALK ME UNTIL YOU HAVE THAT KEY BIT OF INTEL TO HAND CAPTAIN AMERICA?
FIRST, I WANTED TO KNOW YOUR AGENDA--WHY YOU WANTED ECHELON DESTROYED.
AS I CHASED YOU--WATCHED YOU... I STILL WANT TO KNOW WHY, BUT I THINK THAT I MORE WANT TO UNDERSTAND WHY.
THAT'S GREAT! HOW CAN YOU UNDERSTAND? I DON'T UNDERSTAND!
I HAVE SOME IDEAS--
THEN PLEASE, ROBO-STALKER! LET'S HEAR IT!

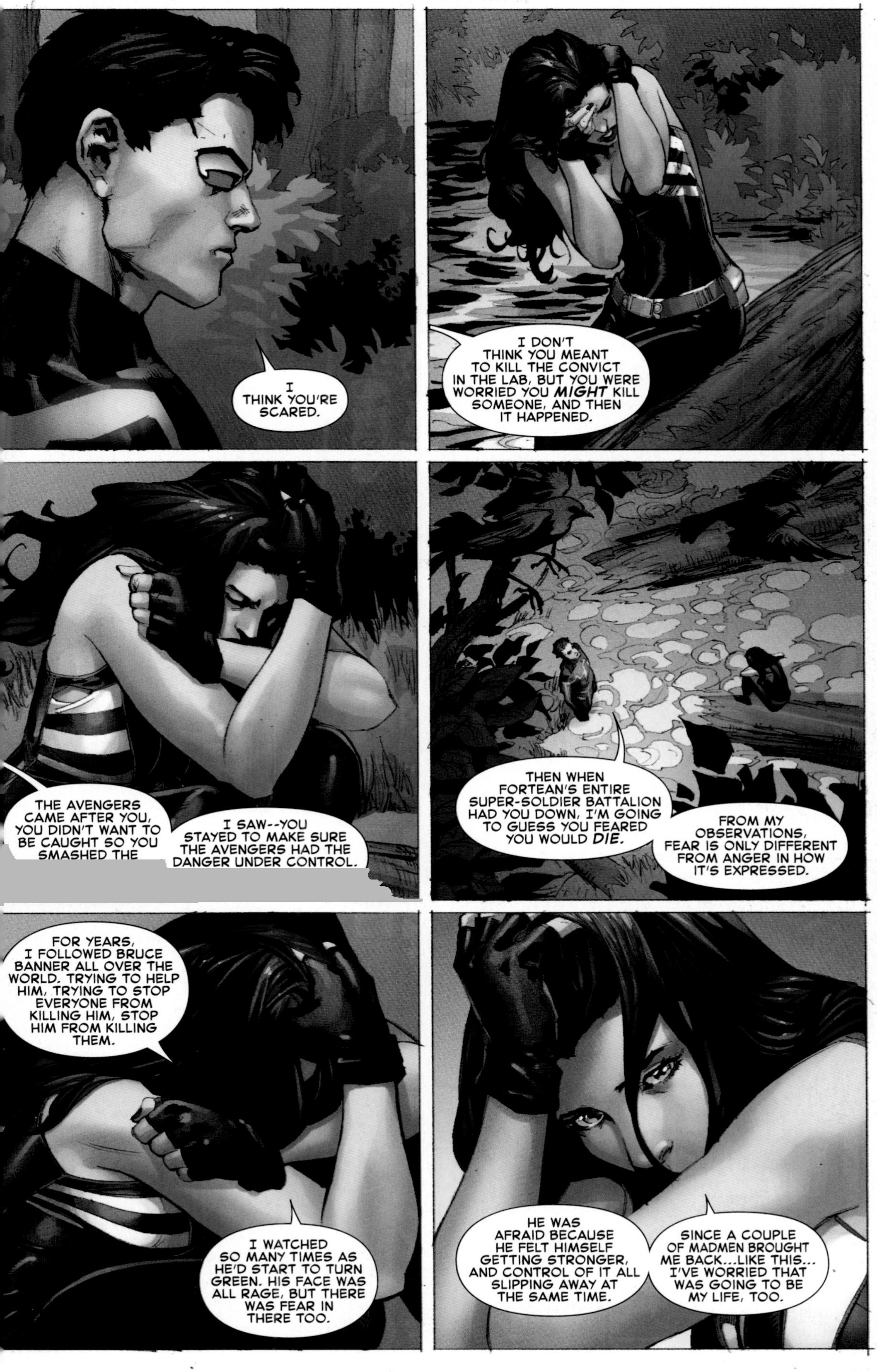
I THINK YOU'RE SCARED.
I DON'T THINK YOU MEANT TO KILL THE CONVICT IN THE LAB, BUT YOU WERE WORRIED YOU *MIGHT* KILL SOMEONE, AND THEN IT HAPPENED.
THE AVENGERS CAME AFTER YOU, YOU DIDN'T WANT TO BE CAUGHT SO YOU SMASHED THE
I SAW--YOU STAYED TO MAKE SURE THE AVENGERS HAD THE DANGER UNDER CONTROL.
THEN WHEN FORTEAN'S ENTIRE SUPER-SOLDIER BATTALION HAD YOU DOWN, I'M GOING TO GUESS YOU FEARED YOU WOULD *DIE.*
FROM MY OBSERVATIONS, FEAR IS ONLY DIFFERENT FROM ANGER IN HOW IT'S EXPRESSED.
FOR YEARS, I FOLLOWED BRUCE BANNER ALL OVER THE WORLD. TRYING TO HELP HIM, TRYING TO STOP EVERYONE FROM KILLING HIM, STOP HIM FROM KILLING THEM.
I WATCHED SO MANY TIMES AS HE'D START TO TURN GREEN. HIS FACE WAS ALL RAGE, BUT THERE WAS FEAR IN THERE TOO.
HE WAS AFRAID BECAUSE HE FELT HIMSELF GETTING STRONGER, AND CONTROL OF IT ALL SLIPPING AWAY AT THE SAME TIME.
SINCE A COUPLE OF MADMEN BROUGHT ME BACK...LIKE THIS... I'VE WORRIED THAT WAS GOING TO BE MY LIFE, TOO.

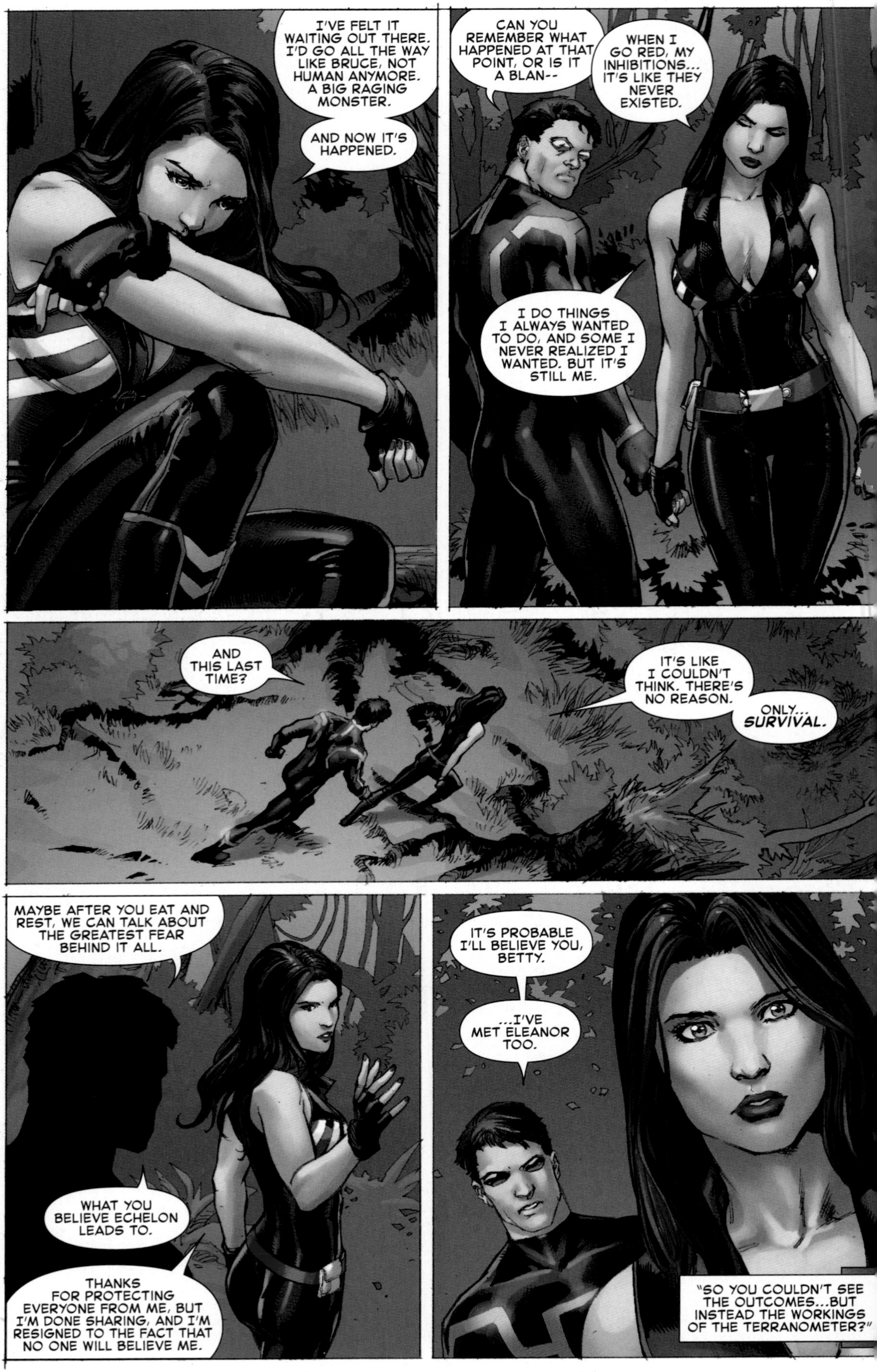
I'VE FELT IT WAITING OUT THERE. I'D GO ALL THE WAY LIKE BRUCE, NOT HUMAN ANYMORE. A BIG RAGING MONSTER.
AND NOW IT'S HAPPENED.
CAN YOU REMEMBER WHAT HAPPENED AT THAT POINT, OR IS IT A BLAN--
WHEN I GO RED, MY INHIBITIONS... IT'S LIKE THEY NEVER EXISTED.
I DO THINGS I ALWAYS WANTED TO DO, AND SOME I NEVER REALIZED I WANTED. BUT IT'S STILL ME.
AND THIS LAST TIME?
IT'S LIKE I COULDN'T THINK. THERE'S NO REASON.
ONLY... SURVIVAL.
MAYBE AFTER YOU EAT AND REST, WE CAN TALK ABOUT THE GREATEST FEAR BEHIND IT ALL.
WHAT YOU BELIEVE ECHELON LEADS TO.
THANKS FOR PROTECTING EVERYONE FROM ME, BUT I'M DONE SHARING, AND I'M RESIGNED TO THE FACT THAT NO ONE WILL BELIEVE ME.
IT'S PROBABLE I'LL BELIEVE YOU, BETTY.
...I'VE MET ELEANOR TOO.
"SO YOU COULDN'T SEE THE OUTCOMES...BUT INSTEAD THE WORKINGS OF THE TERRANOMETER?"

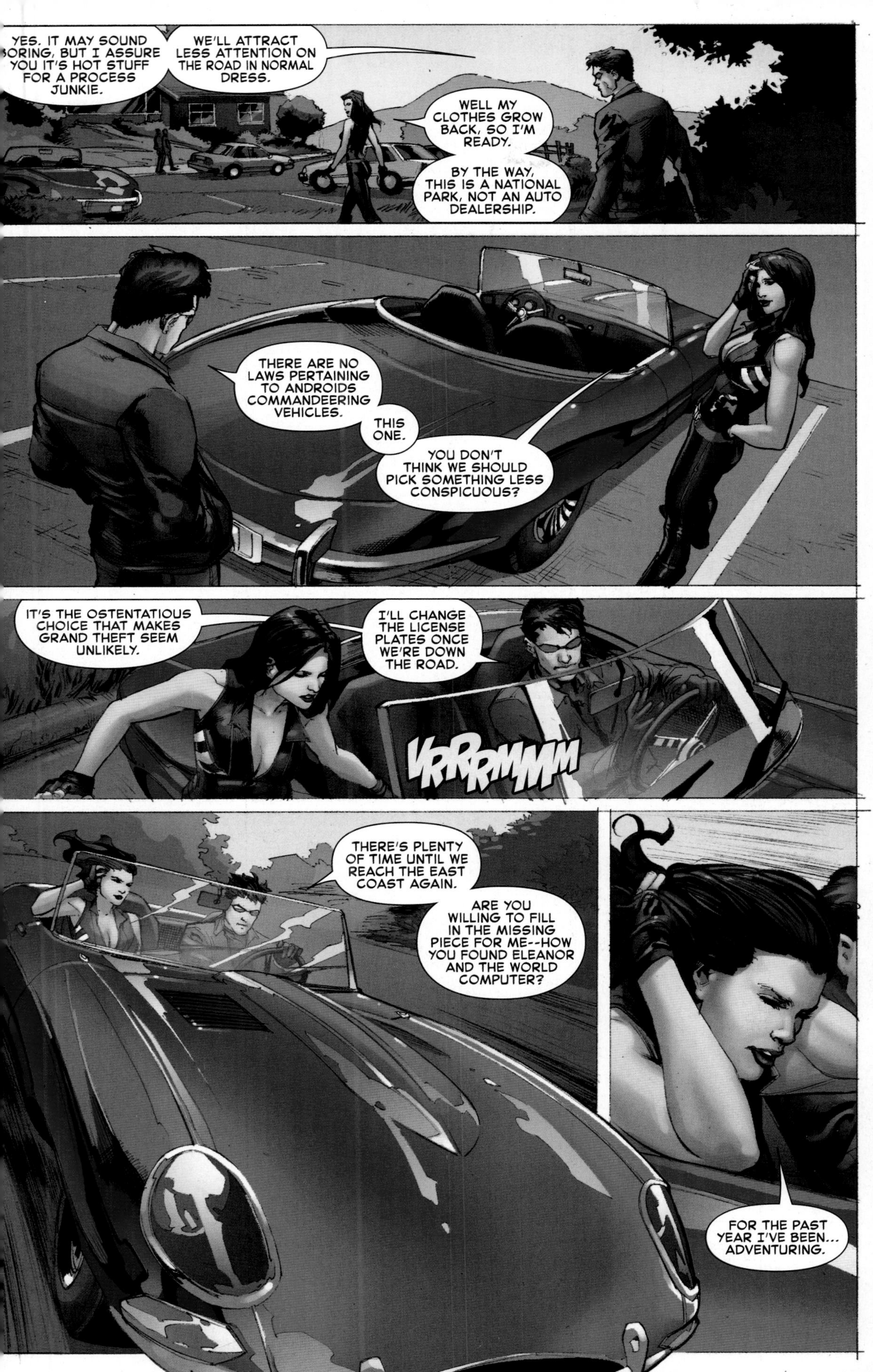
YES. IT MAY SOUND BORING, BUT I ASSURE YOU IT'S HOT STUFF FOR A PROCESS JUNKIE.
WE'LL ATTRACT LESS ATTENTION ON THE ROAD IN NORMAL DRESS.
WELL MY CLOTHES GROW BACK, SO I'M READY.
BY THE WAY, THIS IS A NATIONAL PARK, NOT AN AUTO DEALERSHIP.
THERE ARE NO LAWS PERTAINING TO ANDROIDS COMMANDEERING VEHICLES.
THIS ONE.
YOU DON'T THINK WE SHOULD PICK SOMETHING LESS CONSPICUOUS?
IT'S THE OSTENTATIOUS CHOICE THAT MAKES GRAND THEFT SEEM UNLIKELY.
I'LL CHANGE THE LICENSE PLATES ONCE WE'RE DOWN THE ROAD.
VRRRMMMM
THERE'S PLENTY OF TIME UNTIL WE REACH THE EAST COAST AGAIN.
ARE YOU WILLING TO FILL IN THE MISSING PIECE FOR ME--HOW YOU FOUND ELEANOR AND THE WORLD COMPUTER?
FOR THE PAST YEAR I'VE BEEN... ADVENTURING.

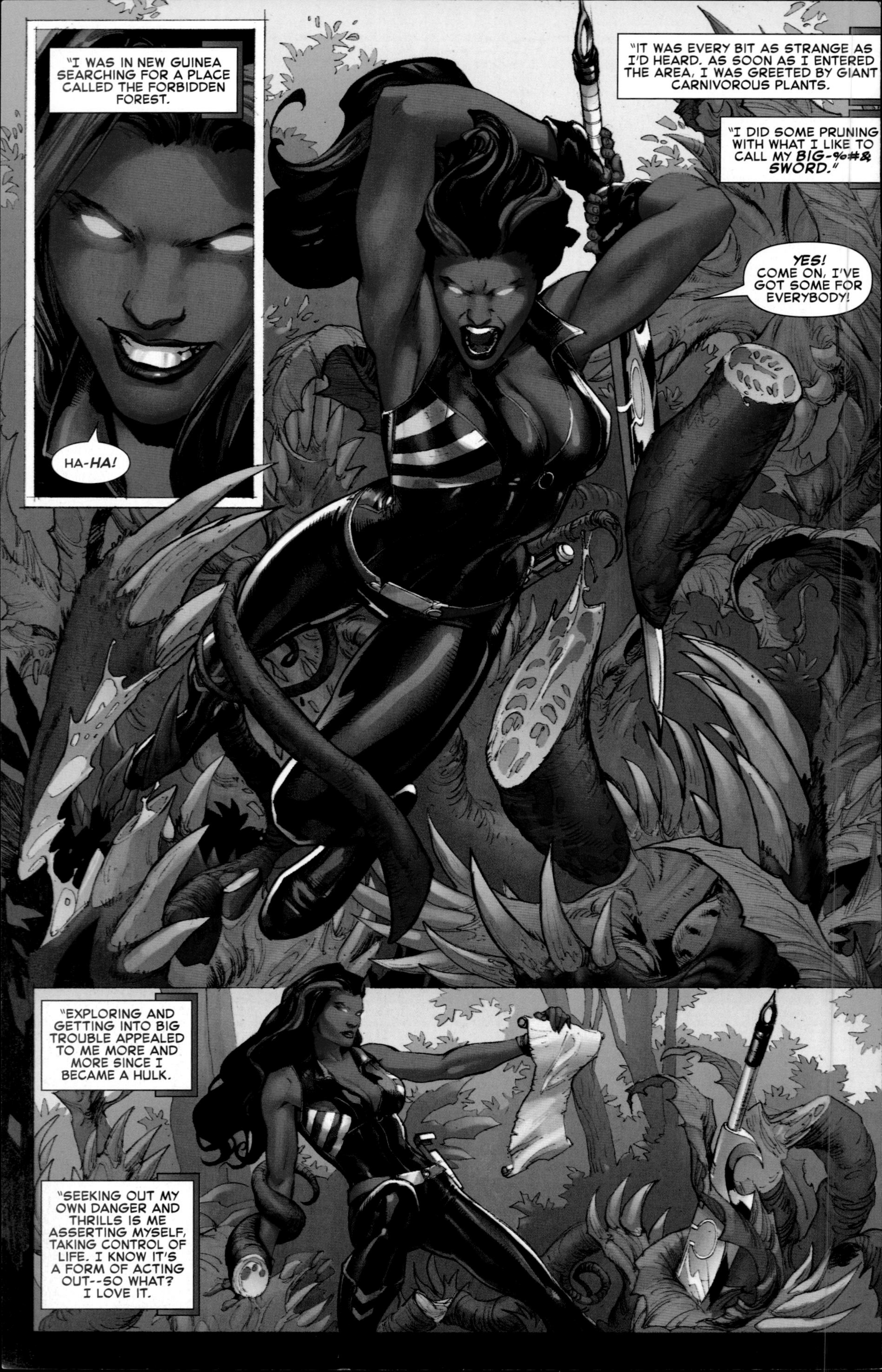
"I WAS IN NEW GUINEA SEARCHING FOR A PLACE CALLED THE FORBIDDEN FOREST.
HA-HA!
"IT WAS EVERY BIT AS STRANGE AS I'D HEARD. AS SOON AS I ENTERED THE AREA, I WAS GREETED BY GIANT CARNIVOROUS PLANTS.
"I DID SOME PRUNING WITH WHAT I LIKE TO CALL MY BIG-%#& SWORD."
YES! COME ON, I'VE GOT SOME FOR EVERYBODY!
"EXPLORING AND GETTING INTO BIG TROUBLE APPEALED TO ME MORE AND MORE SINCE I BECAME A HULK.
"SEEKING OUT MY OWN DANGER AND THRILLS IS ME ASSERTING MYSELF, TAKING CONTROL OF LIFE. I KNOW IT'S A FORM OF ACTING OUT--SO WHAT? I LOVE IT.

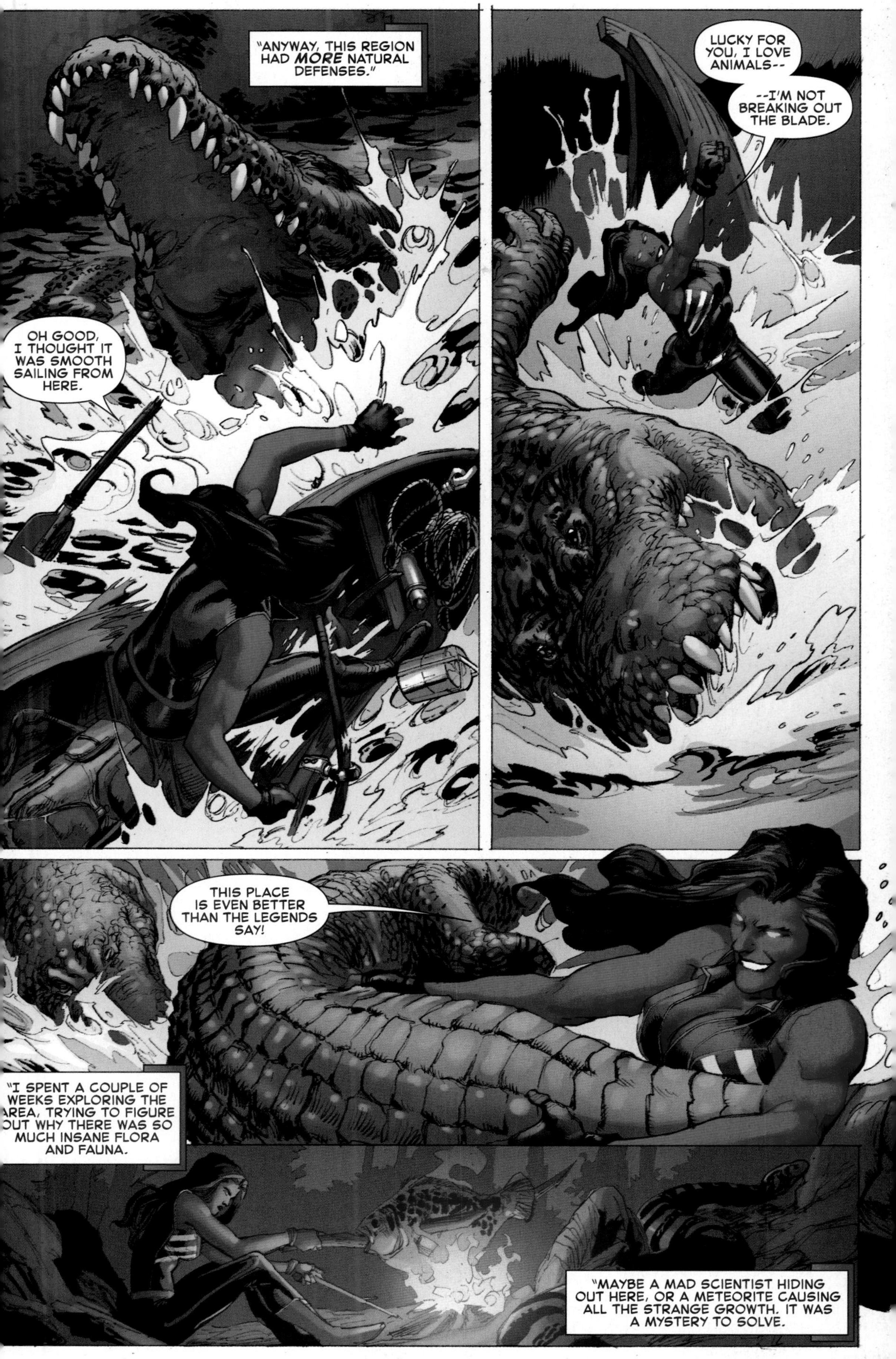
"ANYWAY, THIS REGION HAD MORE NATURAL DEFENSES."
OH GOOD, I THOUGHT IT WAS SMOOTH SAILING FROM HERE.
LUCKY FOR YOU, I LOVE ANIMALS--
--I'M NOT BREAKING OUT THE BLADE.
THIS PLACE IS EVEN BETTER THAN THE LEGENDS SAY!
"I SPENT A COUPLE OF WEEKS EXPLORING THE AREA, TRYING TO FIGURE OUT WHY THERE WAS SO MUCH INSANE FLORA AND FAUNA.
"MAYBE A MAD SCIENTIST HIDING OUT HERE, OR A METEORITE CAUSING ALL THE STRANGE GROWTH. IT WAS A MYSTERY TO SOLVE.

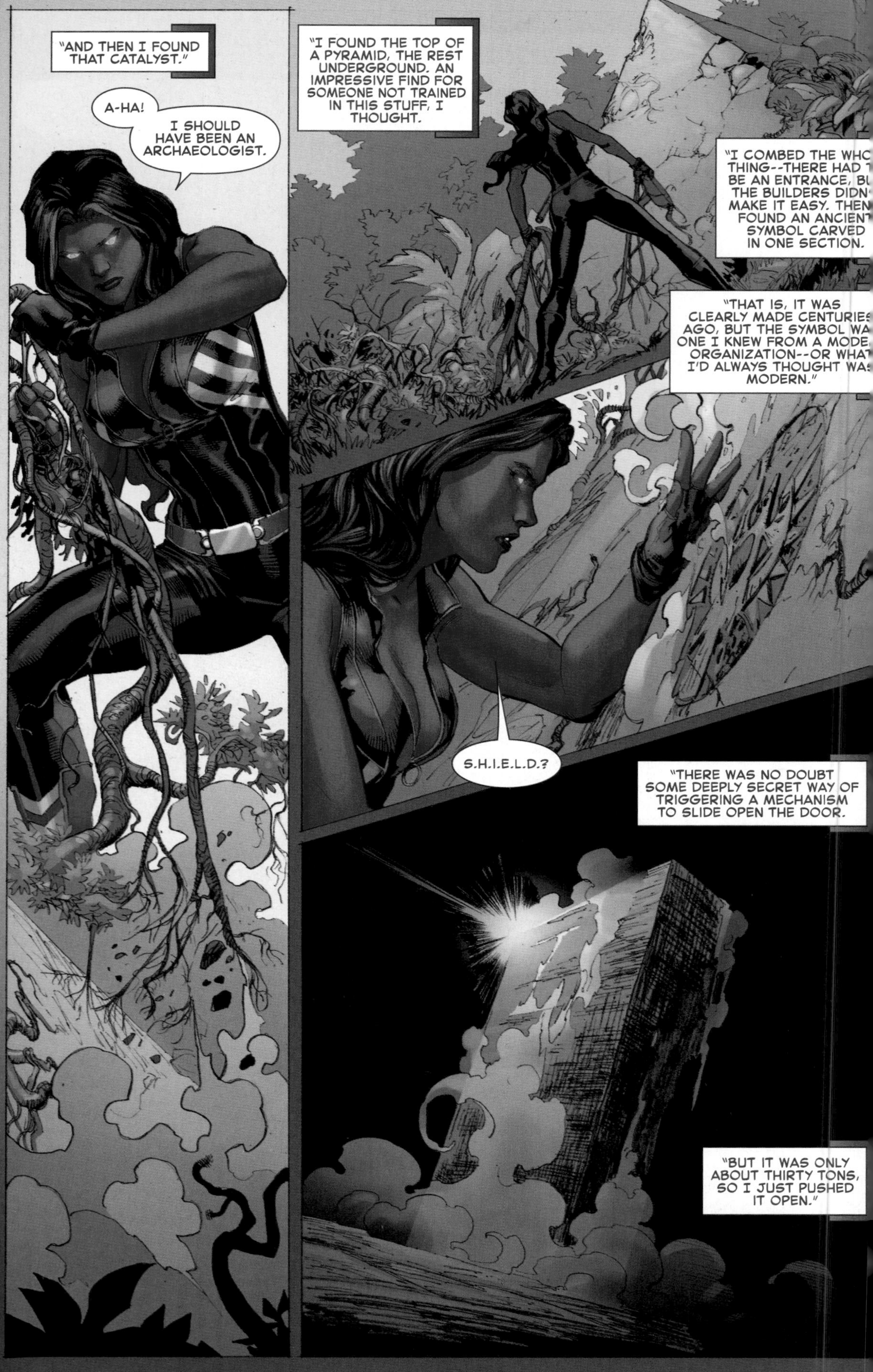
"AND THEN I FOUND THAT CATALYST."
A-HA!
I SHOULD HAVE BEEN AN ARCHAEOLOGIST.
"I FOUND THE TOP OF A PYRAMID, THE REST UNDERGROUND. AN IMPRESSIVE FIND FOR SOMEONE NOT TRAINED IN THIS STUFF, I THOUGHT.
"I COMBED THE WHO THING--THERE HAD BE AN ENTRANCE, BU THE BUILDERS DIDN MAKE IT EASY. THEN FOUND AN ANCIEN SYMBOL CARVED IN ONE SECTION.
"THAT IS, IT WAS CLEARLY MADE CENTURIES AGO, BUT THE SYMBOL WA ONE I KNEW FROM A MODE ORGANIZATION--OR WHAT I'D ALWAYS THOUGHT WAS MODERN."
S.H.I.E.L.D.?
"THERE WAS NO DOUBT SOME DEEPLY SECRET WAY OF TRIGGERING A MECHANISM TO SLIDE OPEN THE DOOR.
"BUT IT WAS ONLY ABOUT THIRTY TONS, SO I JUST PUSHED IT OPEN."

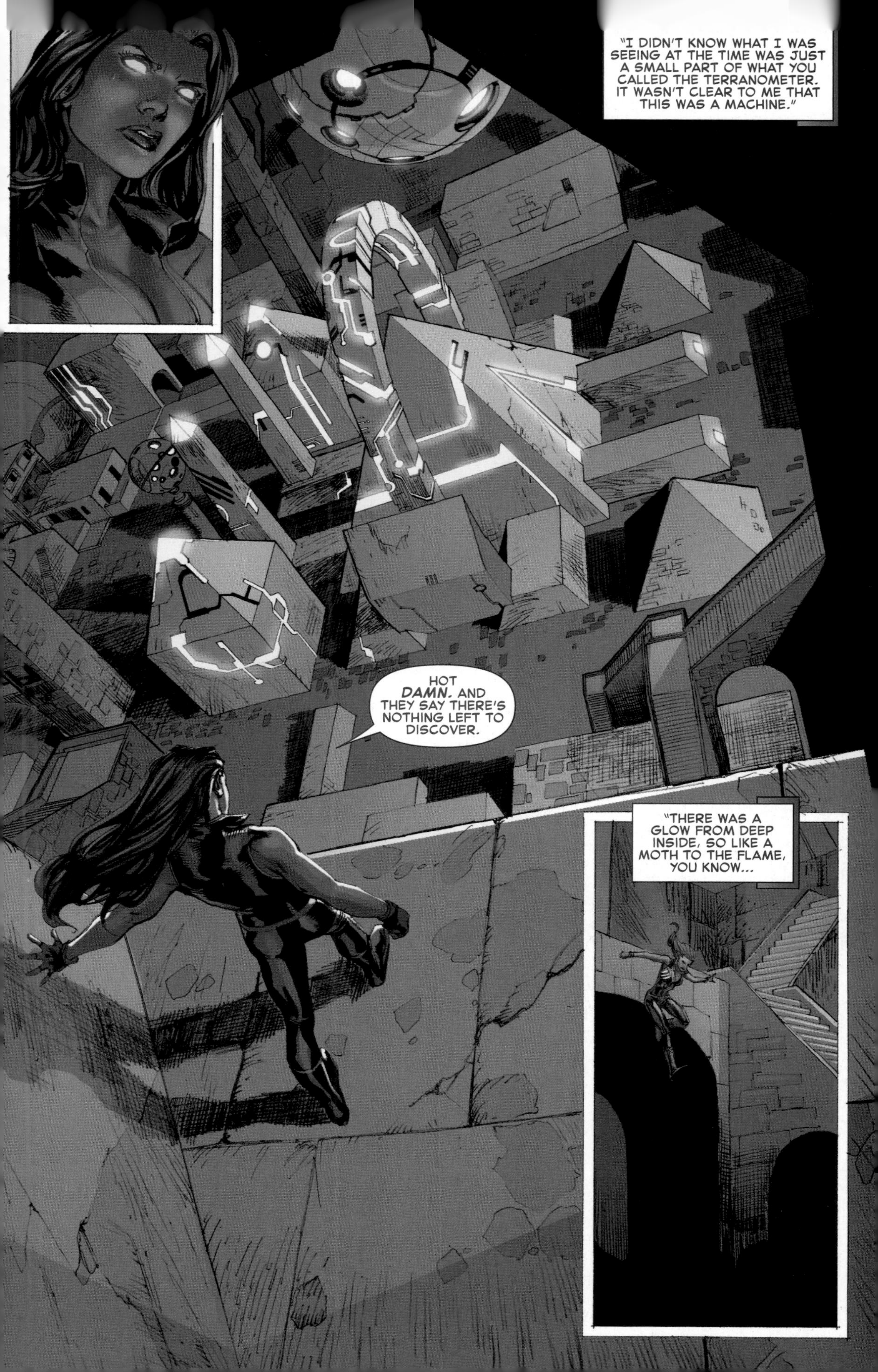
"I DIDN'T KNOW WHAT I WAS SEEING AT THE TIME WAS JUST A SMALL PART OF WHAT YOU CALLED THE TERRANOMETER. IT WASN'T CLEAR TO ME THAT THIS WAS A MACHINE."
HOT *DAMN.* AND THEY SAY THERE'S NOTHING LEFT TO DISCOVER.
"THERE WAS A GLOW FROM DEEP INSIDE, SO LIKE A MOTH TO THE FLAME, YOU KNOW...

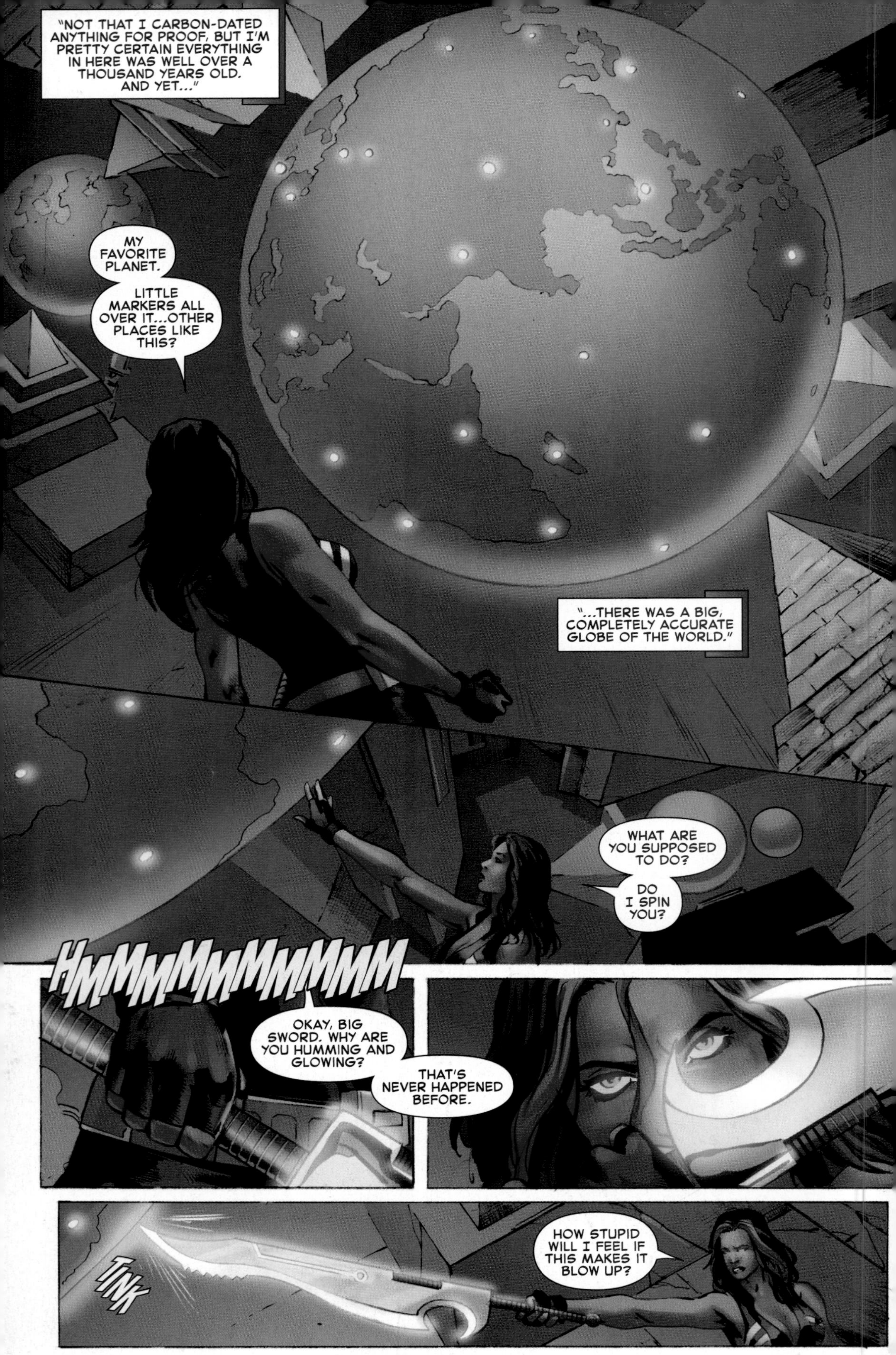
"NOT THAT I CARBON-DATED ANYTHING FOR PROOF, BUT I'M PRETTY CERTAIN EVERYTHING IN HERE WAS WELL OVER A THOUSAND YEARS OLD. AND YET..."
MY FAVORITE PLANET.
LITTLE MARKERS ALL OVER IT...OTHER PLACES LIKE THIS?
"...THERE WAS A BIG, COMPLETELY ACCURATE GLOBE OF THE WORLD."
WHAT ARE YOU SUPPOSED TO DO?
DO I SPIN YOU?
HMMMMMMMMMMMM
OKAY, BIG SWORD. WHY ARE YOU HUMMING AND GLOWING?
THAT'S NEVER HAPPENED BEFORE.
TINK
HOW STUPID WILL I FEEL IF THIS MAKES IT BLOW UP?

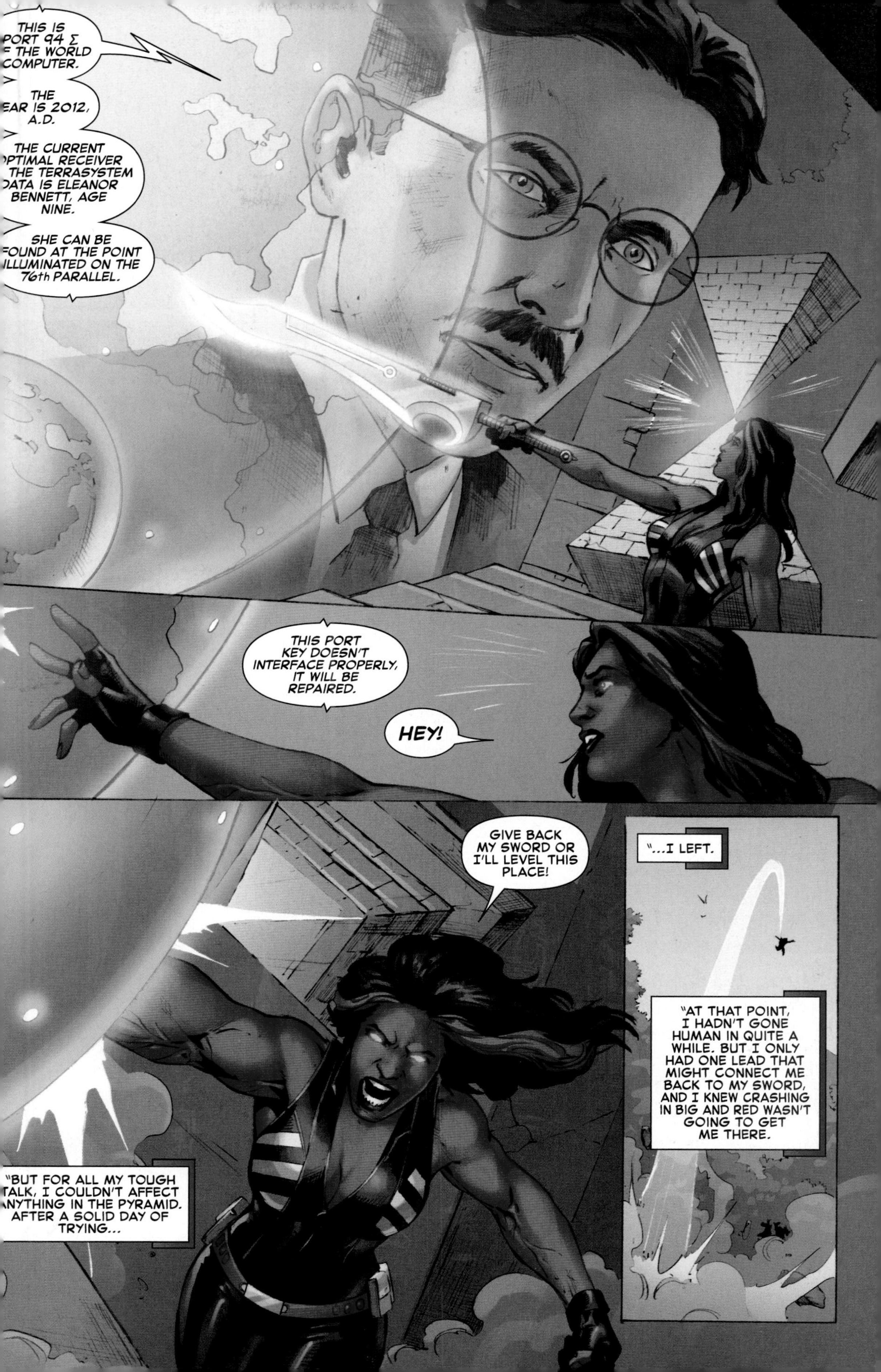
THIS IS
PORT 94 Σ
F THE WORLD
COMPUTER.
THE
EAR IS 2012,
A.D.
THE CURRENT
PTIMAL RECEIVER
THE TERRASYSTEM
DATA IS ELEANOR
BENNETT, AGE
NINE.
SHE CAN BE
FOUND AT THE POINT
ILLUMINATED ON THE
76th PARALLEL.
THIS PORT KEY DOESN'T INTERFACE PROPERLY. IT WILL BE REPAIRED.
HEY!
GIVE BACK MY SWORD OR I'LL LEVEL THIS PLACE!
"BUT FOR ALL MY TOUGH TALK, I COULDN'T AFFECT ANYTHING IN THE PYRAMID. AFTER A SOLID DAY OF TRYING...
"...I LEFT.
"AT THAT POINT, I HADN'T GONE HUMAN IN QUITE A WHILE. BUT I ONLY HAD ONE LEAD THAT MIGHT CONNECT ME BACK TO MY SWORD, AND I KNEW CRASHING IN BIG AND RED WASN'T GOING TO GET ME THERE.

"IT TOOK ME A FEW DAYS ONCE I REACHED THE STATES TO FIND ELEANOR IN ANNAPOLIS. I SHOULD HAVE PAID MORE ATTENTION TO THE PART OF THE GLOBE THAT WAS LIT UP.

"I OBSERVED FOR A WHILE BEFORE APPROACHING, BARGING IN COULD BLOW IT ALL FOR ME. I'M NOT SO OBSESSED WITH THE SWORD WHEN I'M HUMAN, BUT I WAS STILL INTRIGUED BY WHAT WAS CERTAINLY A PROFOUND AND ANCIENT MYSTERY."

"AS YOU DISCOVERED, THE HOUSE IS A CENTER FOR AUTISTIC CHILDREN, BUT THE ONLY LONG-TERM THERAPY PATIENT IS ELLIE.

"FROM WHAT I FOUND, THE NURSES WORKING THERE KNOW NOTHING OF ANY SECRET GLOBAL SOCIETY, THEY ONLY KNOW THE PLACE IS ENDOWED BY A CHARITABLE FOUNDATION CALLED MINDWELL."

"VISITORS FROM MINDWELL STOP BY A FEW TIMES A YEAR SUPPOSEDLY TO CHECK ON ELLIE, SO THAT WAS MY FRONT."

HI, I'M MS. ROSS-- I CALLED EARLIER.

COME IN!

"NOW I KNOW THAT ANY OF THESE VISITORS CHECKING IN ARE REALLY LOOKING FOR FUTURE PREDICTIONS. ELLIE IS A SWEET LITTLE GIRL BUT NOT VERY RESPONSIVE. I WASTED A FAIR AMOUNT OF TIME TRYING TO ASK HER QUESTIONS."

IT'S OKAY IF YOU DON'T WANT TO TALK, I DON'T MEAN TO BOTHER YOU.

I LIKE YOUR STRUCTURE.

"I DECIDED I'D HEARD THE HOLOGRAM MESSAGE WRONG, THIS WAS A DEAD END."

WELL, HAVE A GOOD AFTERNOON, ELLIE.

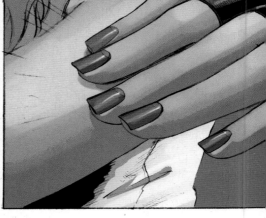

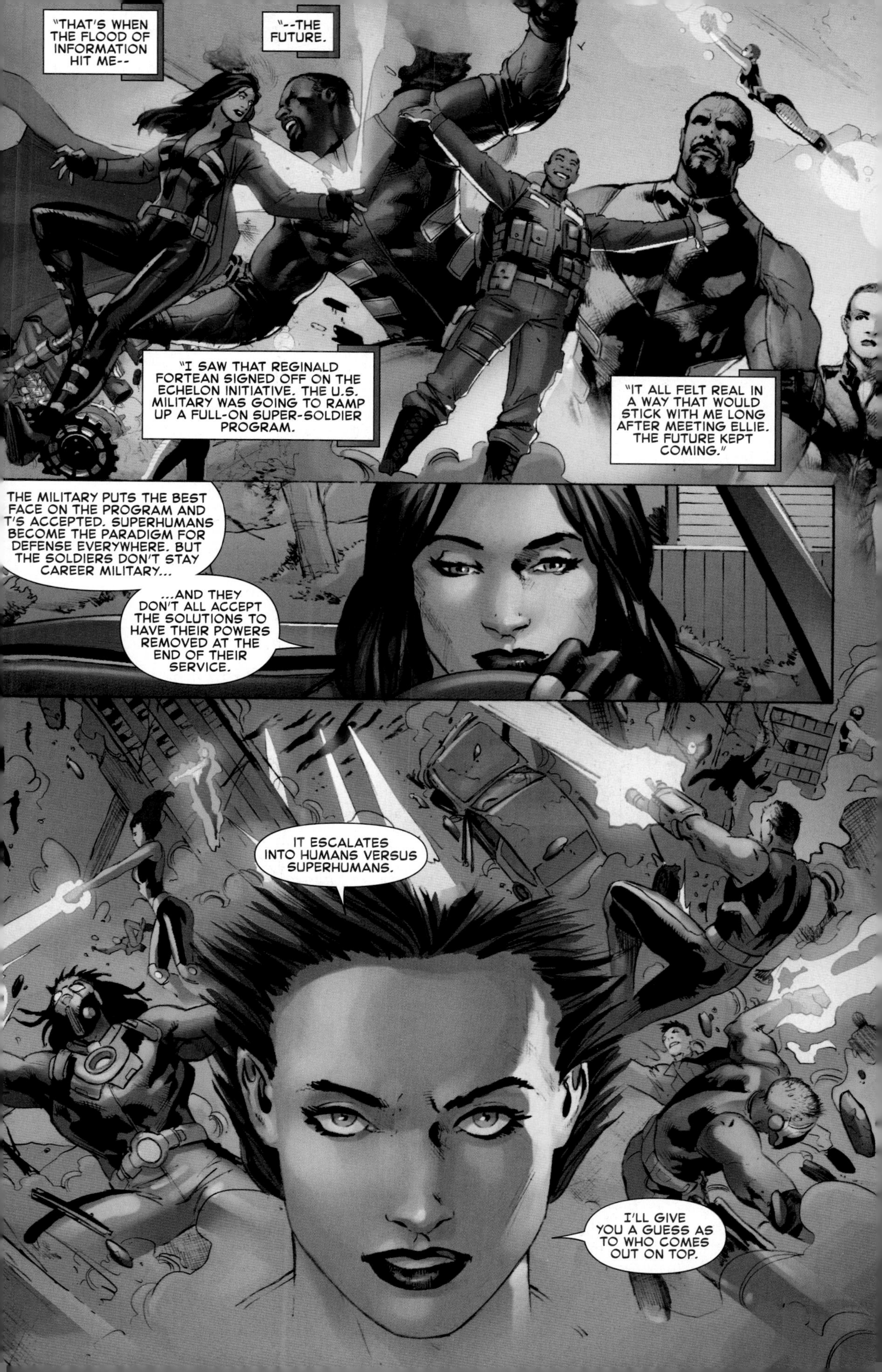
"THAT'S WHEN THE FLOOD OF INFORMATION HIT ME--
"--THE FUTURE.
"I SAW THAT REGINALD FORTEAN SIGNED OFF ON THE ECHELON INITIATIVE. THE U.S. MILITARY WAS GOING TO RAMP UP A FULL-ON SUPER-SOLDIER PROGRAM.
"IT ALL FELT REAL IN A WAY THAT WOULD STICK WITH ME LONG AFTER MEETING ELLIE. THE FUTURE KEPT COMING."
THE MILITARY PUTS THE BEST FACE ON THE PROGRAM AND IT'S ACCEPTED. SUPERHUMANS BECOME THE PARADIGM FOR DEFENSE EVERYWHERE. BUT THE SOLDIERS DON'T STAY CAREER MILITARY...
...AND THEY DON'T ALL ACCEPT THE SOLUTIONS TO HAVE THEIR POWERS REMOVED AT THE END OF THEIR SERVICE.
IT ESCALATES INTO HUMANS VERSUS SUPERHUMANS.
I'LL GIVE YOU A GUESS AS TO WHO COMES OUT ON TOP.

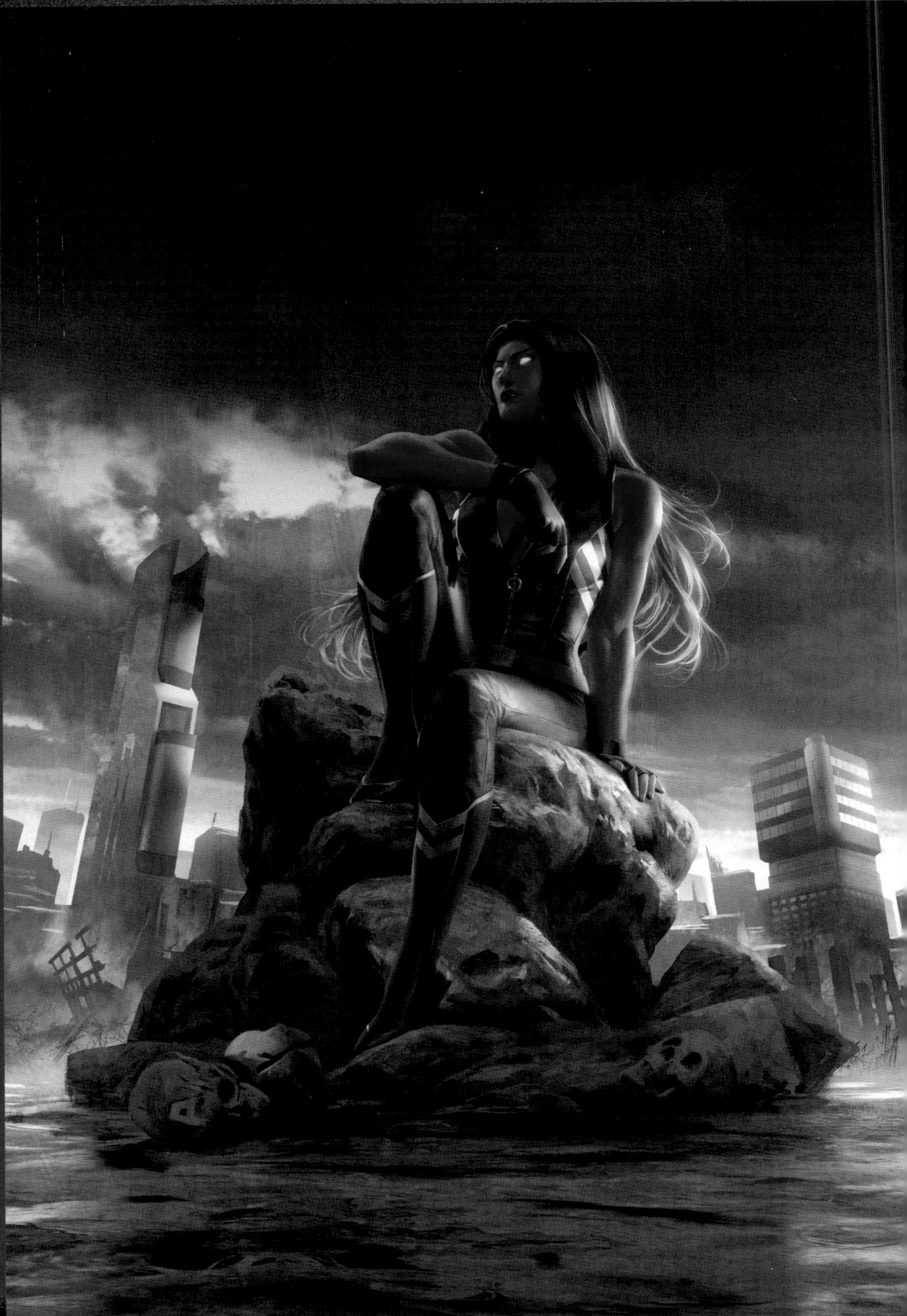

#62

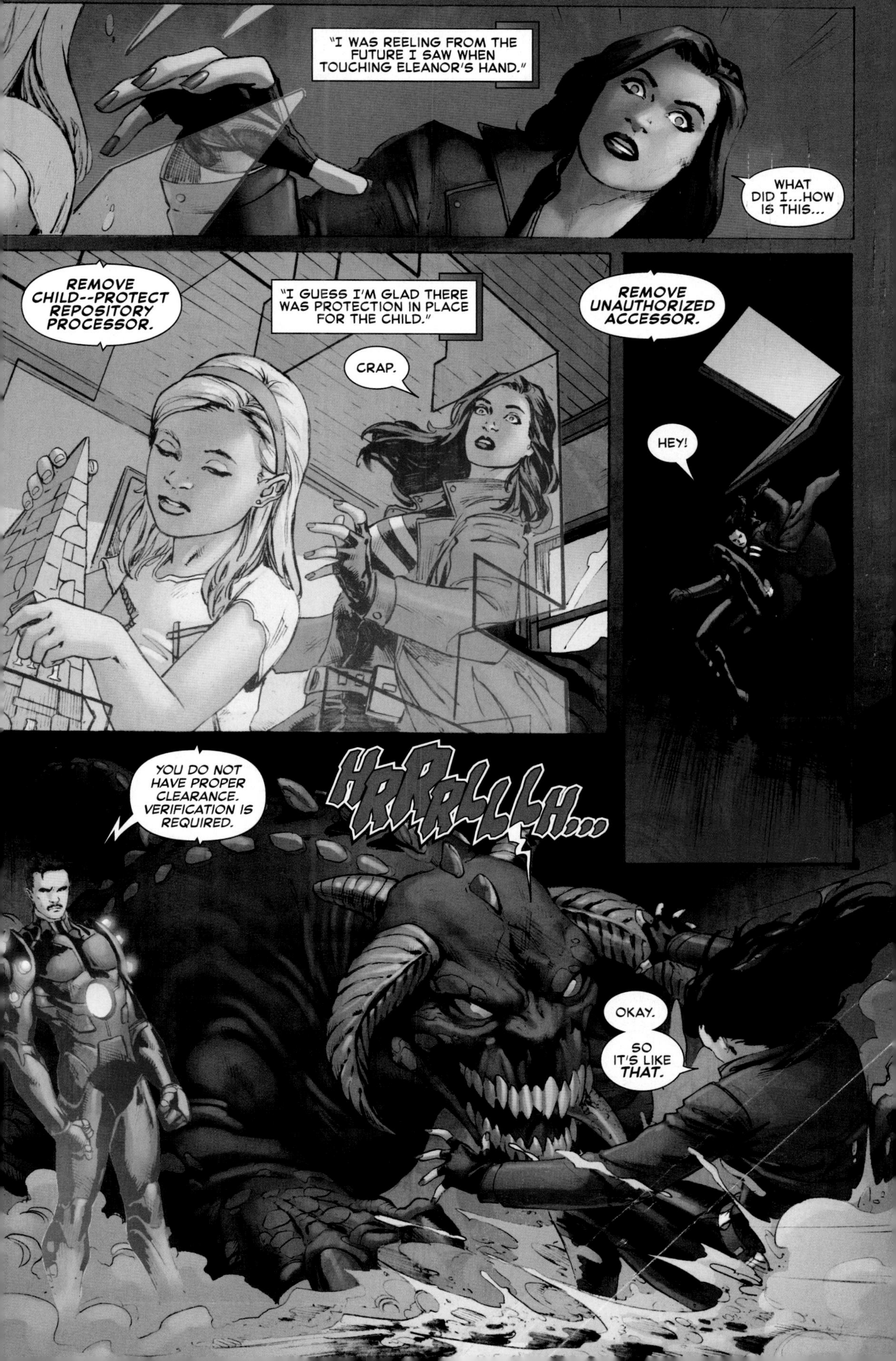

"I WAS REELING FROM THE FUTURE I SAW WHEN TOUCHING ELEANOR'S HAND."
WHAT DID I...HOW IS THIS...
REMOVE CHILD--PROTECT REPOSITORY PROCESSOR.
"I GUESS I'M GLAD THERE WAS PROTECTION IN PLACE FOR THE CHILD."
CRAP.
REMOVE UNAUTHORIZED ACCESSOR.
HEY!
YOU DO NOT HAVE PROPER CLEARANCE. VERIFICATION IS REQUIRED.
HRRRLLLH...
OKAY.
SO IT'S LIKE THAT.

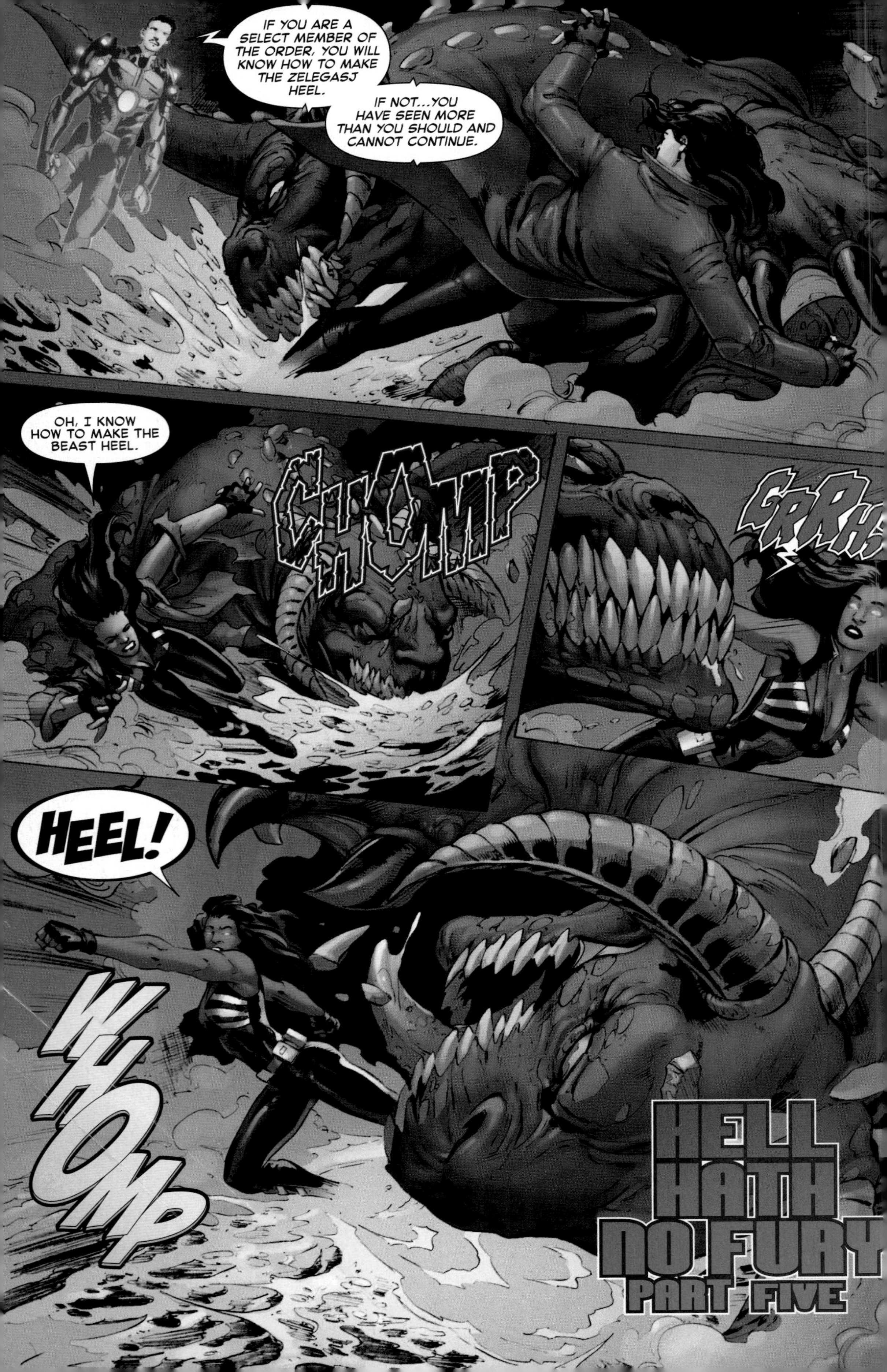

IF YOU ARE A SELECT MEMBER OF THE ORDER, YOU WILL KNOW HOW TO MAKE THE ZELEGASJ HEEL.
IF NOT...YOU HAVE SEEN MORE THAN YOU SHOULD AND CANNOT CONTINUE.
OH, I KNOW HOW TO MAKE THE BEAST HEEL.
CHOMP
GRRH
HEEL!
WHOMP
HELL HATH NO FURY
PART FIVE

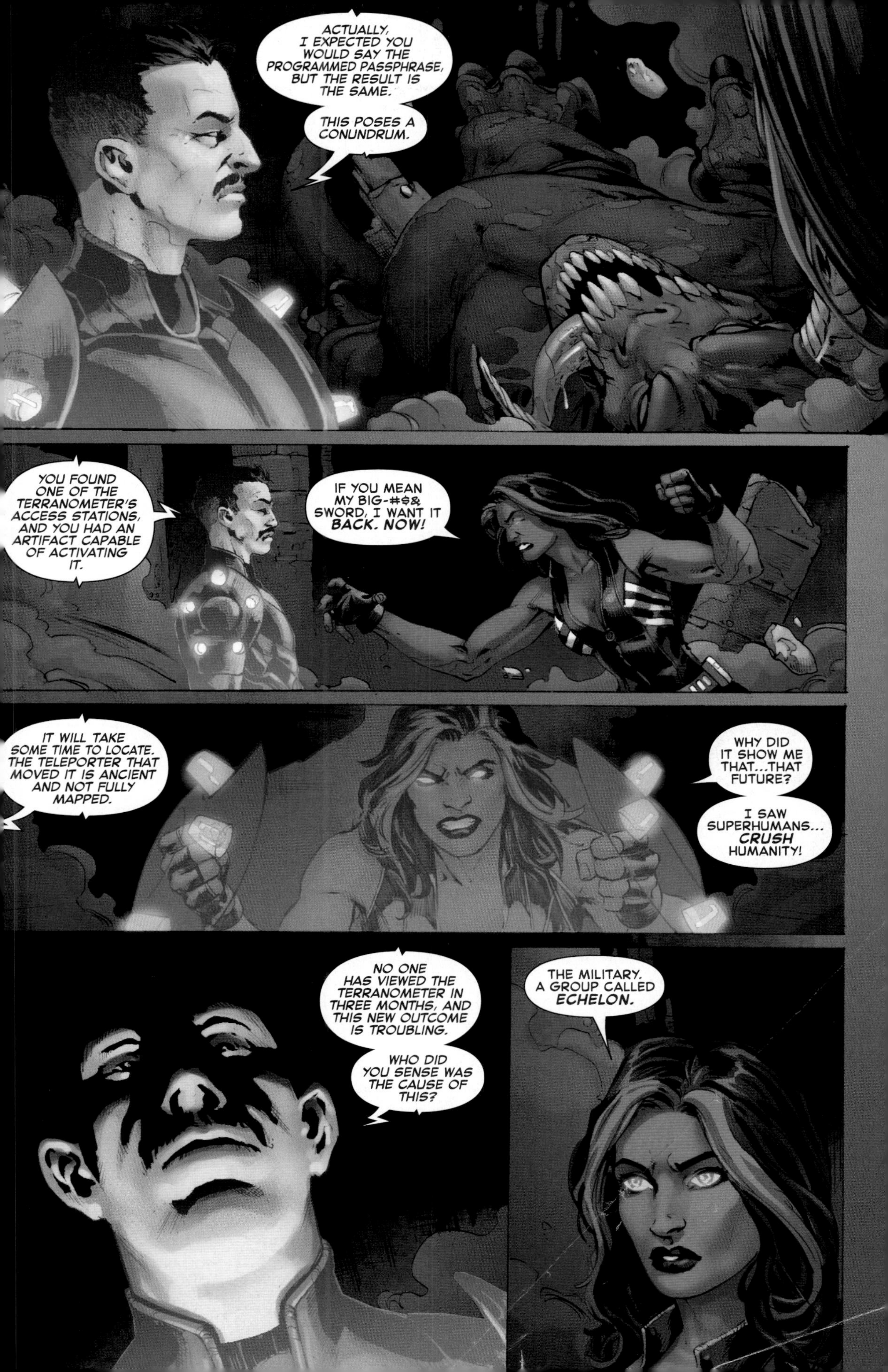
ACTUALLY, I EXPECTED YOU WOULD SAY THE PROGRAMMED PASSPHRASE, BUT THE RESULT IS THE SAME.
THIS POSES A CONUNDRUM.
YOU FOUND ONE OF THE TERRANOMETER'S ACCESS STATIONS, AND YOU HAD AN ARTIFACT CAPABLE OF ACTIVATING IT.
IF YOU MEAN MY BIG-#$& SWORD, I WANT IT BACK. NOW!
IT WILL TAKE SOME TIME TO LOCATE. THE TELEPORTER THAT MOVED IT IS ANCIENT AND NOT FULLY MAPPED.
WHY DID IT SHOW ME THAT...THAT FUTURE?
I SAW SUPERHUMANS... CRUSH HUMANITY!
NO ONE HAS VIEWED THE TERRANOMETER IN THREE MONTHS, AND THIS NEW OUTCOME IS TROUBLING.
WHO DID YOU SENSE WAS THE CAUSE OF THIS?
THE MILITARY. A GROUP CALLED ECHELON.

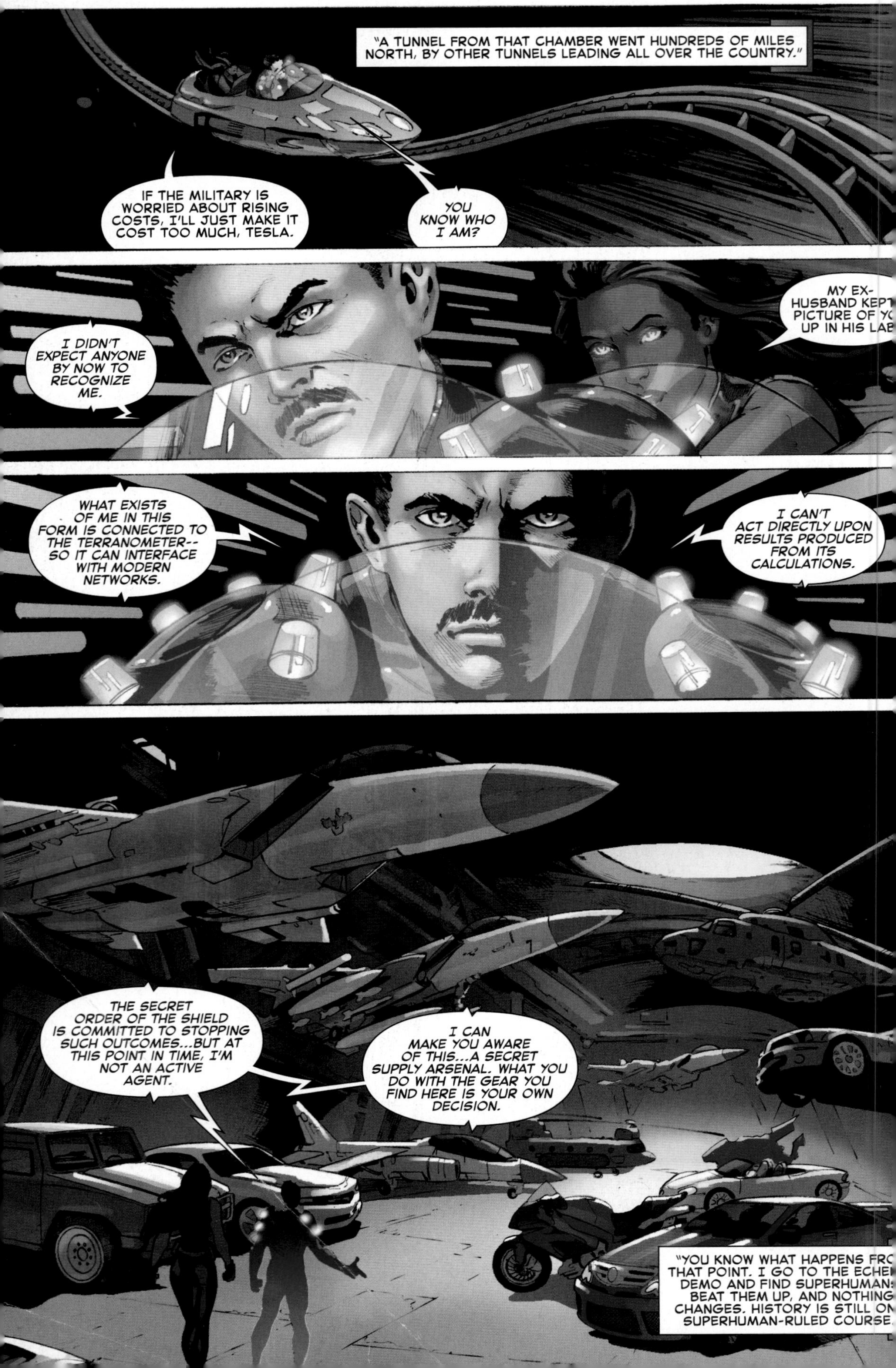

"A TUNNEL FROM THAT CHAMBER WENT HUNDREDS OF MILES NORTH, BY OTHER TUNNELS LEADING ALL OVER THE COUNTRY."
IF THE MILITARY IS WORRIED ABOUT RISING COSTS, I'LL JUST MAKE IT COST TOO MUCH, TESLA.
YOU KNOW WHO I AM?
I DIDN'T EXPECT ANYONE BY NOW TO RECOGNIZE ME.
MY EX-HUSBAND KEPT PICTURE OF YO UP IN HIS LAB
WHAT EXISTS OF ME IN THIS FORM IS CONNECTED TO THE TERRANOMETER--SO IT CAN INTERFACE WITH MODERN NETWORKS.
I CAN'T ACT DIRECTLY UPON RESULTS PRODUCED FROM ITS CALCULATIONS.
THE SECRET ORDER OF THE SHIELD IS COMMITTED TO STOPPING SUCH OUTCOMES...BUT AT THIS POINT IN TIME, I'M NOT AN ACTIVE AGENT.
I CAN MAKE YOU AWARE OF THIS...A SECRET SUPPLY ARSENAL. WHAT YOU DO WITH THE GEAR YOU FIND HERE IS YOUR OWN DECISION.
"YOU KNOW WHAT HAPPENS FRO THAT POINT. I GO TO THE ECHE DEMO AND FIND SUPERHUMAN BEAT THEM UP, AND NOTHING CHANGES. HISTORY IS STILL ON SUPERHUMAN-RULED COURSE.

#62

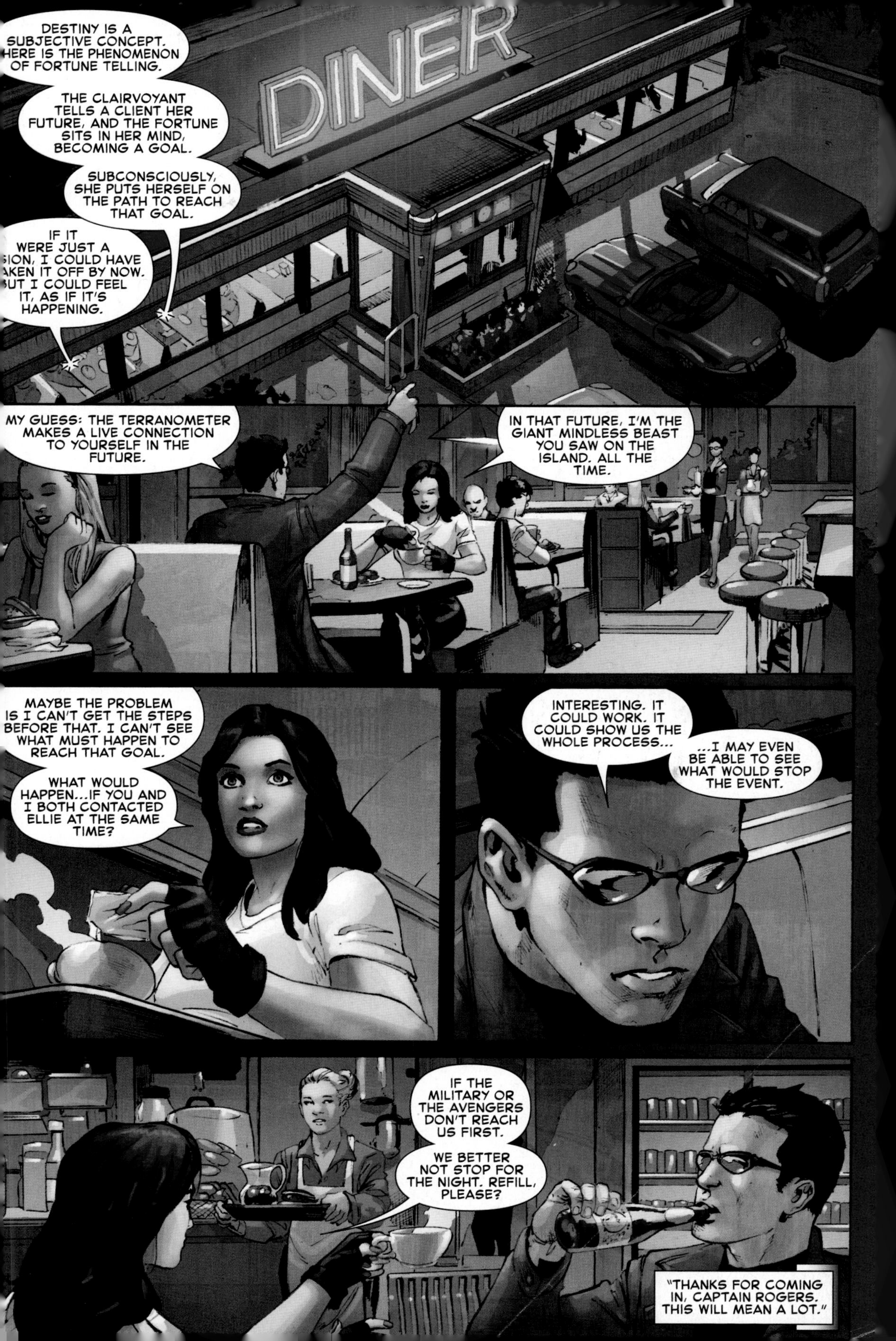
DINER
DESTINY IS A SUBJECTIVE CONCEPT. HERE IS THE PHENOMENON OF FORTUNE TELLING.
THE CLAIRVOYANT TELLS A CLIENT HER FUTURE, AND THE FORTUNE SITS IN HER MIND, BECOMING A GOAL.
SUBCONSCIOUSLY, SHE PUTS HERSELF ON THE PATH TO REACH THAT GOAL.
IF IT WERE JUST A VISION, I COULD HAVE SHAKEN IT OFF BY NOW. BUT I COULD FEEL IT, AS IF IT'S HAPPENING.
MY GUESS: THE TERRANOMETER MAKES A LIVE CONNECTION TO YOURSELF IN THE FUTURE.
IN THAT FUTURE, I'M THE GIANT MINDLESS BEAST YOU SAW ON THE ISLAND. ALL THE TIME.
MAYBE THE PROBLEM IS I CAN'T GET THE STEPS BEFORE THAT. I CAN'T SEE WHAT MUST HAPPEN TO REACH THAT GOAL.
WHAT WOULD HAPPEN...IF YOU AND I BOTH CONTACTED ELLIE AT THE SAME TIME?
INTERESTING. IT COULD WORK. IT COULD SHOW US THE WHOLE PROCESS...
...I MAY EVEN BE ABLE TO SEE WHAT WOULD STOP THE EVENT.
IF THE MILITARY OR THE AVENGERS DON'T REACH US FIRST.
WE BETTER NOT STOP FOR THE NIGHT. REFILL, PLEASE?
"THANKS FOR COMING IN, CAPTAIN ROGERS. THIS WILL MEAN A LOT."

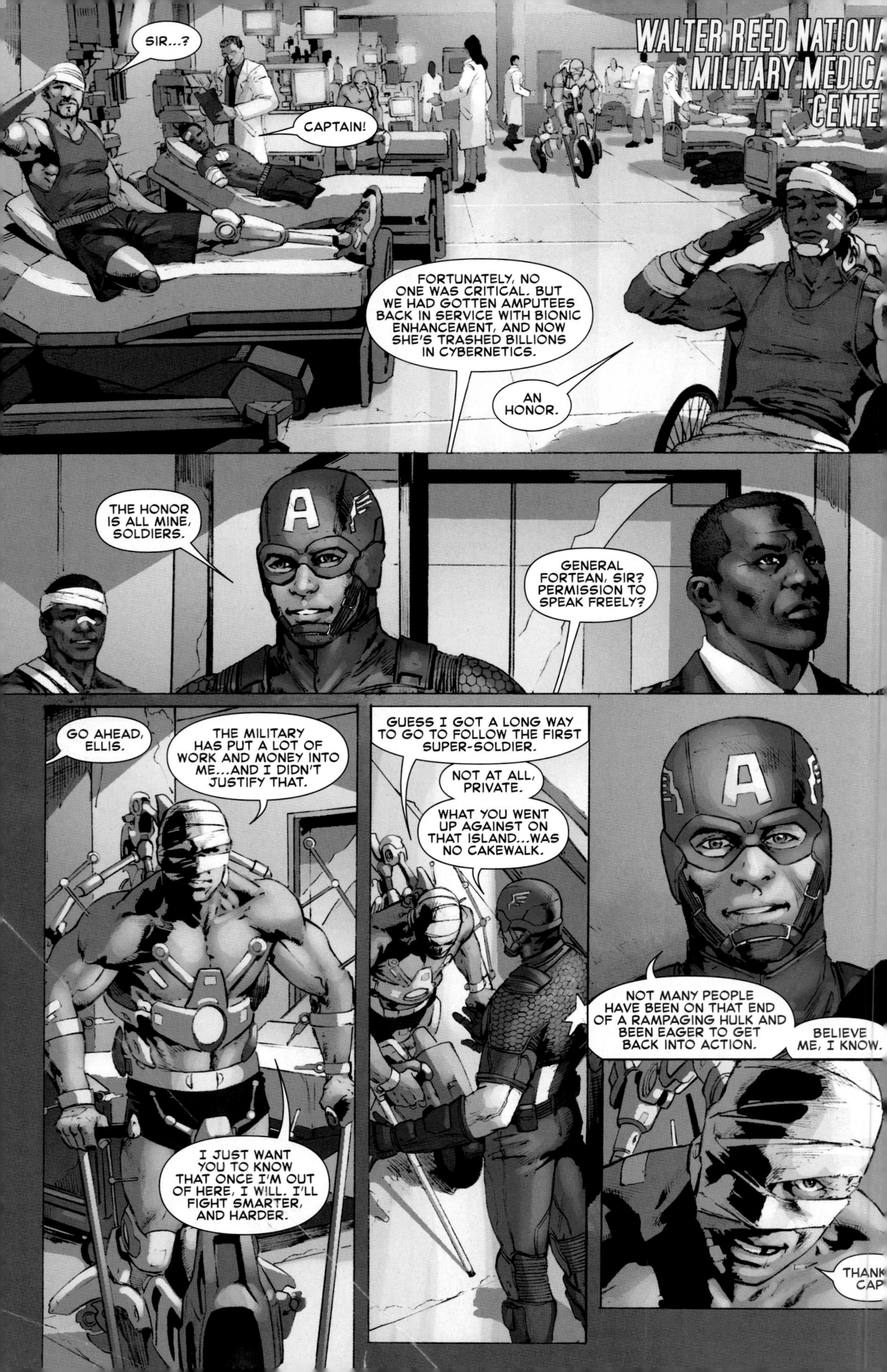
WALTER REED NATIONA
MILITARY MEDICA
CENTE
SIR...?
CAPTAIN!
FORTUNATELY, NO ONE WAS CRITICAL. BUT WE HAD GOTTEN AMPUTEES BACK IN SERVICE WITH BIONIC ENHANCEMENT, AND NOW SHE'S TRASHED BILLIONS IN CYBERNETICS.
AN HONOR.
THE HONOR IS ALL MINE, SOLDIERS.
GENERAL FORTEAN, SIR? PERMISSION TO SPEAK FREELY?
GO AHEAD, ELLIS.
THE MILITARY HAS PUT A LOT OF WORK AND MONEY INTO ME...AND I DIDN'T JUSTIFY THAT.
I JUST WANT YOU TO KNOW THAT ONCE I'M OUT OF HERE, I WILL. I'LL FIGHT SMARTER, AND HARDER.
GUESS I GOT A LONG WAY TO GO TO FOLLOW THE FIRST SUPER-SOLDIER.
NOT AT ALL, PRIVATE.
WHAT YOU WENT UP AGAINST ON THAT ISLAND...WAS NO CAKEWALK.
NOT MANY PEOPLE HAVE BEEN ON THAT END OF A RAMPAGING HULK AND BEEN EAGER TO GET BACK INTO ACTION.
BELIEVE ME, I KNOW.
THANK
CAP

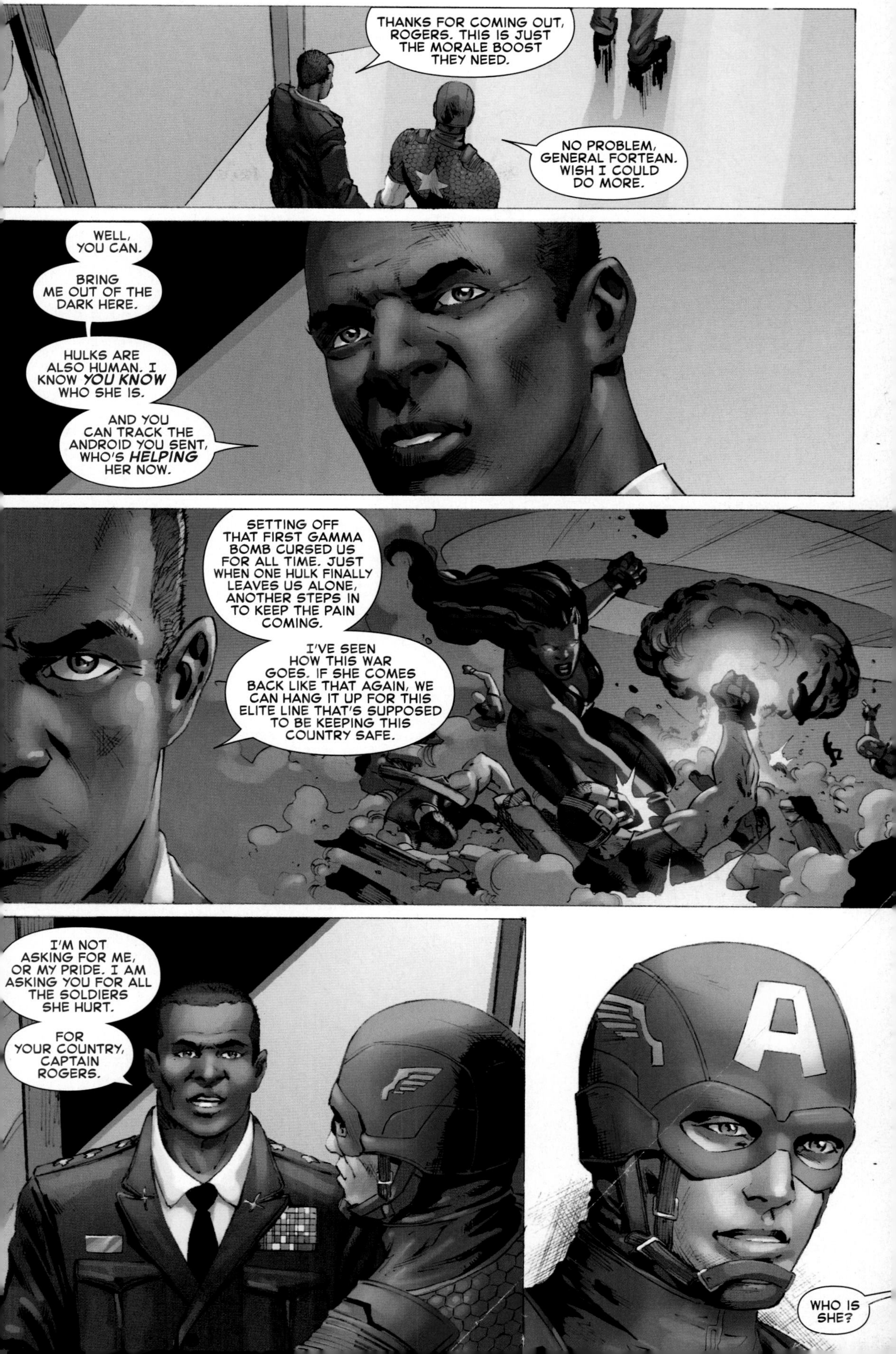
THANKS FOR COMING OUT, ROGERS. THIS IS JUST THE MORALE BOOST THEY NEED.
NO PROBLEM, GENERAL FORTEAN. WISH I COULD DO MORE.
WELL, YOU CAN.
BRING ME OUT OF THE DARK HERE.
HULKS ARE ALSO HUMAN. I KNOW *YOU KNOW* WHO SHE IS.
AND YOU CAN TRACK THE ANDROID YOU SENT, WHO'S *HELPING* HER NOW.
SETTING OFF THAT FIRST GAMMA BOMB CURSED US FOR ALL TIME. JUST WHEN ONE HULK FINALLY LEAVES US ALONE, ANOTHER STEPS IN TO KEEP THE PAIN COMING.
I'VE SEEN HOW THIS WAR GOES. IF SHE COMES BACK LIKE THAT AGAIN, WE CAN HANG IT UP FOR THIS ELITE LINE THAT'S SUPPOSED TO BE KEEPING THIS COUNTRY SAFE.
I'M NOT ASKING FOR ME, OR MY PRIDE. I AM ASKING YOU FOR ALL THE SOLDIERS SHE HURT.
FOR YOUR COUNTRY, CAPTAIN ROGERS.
WHO IS SHE?

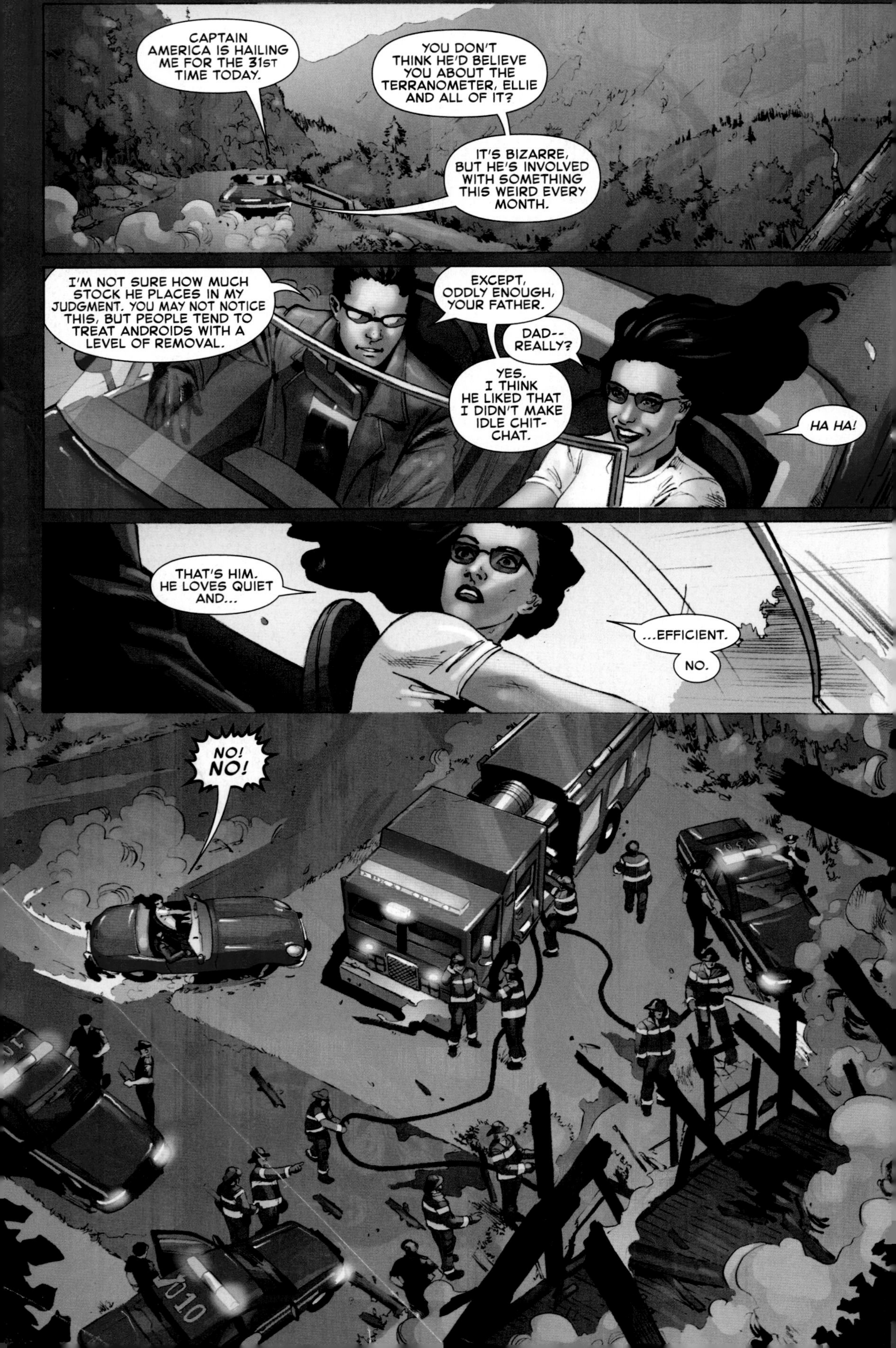
CAPTAIN AMERICA IS HAILING ME FOR THE 31ST TIME TODAY.
YOU DON'T THINK HE'D BELIEVE YOU ABOUT THE TERRANOMETER, ELLIE AND ALL OF IT?
IT'S BIZARRE, BUT HE'S INVOLVED WITH SOMETHING THIS WEIRD EVERY MONTH.
I'M NOT SURE HOW MUCH STOCK HE PLACES IN MY JUDGMENT. YOU MAY NOT NOTICE THIS, BUT PEOPLE TEND TO TREAT ANDROIDS WITH A LEVEL OF REMOVAL.
EXCEPT, ODDLY ENOUGH, YOUR FATHER.
DAD-- REALLY?
YES. I THINK HE LIKED THAT I DIDN'T MAKE IDLE CHIT-CHAT.
HA HA!
THAT'S HIM. HE LOVES QUIET AND...
...EFFICIENT.
NO.
NO! NO!

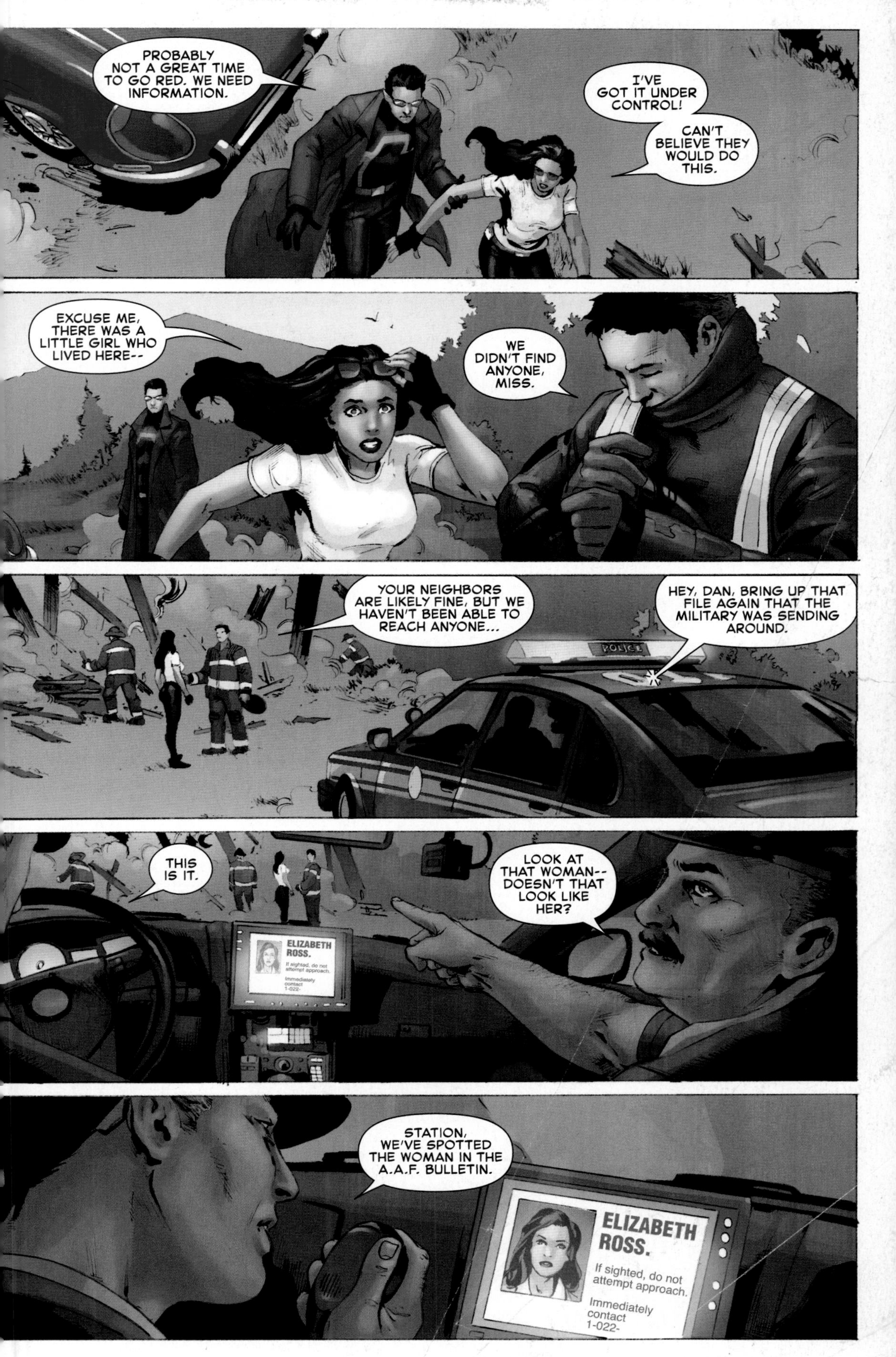
PROBABLY NOT A GREAT TIME TO GO RED. WE NEED INFORMATION.
I'VE GOT IT UNDER CONTROL!
CAN'T BELIEVE THEY WOULD DO THIS.
EXCUSE ME, THERE WAS A LITTLE GIRL WHO LIVED HERE--
WE DIDN'T FIND ANYONE, MISS.
YOUR NEIGHBORS ARE LIKELY FINE, BUT WE HAVEN'T BEEN ABLE TO REACH ANYONE...
HEY, DAN, BRING UP THAT FILE AGAIN THAT THE MILITARY WAS SENDING AROUND.
POLICE
THIS IS IT.
LOOK AT THAT WOMAN--DOESN'T THAT LOOK LIKE HER?
ELIZABETH ROSS.
If sighted, do not attempt approach.
Immediately contact 1-022-
STATION, WE'VE SPOTTED THE WOMAN IN THE A.A.F. BULLETIN.
ELIZABETH ROSS.
If sighted, do not attempt approach.
Immediately contact 1-022-

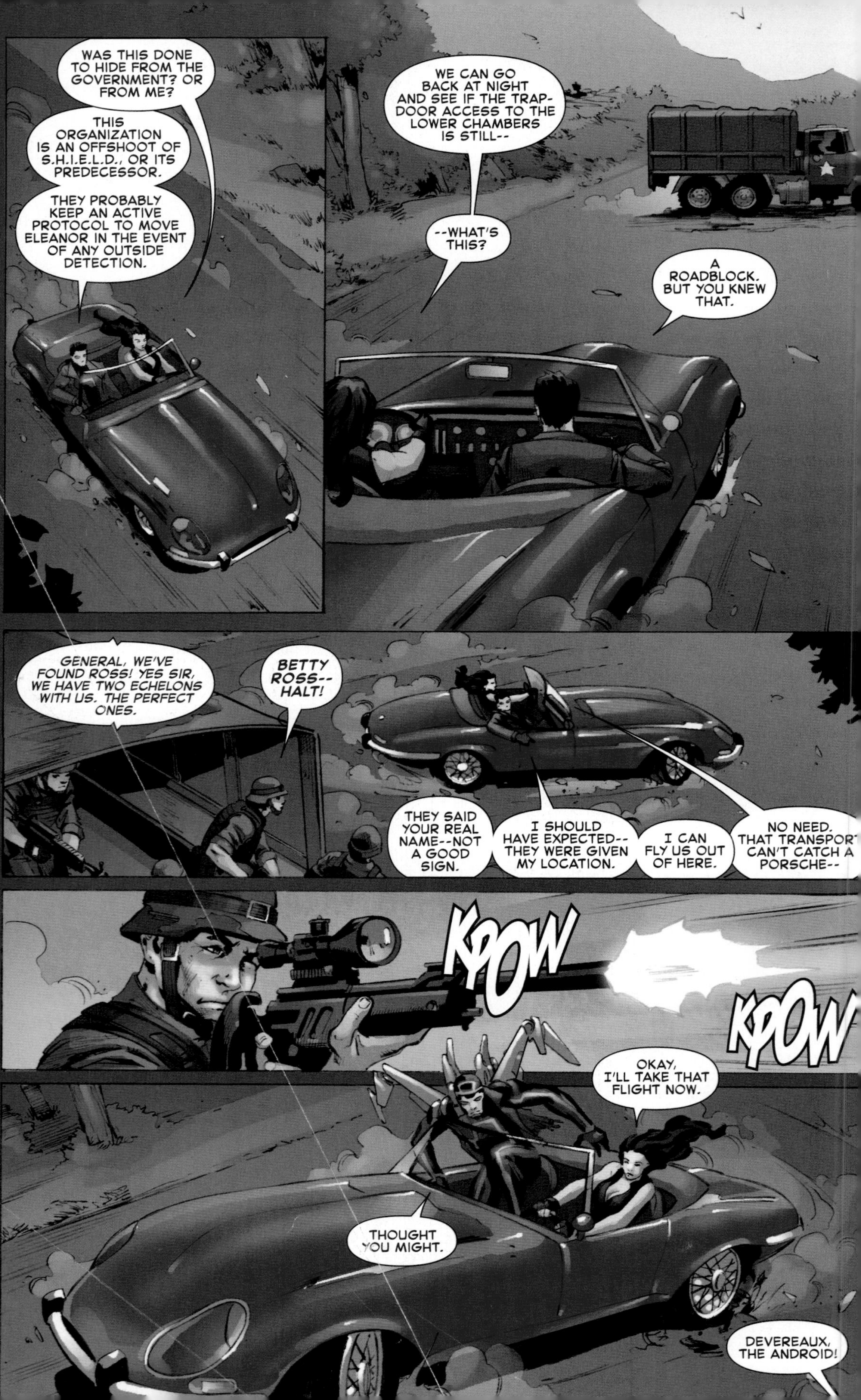
WAS THIS DONE TO HIDE FROM THE GOVERNMENT? OR FROM ME?
THIS ORGANIZATION IS AN OFFSHOOT OF S.H.I.E.L.D., OR ITS PREDECESSOR.
THEY PROBABLY KEEP AN ACTIVE PROTOCOL TO MOVE ELEANOR IN THE EVENT OF ANY OUTSIDE DETECTION.
WE CAN GO BACK AT NIGHT AND SEE IF THE TRAP-DOOR ACCESS TO THE LOWER CHAMBERS IS STILL--
--WHAT'S THIS?
A ROADBLOCK. BUT YOU KNEW THAT.
GENERAL, WE'VE FOUND ROSS! YES SIR, WE HAVE TWO ECHELONS WITH US. THE PERFECT ONES.
BETTY ROSS--HALT!
THEY SAID YOUR REAL NAME--NOT A GOOD SIGN.
I SHOULD HAVE EXPECTED--THEY WERE GIVEN MY LOCATION.
I CAN FLY US OUT OF HERE.
NO NEED. THAT TRANSPORT CAN'T CATCH A PORSCHE--
KPOW
KPOW
OKAY, I'LL TAKE THAT FLIGHT NOW.
THOUGHT YOU MIGHT.
DEVEREAUX, THE ANDROID!

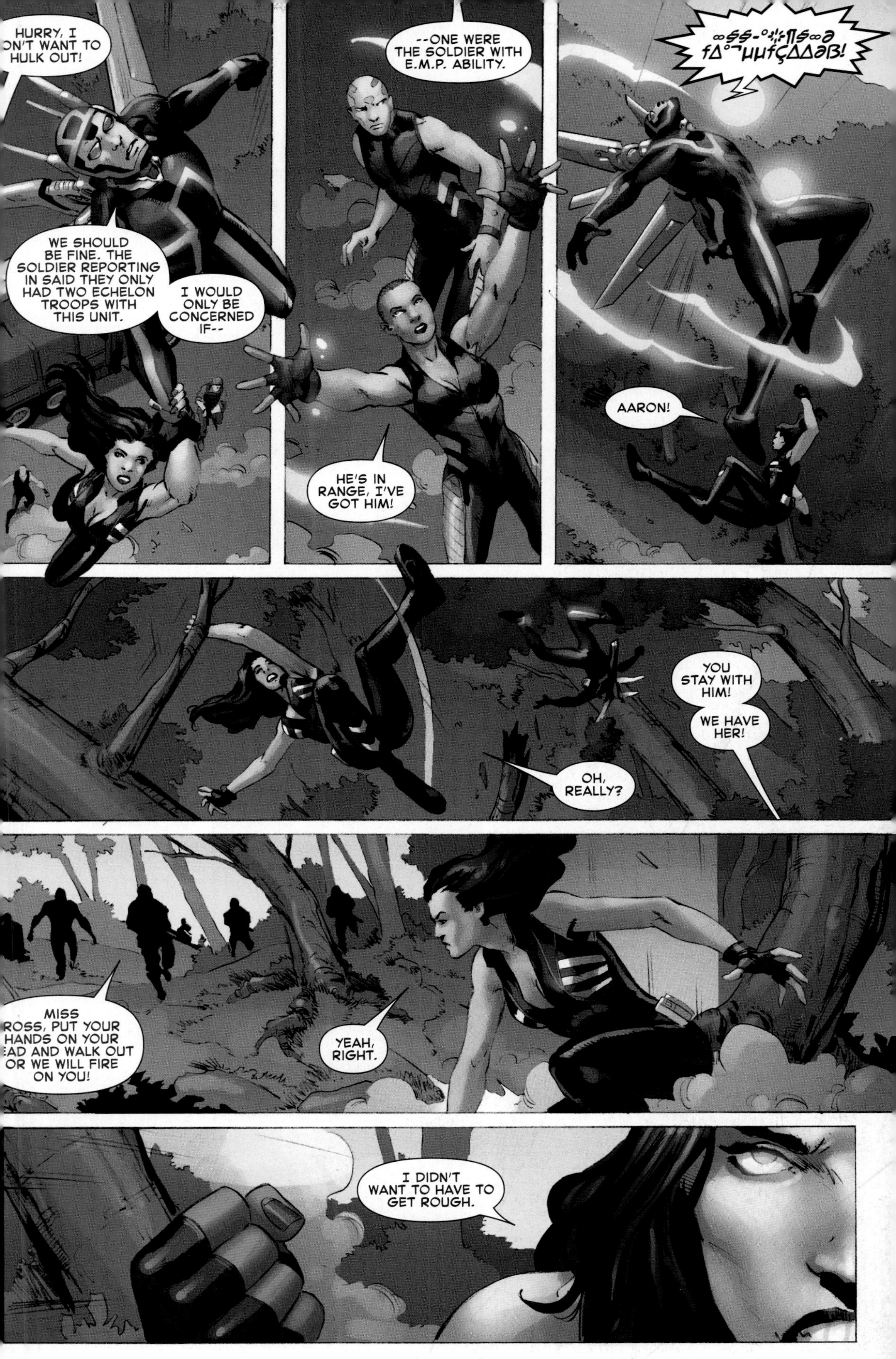
HURRY, I ON'T WANT TO HULK OUT!
WE SHOULD BE FINE. THE SOLDIER REPORTING IN SAID THEY ONLY HAD TWO ECHELON TROOPS WITH THIS UNIT.
I WOULD ONLY BE CONCERNED IF--
--ONE WERE THE SOLDIER WITH E.M.P. ABILITY.
HE'S IN RANGE, I'VE GOT HIM!
AARON!
YOU STAY WITH HIM!
WE HAVE HER!
OH, REALLY?
MISS ROSS, PUT YOUR HANDS ON YOUR EAD AND WALK OUT OR WE WILL FIRE ON YOU!
YEAH, RIGHT.
I DIDN'T WANT TO HAVE TO GET ROUGH.

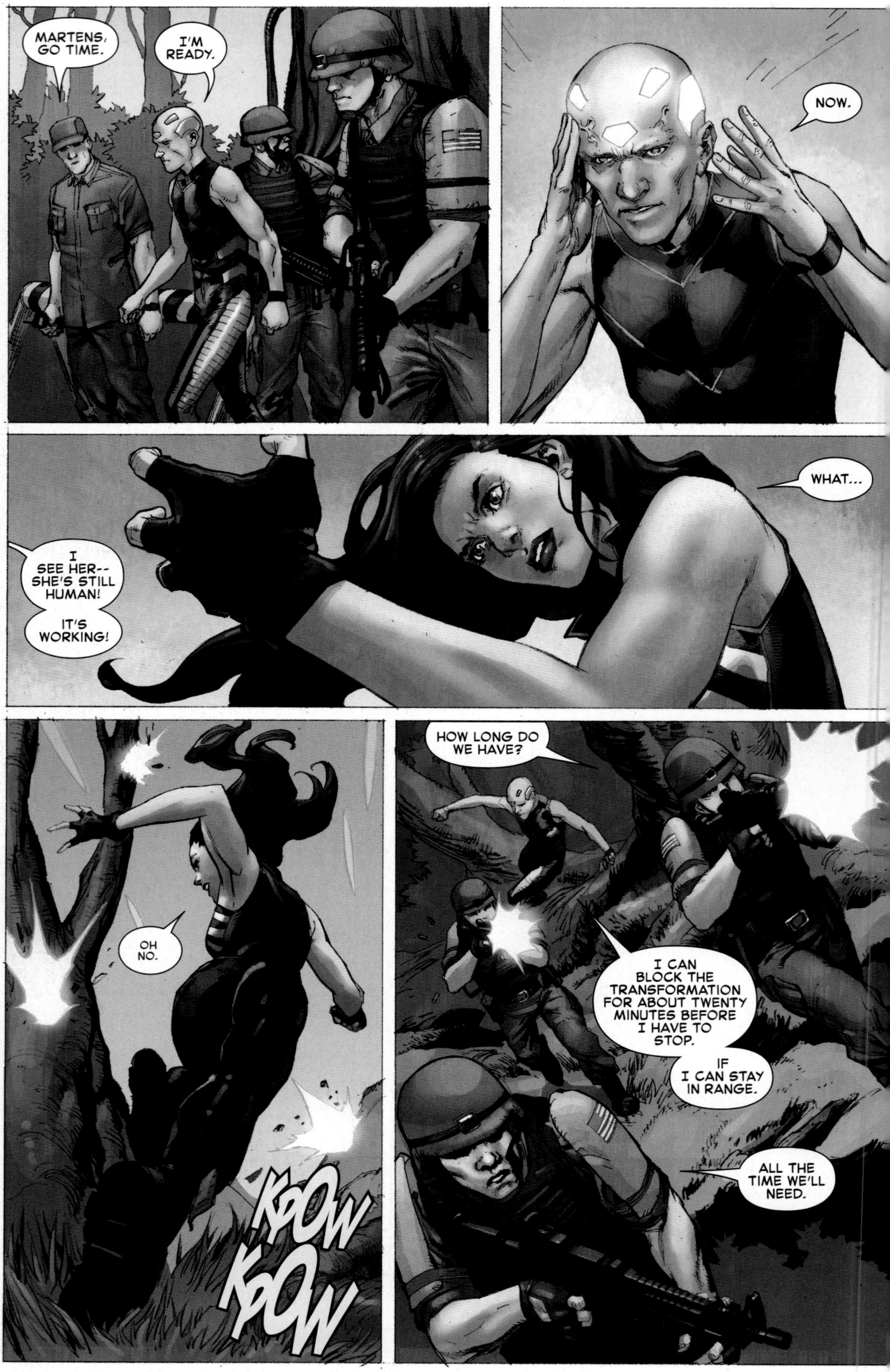
MARTENS, GO TIME.
I'M READY.
NOW.
WHAT...
I SEE HER-- SHE'S STILL HUMAN!
IT'S WORKING!
OH NO.
KDOW KDOW
HOW LONG DO WE HAVE?
I CAN BLOCK THE TRANSFORMATION FOR ABOUT TWENTY MINUTES BEFORE I HAVE TO STOP.
IF I CAN STAY IN RANGE.
ALL THE TIME WE'LL NEED.

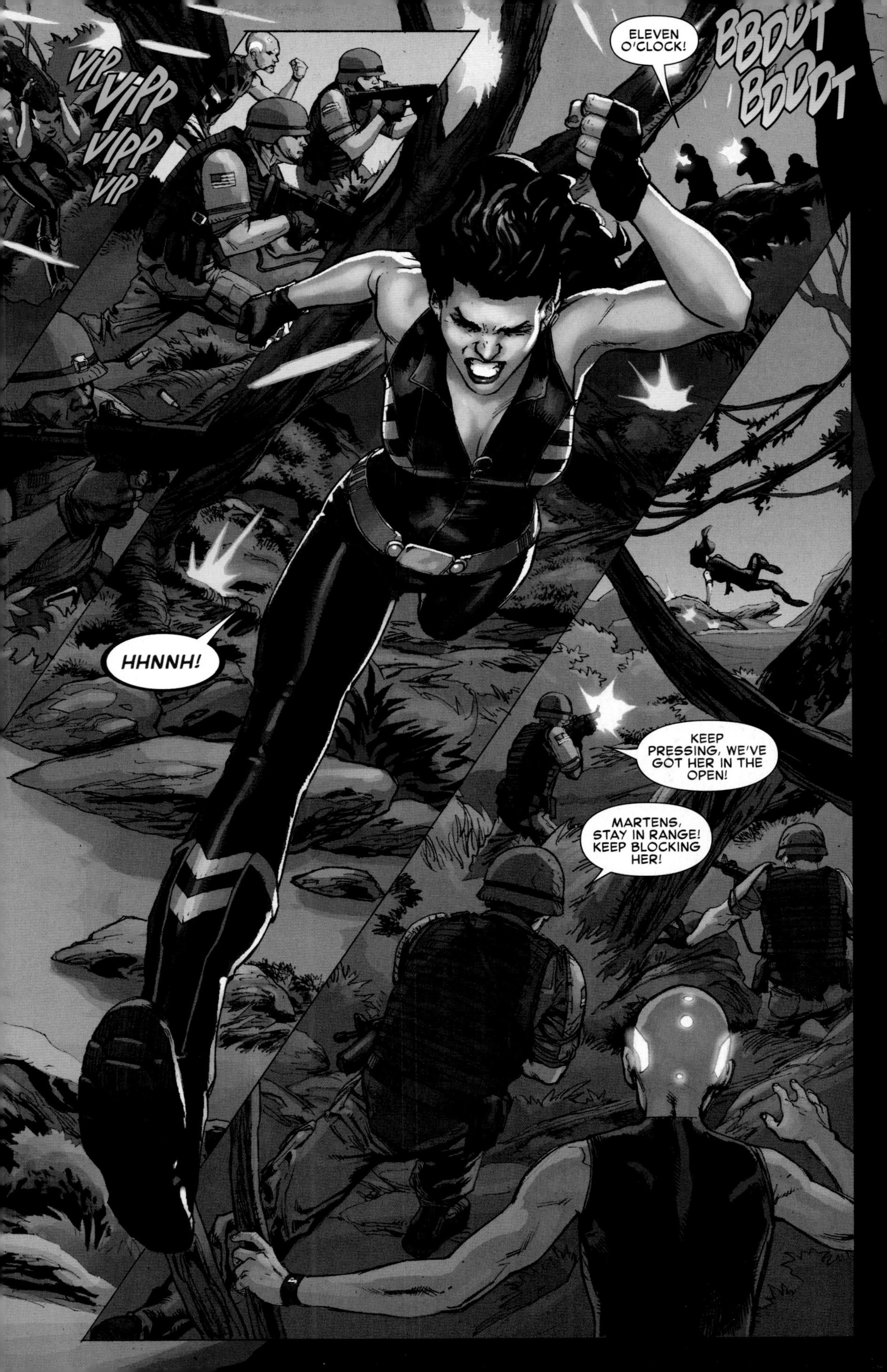
VIP VIPP VIPP VIP
ELEVEN O'CLOCK!
BBDDT BDDDT
HHNNH!
KEEP PRESSING, WE'VE GOT HER IN THE OPEN!
MARTENS, STAY IN RANGE! KEEP BLOCKING HER!

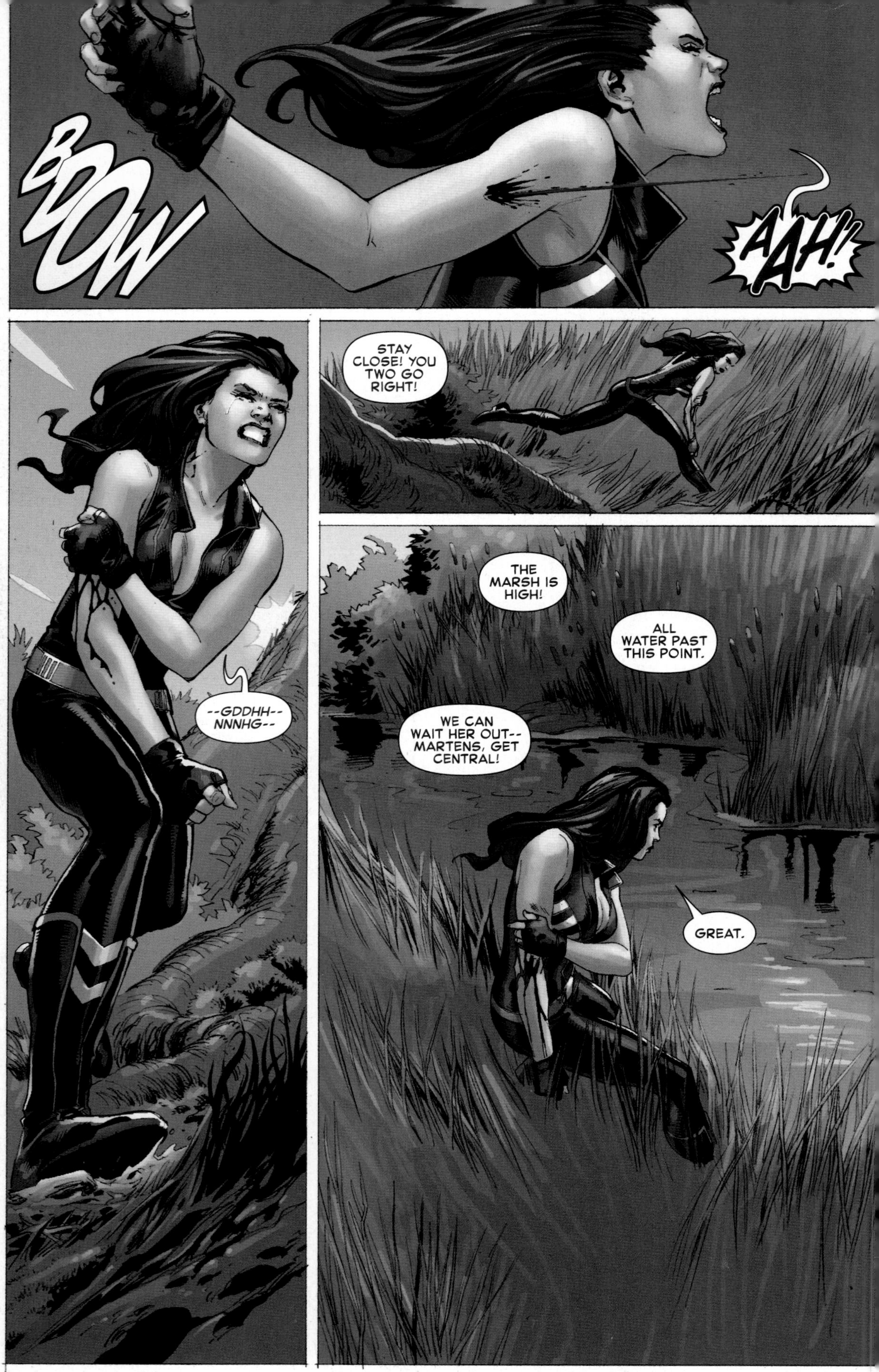
BDOW
AAH!
--GDDHH-- NNNHG--
STAY CLOSE! YOU TWO GO RIGHT!
THE MARSH IS HIGH!
ALL WATER PAST THIS POINT.
WE CAN WAIT HER OUT-- MARTENS, GET CENTRAL!
GREAT.

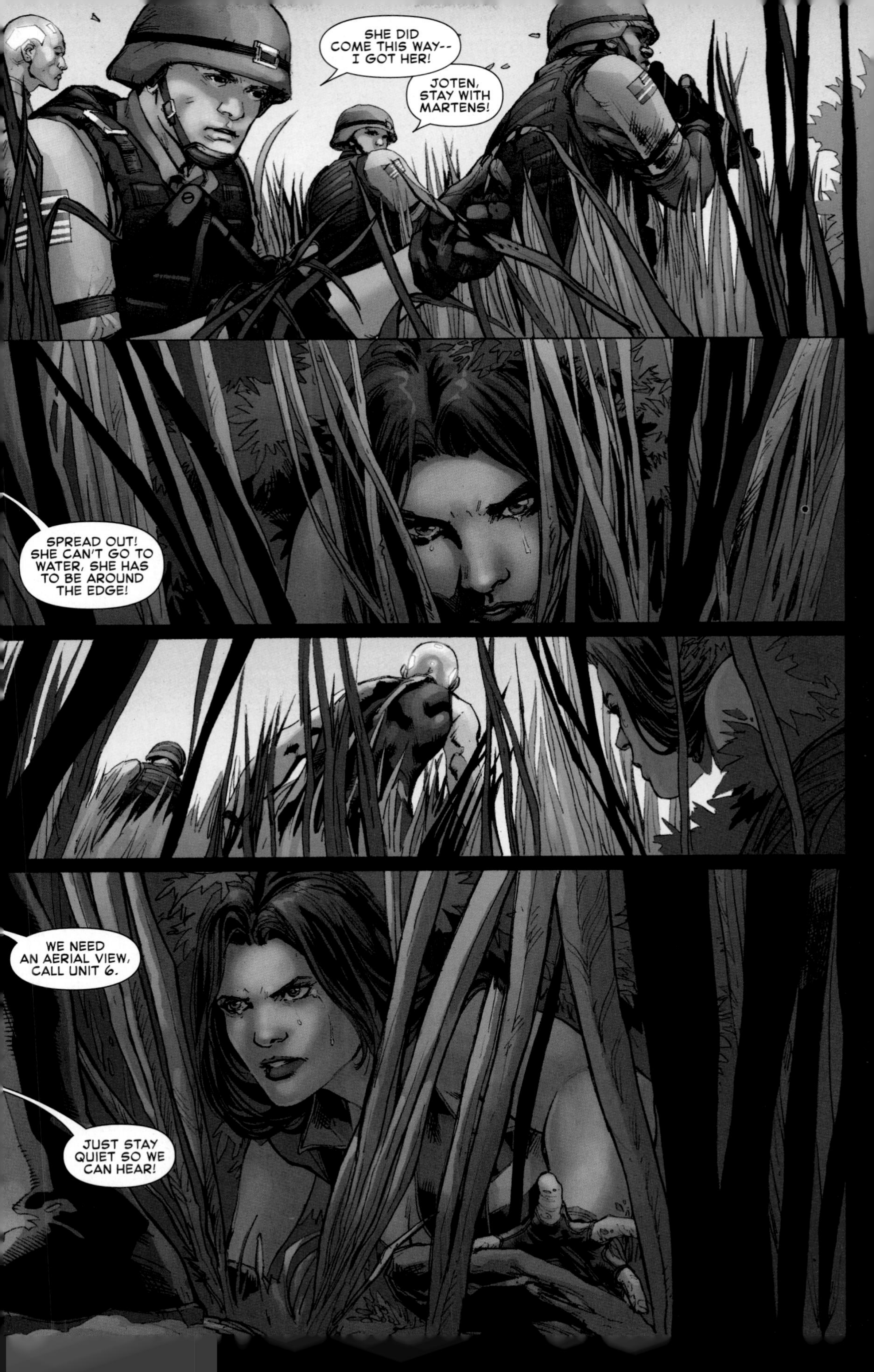
SHE DID COME THIS WAY-- I GOT HER!
JOTEN, STAY WITH MARTENS!
SPREAD OUT! SHE CAN'T GO TO WATER, SHE HAS TO BE AROUND THE EDGE!
WE NEED AN AERIAL VIEW, CALL UNIT 6.
JUST STAY QUIET SO WE CAN HEAR!

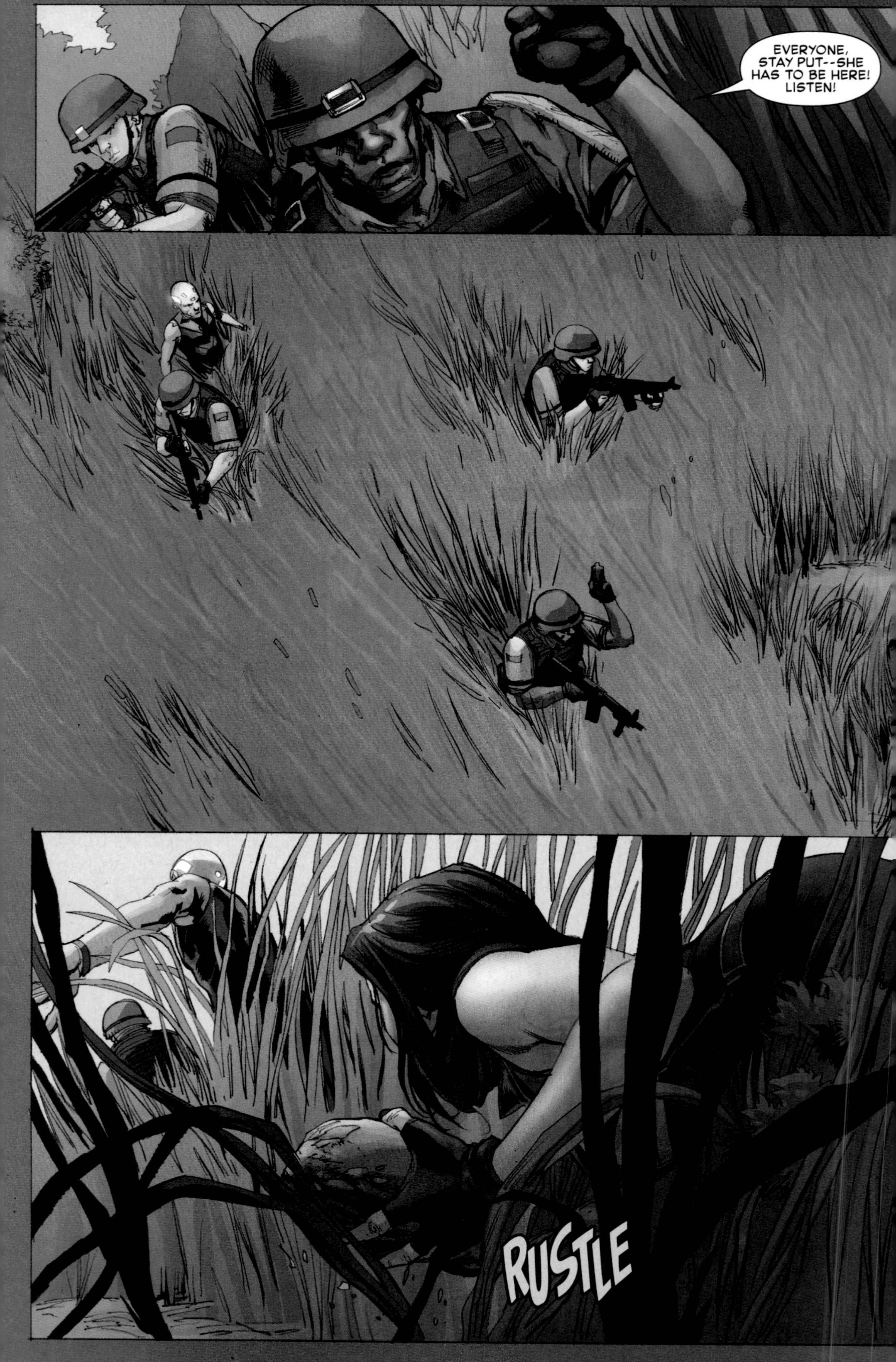
EVERYONE, STAY PUT--SHE HAS TO BE HERE! LISTEN!
RUSTLE

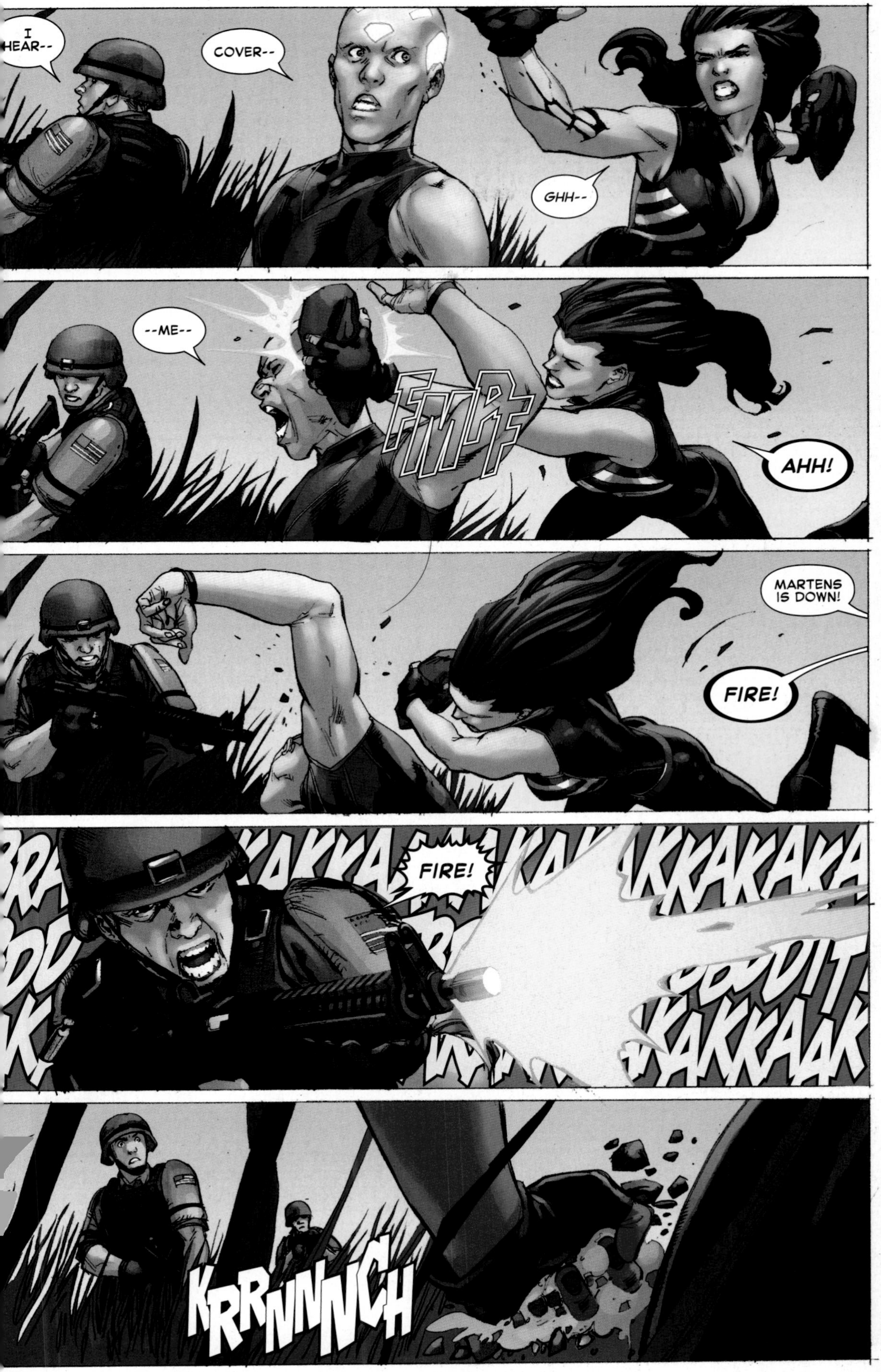
I HEAR--
COVER--
GHH--
--ME--
FMPF
AHH!
MARTENS IS DOWN!
FIRE!
FIRE!
KRRNNNCH

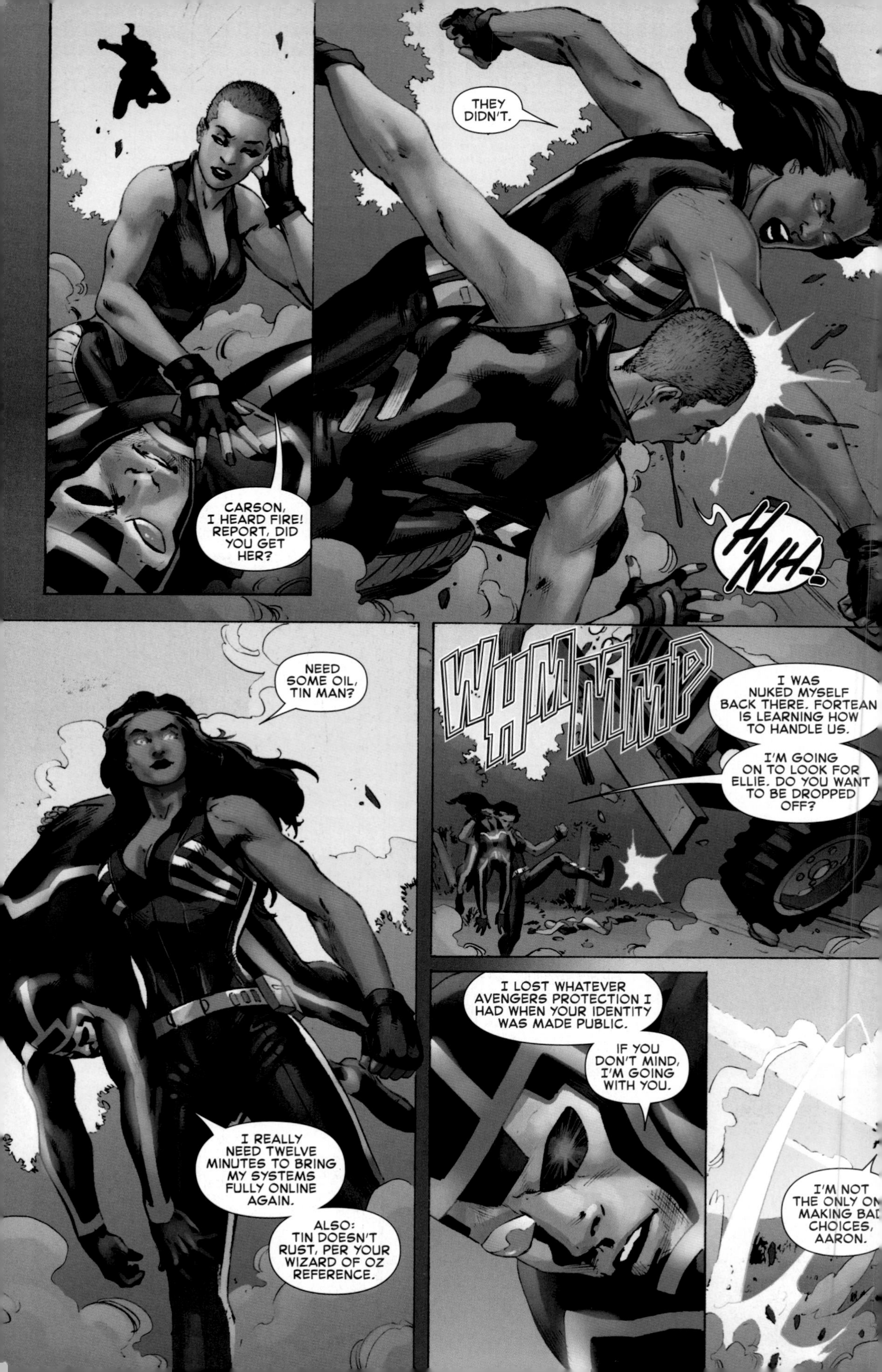
CARSON, I HEARD FIRE! REPORT, DID YOU GET HER?
THEY DIDN'T.
HNH-
NEED SOME OIL, TIN MAN?
I REALLY NEED TWELVE MINUTES TO BRING MY SYSTEMS FULLY ONLINE AGAIN.
ALSO: TIN DOESN'T RUST, PER YOUR WIZARD OF OZ REFERENCE.
WHMMMMP
I WAS NUKED MYSELF BACK THERE. FORTEAN IS LEARNING HOW TO HANDLE US.
I'M GOING ON TO LOOK FOR ELLIE. DO YOU WANT TO BE DROPPED OFF?
I LOST WHATEVER AVENGERS PROTECTION I HAD WHEN YOUR IDENTITY WAS MADE PUBLIC.
IF YOU DON'T MIND, I'M GOING WITH YOU.
I'M NOT THE ONLY O MAKING BA CHOICES, AARON.

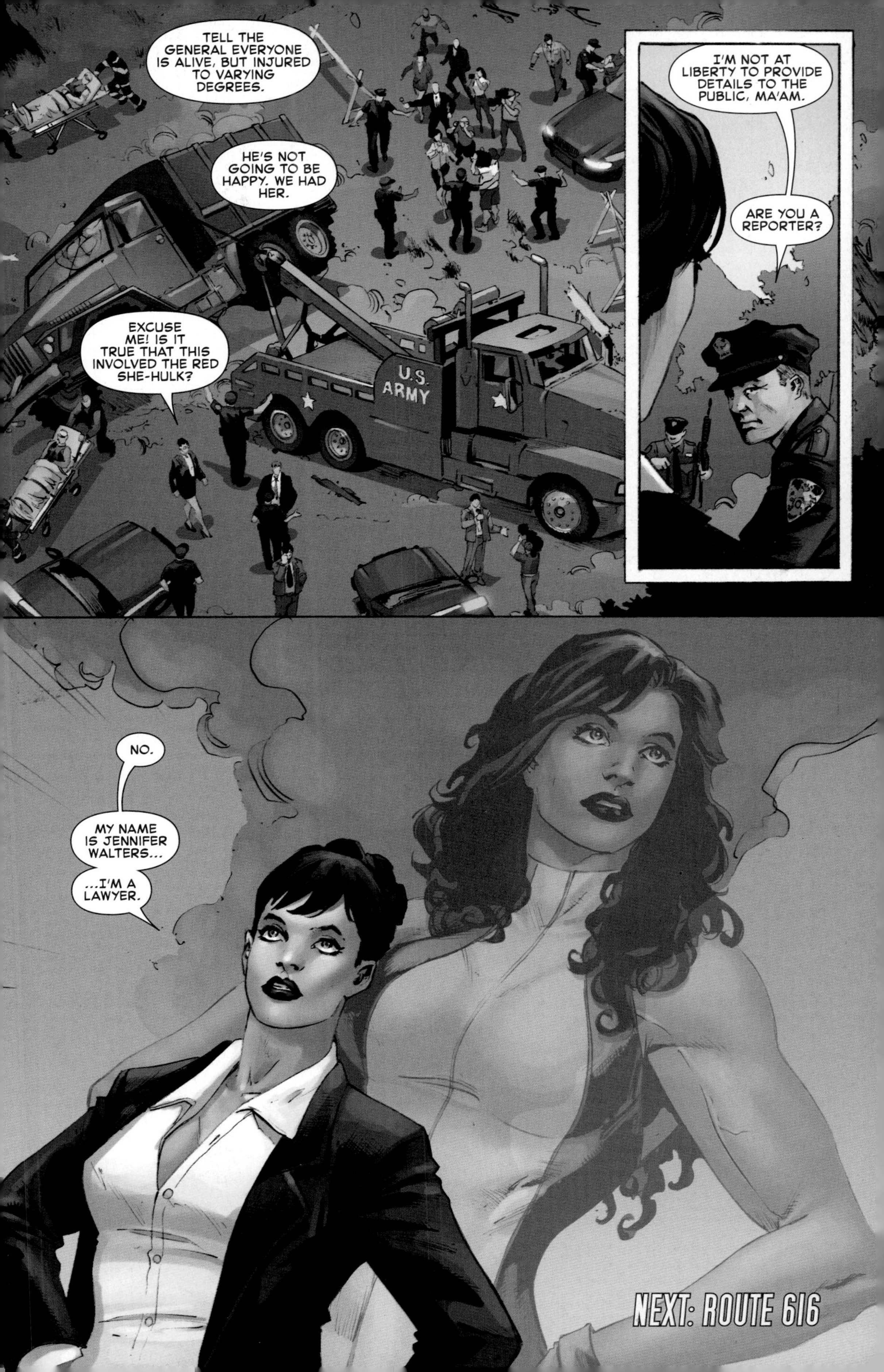
TELL THE GENERAL EVERYONE IS ALIVE, BUT INJURED TO VARYING DEGREES.
HE'S NOT GOING TO BE HAPPY. WE HAD HER.
EXCUSE ME! IS IT TRUE THAT THIS INVOLVED THE RED SHE-HULK?
U.S. ARMY
I'M NOT AT LIBERTY TO PROVIDE DETAILS TO THE PUBLIC, MA'AM.
ARE YOU A REPORTER?
NO.
MY NAME IS JENNIFER WALTERS...
...I'M A LAWYER.
NEXT: ROUTE 616

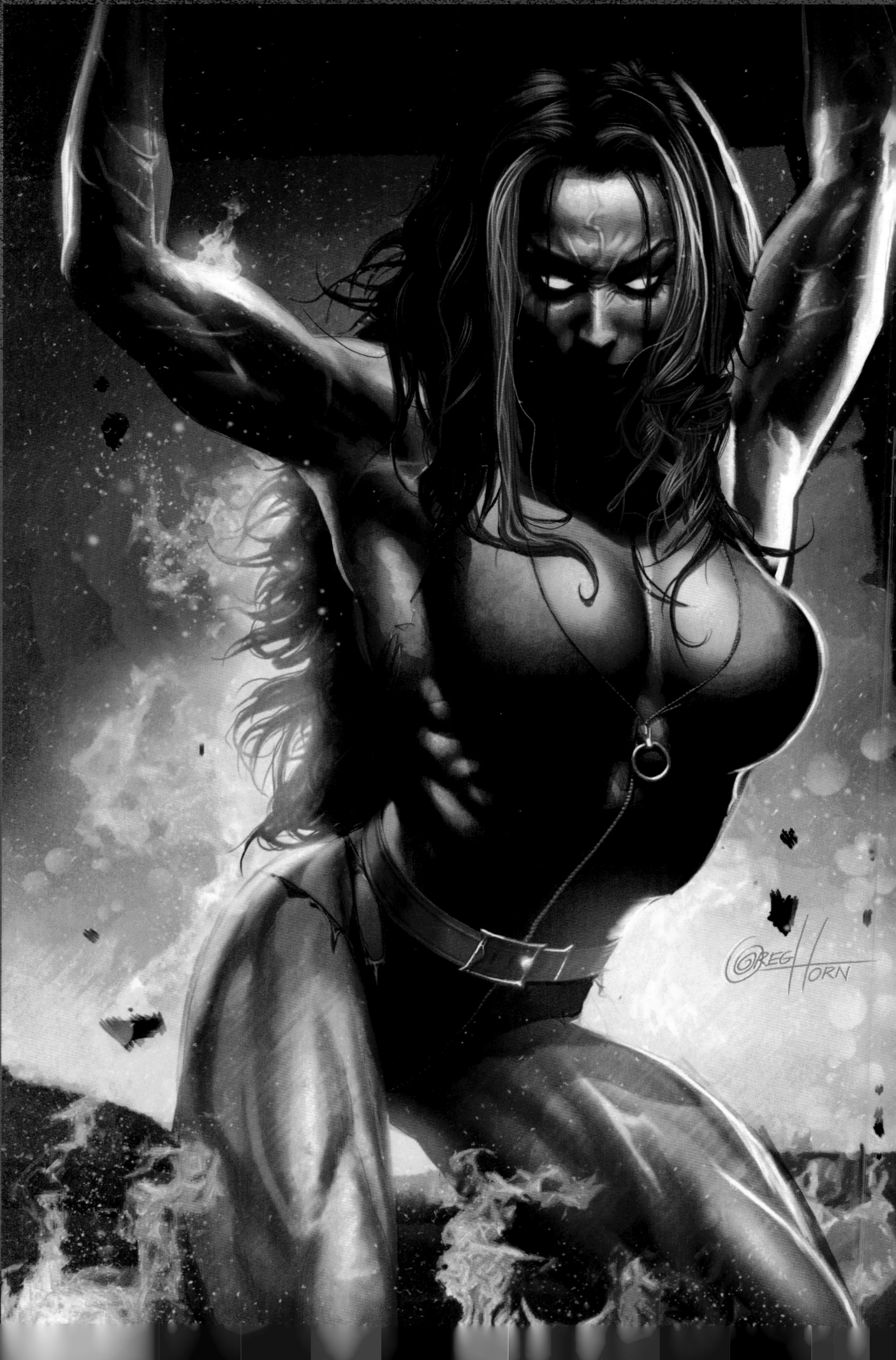
GREG HORN

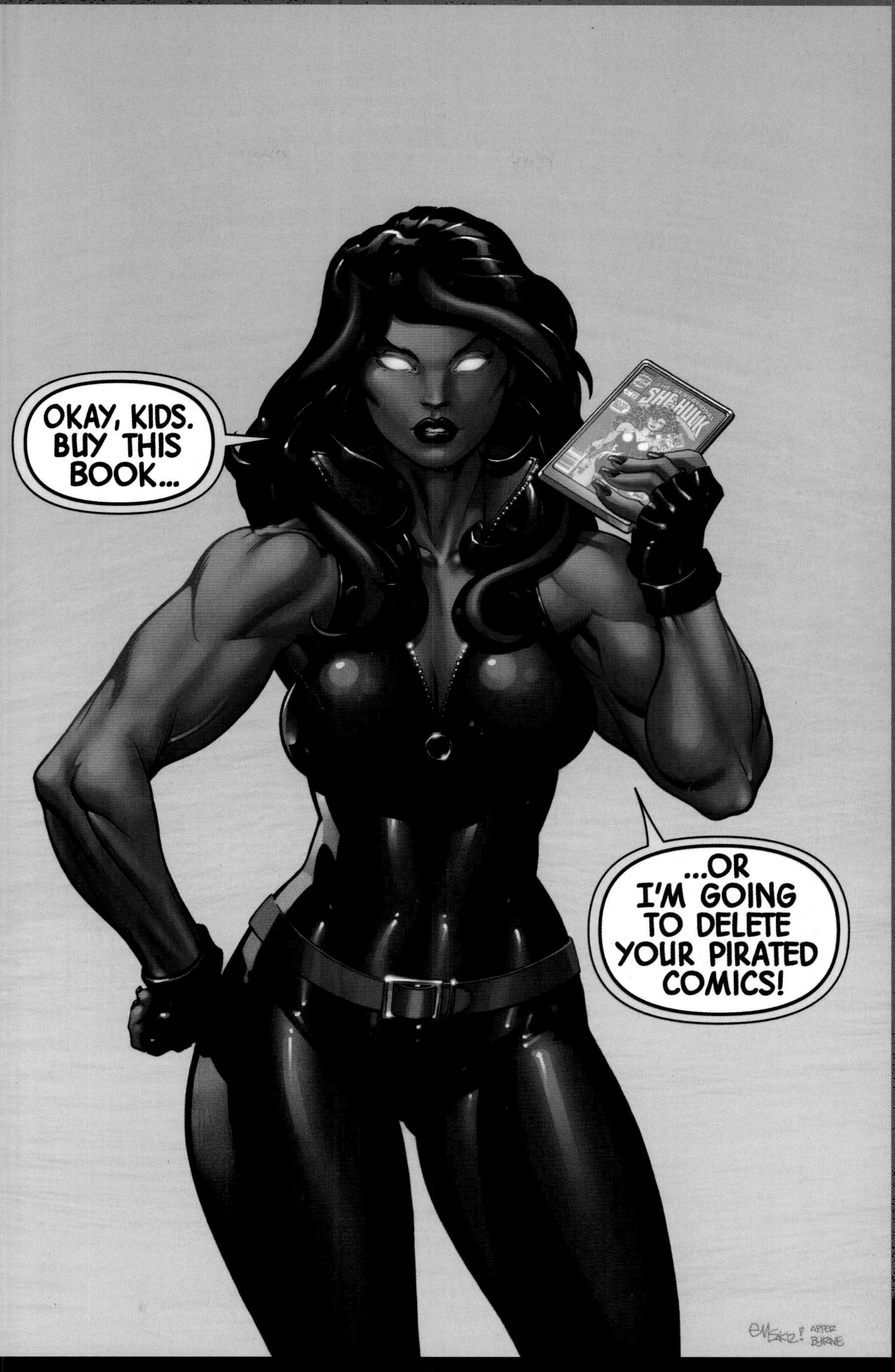
OKAY, KIDS. BUY THIS BOOK...
...OR I'M GOING TO DELETE YOUR PIRATED COMICS!

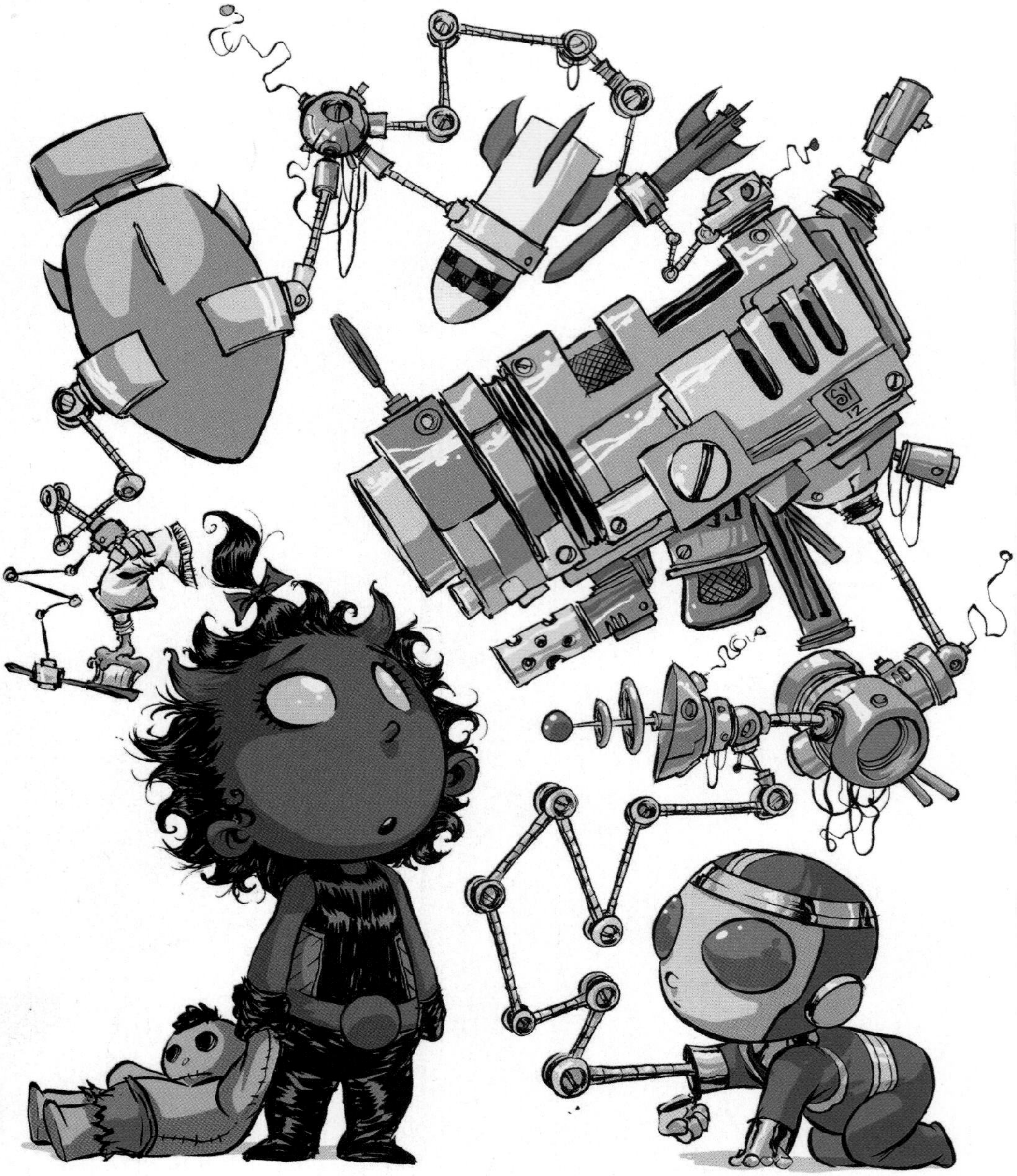

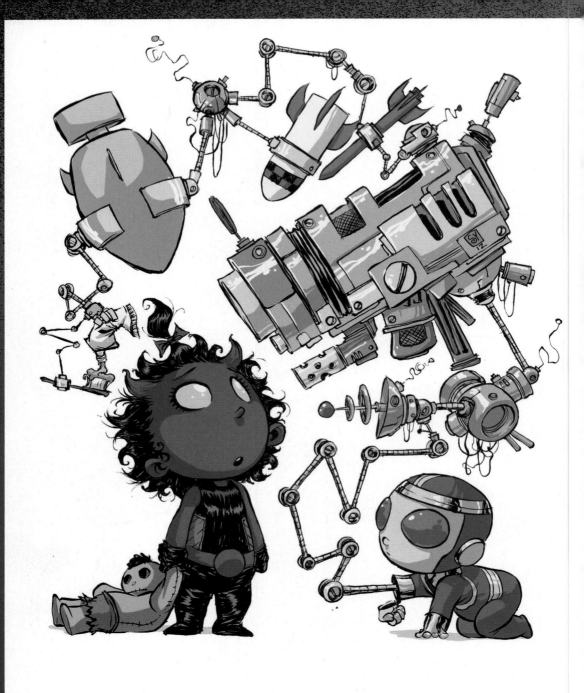

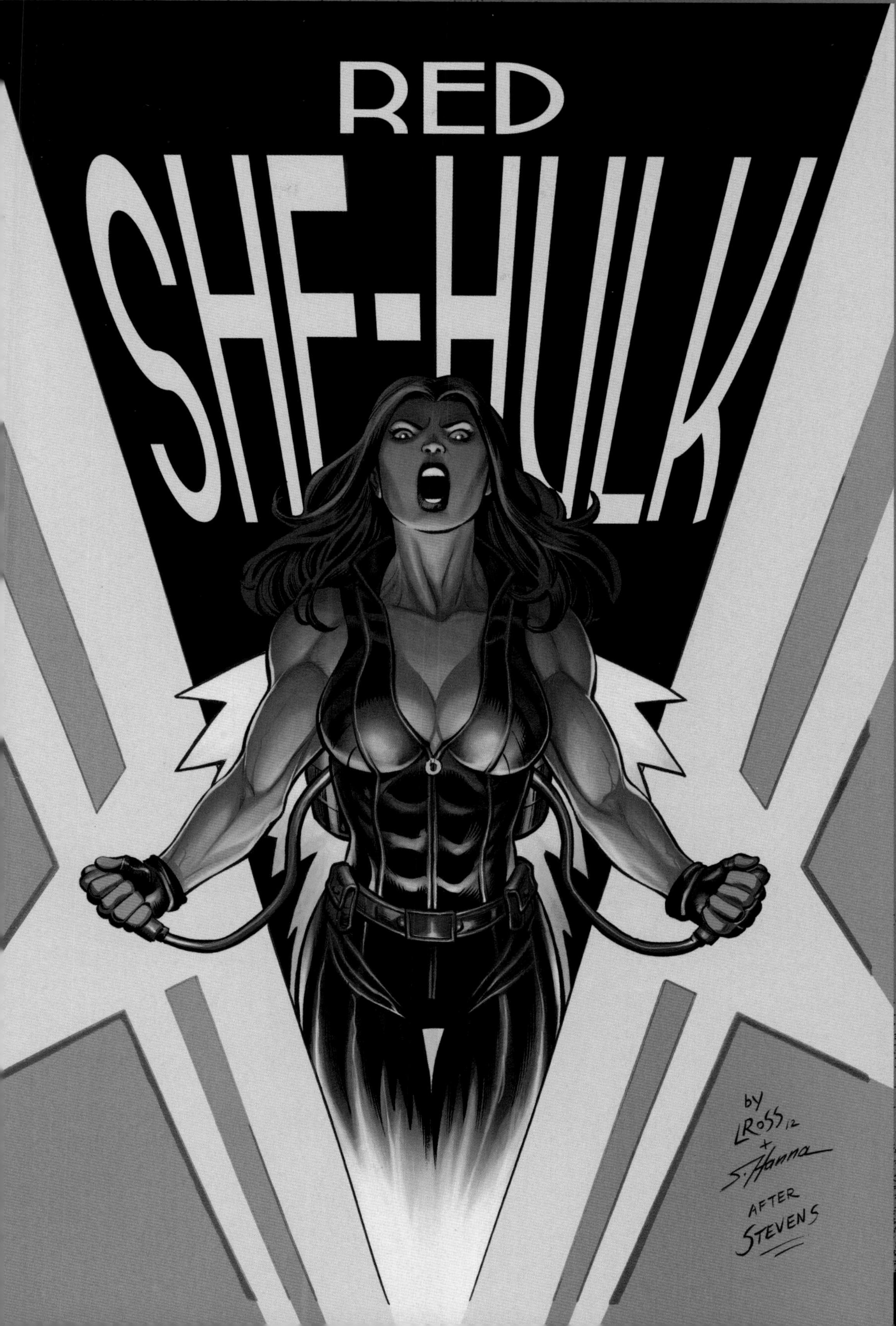
RED
SHE-HULK
by
LRoss 12
+
S. Hanna
AFTER
STEVENS

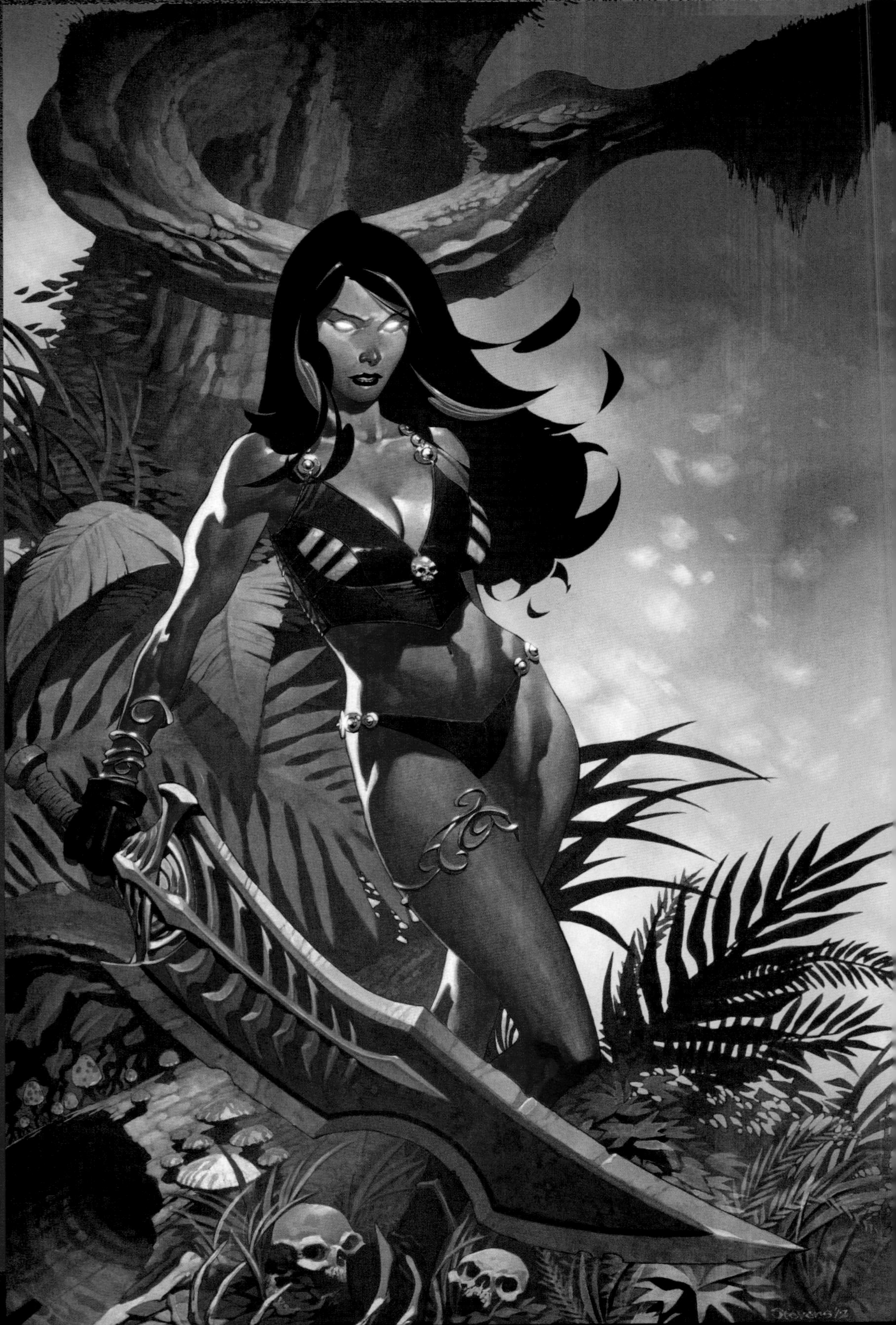

#60 VARIANT BY CHRIS STEVENS

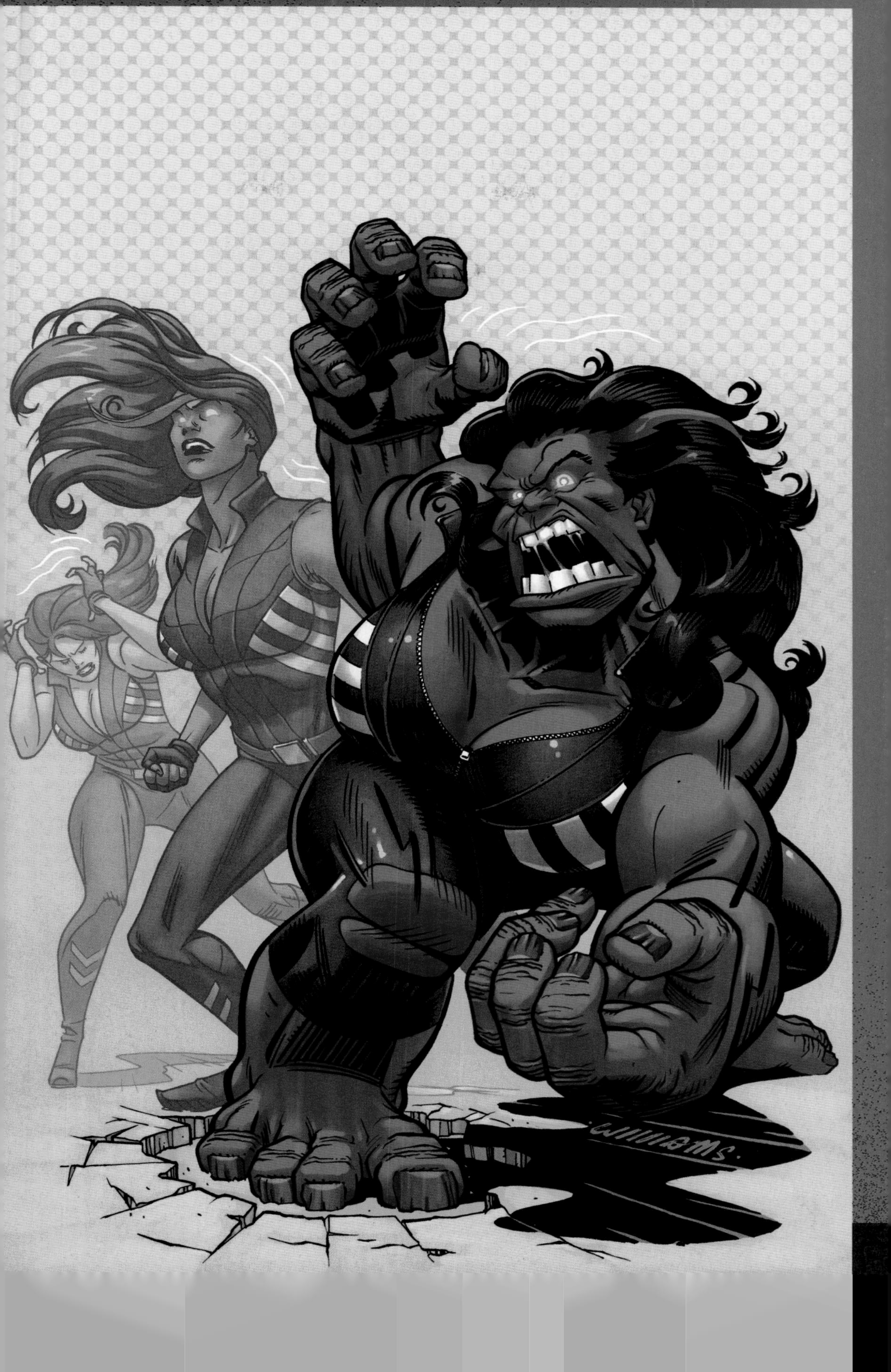
WILLIAMS.

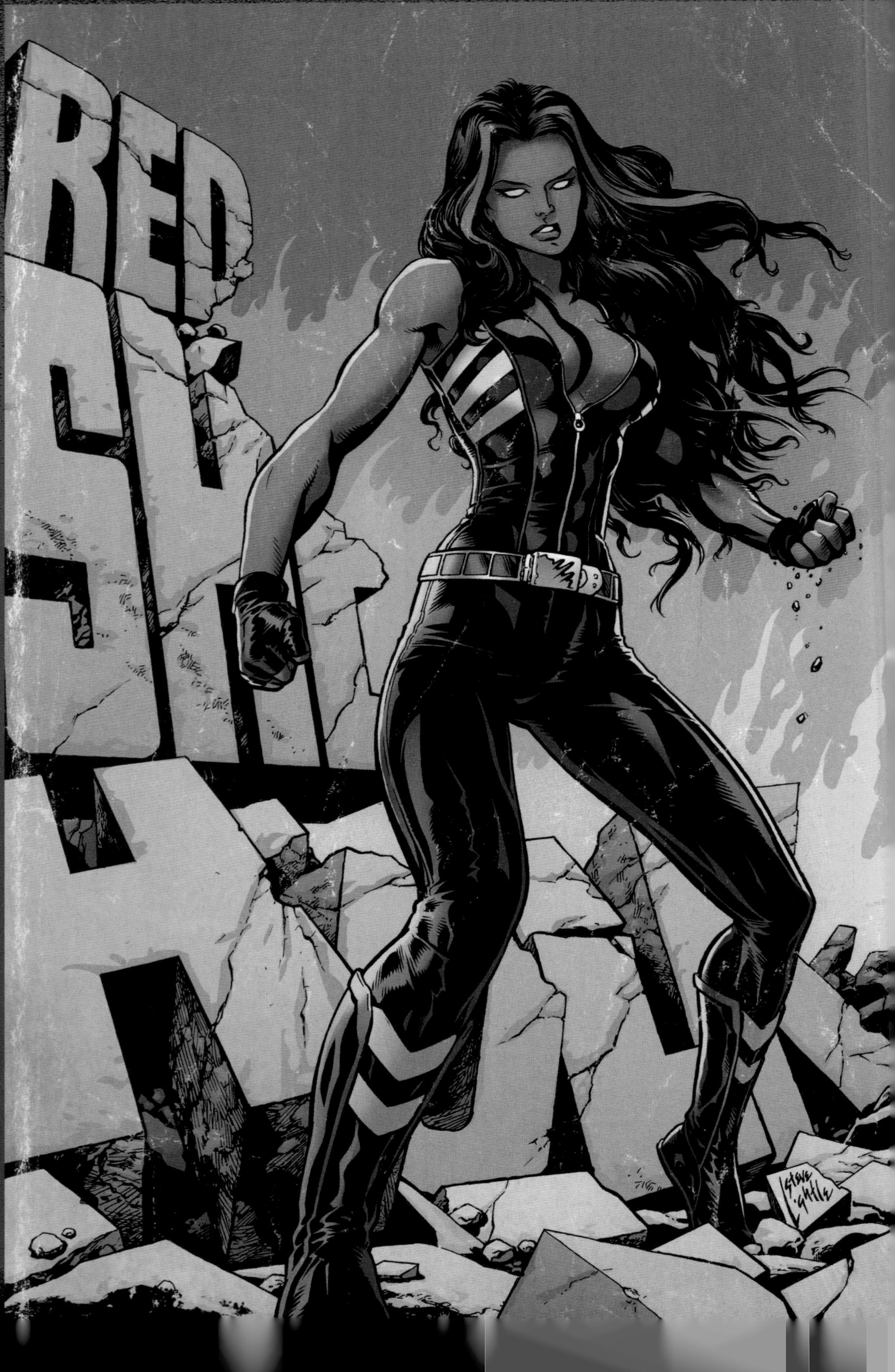
RED

ELIZABETH "BETTY" ROSS
AKA
RED SHE-HULK
SECTION B

BETTY'S FATHER WAS INSTRUMENTAL IN HER BECOMING ONE OF THE SECONDARY HULKS. THE GENERAL ALLOWED THE MASTERMIND FELONS THE LEADER AND M.O.D.O.K. TO INITIATE A METAMORPHOSIS LIKE BANNER'S WITH A MIXTURE OF GAMMA AND COSMIC RAYS. AS THE RED HULK, HE AGREED TO HELP THEM KILL BANNER IN EXCHANGE FOR THEM REVIVING HIS PHYSICALLY-TERMINAL DAUGHTER BEING KEPT IN CRYOGENIC STASIS AFTER POISONING BY THE HOSTILE KNOWN AS THE ABOMINATION.

UNKNOWN TO THE GENERAL, THE CRIMINAL SCIENTISTS USED A MORE REFINED VERSION OF THE RED HULK PROCESS ON HIS DAUGHTER. THIS DID RESTORE HER TO FULL HEALTH WHILE MAKING HER A HULK. THEIR ATTEMPTS AT CREATING IMPRINTED LOYALTY TO THEMSELVES WERE LESS SUCCESSFUL WITH THE RED HULKS * AND BOTH SOON REGAINED AUTONOMY.

X-51 CAPSULE PROFILE:

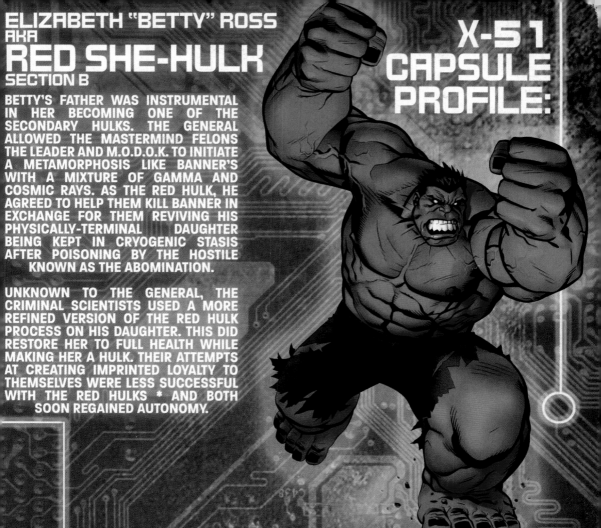

RECENT ACTIVITY

LATER WORKED WITH THE RED HULK AT THE INITIAL REQUEST OF CAPTAIN AMERICA, AND DURING THAT TIME I MET RED SHE-HULK. SHE ARRIVED FIRST AS AN ADVERSARY, BUT HELPED US SHUT DOWN AN OPERATION BY THE HOSTILE KNOWN AS ZERO/ONE, SAVING BOTH OF OUR LIVES (THIS IS QUALIFIED FOR THOSE WHO CONSIDER ME ALIVE).

FROM WHAT LITTLE I'VE FOUND, SHE WAS CONCURRENTLY WORKING WITH OTHER POWERFUL AGENTS, AMONG THEM DR. STEPHEN STRANGE, IRON FIST AND THE ALIEN ENTITY CALLED SILVER SURFER. GIVEN THE PAST HISTORY OF THESE FIGURES, THE ASSUMPTION IS SHE HAS NOT ACTED IN A MALEVOLENT FASHION. THIS MAKES THE RECENT ATTACK ON THE ECHELON DEMONSTRATION MORE PUZZLING.

BETTY ROSS CAN TRANSFORM INTO HER HULK FORM AT WILL, AND THE UPPER RANGE OF HER POWER IS UNDETERMINED. MY LIMITED EXPERIENCE WITH HER SUGGESTS SHE DOESN'T HAVE MULTIPLE PERSONALITIES, BUT BECOMES MORE ERRATIC AND EMOTION-DRIVEN WHEN RED. I PLACE HER THREAT LEVEL AT 4 OF 5. 5 IS RESERVED FOR THE PURPOSEFULLY LETHAL, AND FROM ALL ACCOUNTS THE RED SHE-HULK IS NOT A KILLER.

ND AGAIN WITH RICK JONES WHO WAS ALTERED INTO THE
ERATIVE CALLED A-BOMB.

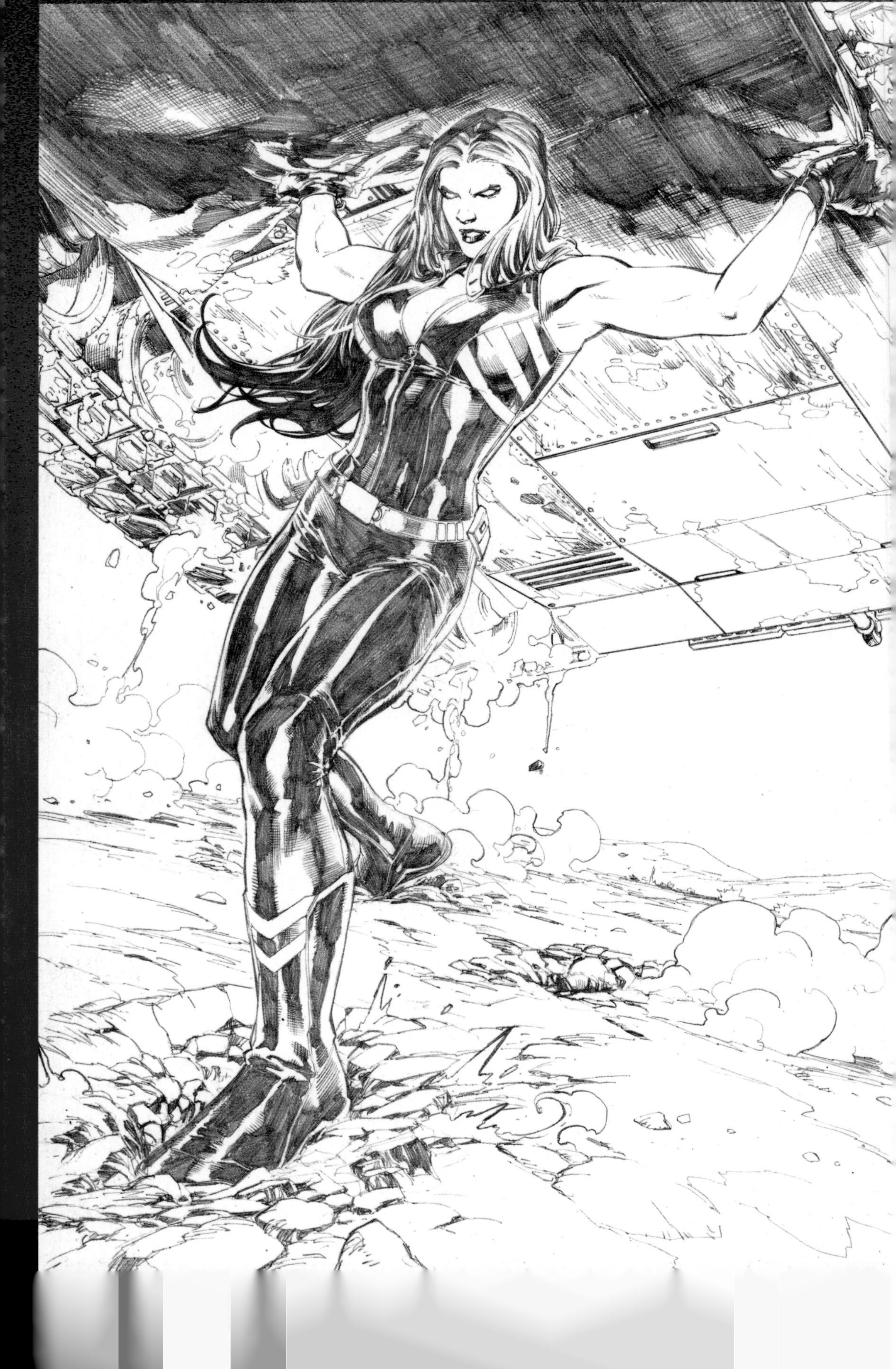

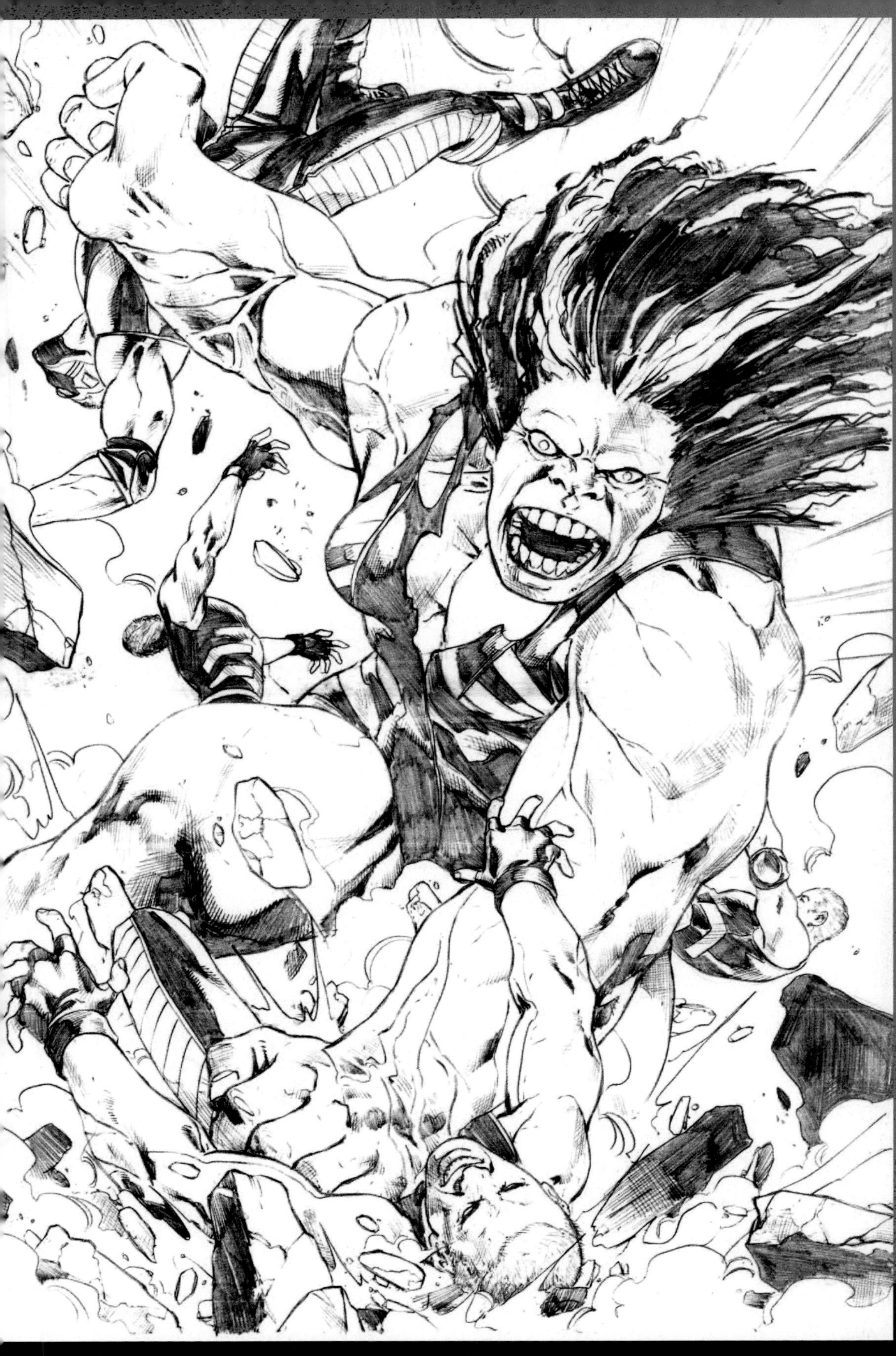

#60 PAGE 20 PENCILS BY CARLO PAGULAYAN